GLOBALIZATION UNPLUGGED:
SOVEREIGNTY AND THE CANADIAN
STATE IN THE TWENTY-FIRST CENTURY

The debate over economic globalization has reached a fever pitch in the past decade and a half with Western governments and multinational corporations trumpeting its virtues and a multitude of activists and developing-world citizens vociferously denouncing it. For better or worse, globalization is changing the way people and nations do business, but to what extent? In *Globalization Unplugged*, Peter Urmetzer questions whether national economies are indeed losing their sovereignty and whether the topic of globalization merits as much discussion as it receives.

Focusing specifically on Canada, Urmetzer demonstrates that current levels of trade are not unprecedented and, further, that as the economy becomes more service oriented, it will also become less trade dependent. He points out that only a small percentage of Canada's wealth is owned by foreign investors and, likewise, that only a small portion of the country's wealth is invested outside of its borders.

Disputing claims that the nation-state is weakening or disappearing altogether, Urmetzer shows how the welfare-state side of government spending – conveniently ignored in the anti-globalization literature yet arguably the most significant development in the political economy of the nation-state in the twentieth century – remains remarkably stable. A compelling and accessible work of scholarship, *Globalization Unplugged* will spark controversy on both sides of the globalization debate and help deflate the rhetoric of both advocates and detractors.

(Studies in Comparative Political Economy and Public Policy)

PETER URMETZER is an assistant professor in the Department of Sociology at the University of British Columbia, Okanagan.

Studies in Comparative Political Economy and Public Policy

Editors: MICHAEL HOWLETT, DAVID LAYCOCK, STEPHEN MCBRIDE, Simon Fraser University

Studies in Comparative Political Economy and Public Policy is designed to showcase innovative approaches to political economy and public policy from a comparative perspective. While originating in Canada, the series will provide attractive offerings to a wide international audience, featuring studies with local, subnational, cross-national, and international empirical bases and theoretical frameworks.

Editorial Advisory Board

For a list of books published in the series, see pp. 233–4.

Globalization Unplugged

Sovereignty and
the Canadian State
in the Twenty-first Century

Peter Urmetzer

UNIVERSITY OF TORONTO PRESS
Toronto Buffalo London

© University of Toronto Press Incorporated 2005
Toronto Buffalo London
Printed in Canada

ISBN 0-8020-3855-7 (cloth)
ISBN 0-8020-3799-2 (paper)

Library and Archives Canada Cataloguing in Publication

Urmetzer, Peter, 1955–
    Globalization unplugged : sovereignty and the Canadian state in the
    twenty-first century / Peter Urmetzer.

    (Studies in comparative political economy and public policy)
    Includes bibliographical references and index.
    ISBN 0-8020-3855-7 (bound).   ISBN 0-8020-3799-2 (pbk.)

    1. Globalization – Economic aspects – Canada.   2. Canada – Economic
    policy – 1991–   3. Globalization.   I. Title.   II. Series.

    HC115.U74 2005   330.971′ 072   C2005-900389-8

University of Toronto Press acknowledges the financial assistance to its
publishing program of the Canada Council for the Arts and the Ontario
Arts Council.

University of Toronto Press acknowledges the financial support for its
publishing activities of the Government of Canada through the Book
Publishing Industry Development Program (BPIDP).

To my father,
Martin Urmetzer

Contents

Acknowledgments

There is a long list of people I wish to thank for their contribution in the writing and publication of this book. First and foremost, I owe a debt of gratitude to the anonymous reviewers for their careful reading of the manuscript. They made many helpful suggestions and directed me to a variety of valuable sources. At the University of Toronto Press, I would particularly like to thank Virgil Duff for his persistent effort and patience in bringing this book to publication. Thanks must also go to Stephen Kotowych, the editor responsible for putting this project together, and Margaret Allen, for copy editing. I would also like to thank Okanagan University College and the Grant in Aid program, and in particular Dean Bob Belton, for funds provided. Peter Wylie, the chair of economics at Okanagan University College, offered helpful sources and advice on the history of the world economy. Faith Peyton at the OUC library reliably and promptly answered my interlibrary requests and brought in books from across the country. Kathleen Benson, Kristin Dunlop, Starleigh Grass, and Colin Wiseman all provided invaluable help in the final stages of this document. I would also like to thank Professors Neil Guppy, Gillian Creese, and Brian Elliott at the University of British Columbia and Gordon Laxer of the University of Alberta, who served on the PhD committee for the dissertation on which this manuscript is based; as well, I am grateful for their ongoing career advice. Bridget Donald had many insightful comments and provided encouragement when my enthusiasm ebbed. Mark Lowes and Paul Champ engaged me in helpful discussions about the topic and about writing in general. I would also like to thank a number of people at Green College at the University of British Columbia for intellectual engagement and humour during my stay there as a graduate student:

Dr Dawna Tong, Heidi Peterson, Dr Andrew McKinnon, Dr Scott Hazelhurst, Dr Victoria Beard, Andrew Hare, Jennifer Giovannitti, and Karen Smallwood. Special thanks must also go to Professor Richard Ericson, the principal of Green College from 1993 to 2003, who was instrumental in getting this manuscript to press.

GLOBALIZATION UNPLUGGED

Introduction

The concept of globalization has been the subject of considerable commentary and speculation among academics, politicians, and the general public. It has successfully served as a 'catch-all' term to explain everything from rapidly changing communications technology to increased unemployment. Globalization has also been perceived as an overwhelmingly powerful force, so much so that even governments are unable to escape its grip. In this new global era the nation-state is, we are told, fast becoming an antiquated institution. Considered only a minor player in the global economy, state action is frequently presented as reactive rather than proactive. Yet despite globalization's purportedly pervasive and unrestrained power, the empirical foundations of how it has affected Canada remain largely unexamined. Through detailed investigation of Canada's foreign trade and investment patterns, as well as an assessment of government involvement in the economy, this book challenges claims made about both the power and the novelty of globalization, and especially about how it relates to the fortunes of the nation-state.

Globalization has proven an attractive concept precisely because it provides a plausible explanation for many of the changes that Canadians have been able to observe in the past few decades: the onslaught of consumer products manufactured abroad, persistent and high unemployment, expanding computer technology and global communication, and a seemingly interminable string of trade agreements including the North American Free Trade Agreement (NAFTA), the General Agreement on Tariffs and Trade (GATT), and Trade Related Investment Measures (TRIMs). Collectively, these developments appear as irrefutable evidence in support of the 'coming down of borders' and end-of-nation-state arguments made by both globalization advocates and opponents alike. On the other hand, after two decades of globalization newspeak (according to Orwell, language 'designed to diminish the range of thought'), Canada seems to be pretty much intact and, if anything – given the persistent threat of Quebec sovereignty and western alienation – the more pressing issue this country is facing is one of more borders, not fewer.

Nevertheless, terms like 'globalization' and 'globalism' not only remain an incessant feature of the news but are also widely discussed among a broad range of disciplines in academia. In this respect, particularly when contrasted to recent academic debates on post-Fordism, postmodernism, and postindustrialism, globalization is unique in that it straddles the academic and popular realms. Despite this unprecedented exposure, the concept has come under little scrutiny. For the most part, and this holds true for both academic and public debates, globalization is widely accepted by both left and right, leaving the validity of its premises often unchallenged.[1] Consequently, people are generally accepting when changes such as welfare-program cutbacks and high unemployment are blamed on globalization.

Everything and anything is blamed on or related to globalization in some way. One has to go no further than the local paper to find evidence of this uncritical stance. An article about dating observes that 'intimacy has fallen victim to globalization ...'(*Globe and Mail*, 26 Sept. 2002: R5), and a headline in Canada's national newspaper strangely proclaims the advent of 'the globalization of gardening' (*Globe and Mail*, 7 Aug. 1999: D7). But mostly the focus of globalization talk is on economics. Anne Golden of the Conference Board of Canada writes that, 'Globalization has been accompanied by growing wealth-poverty gaps among and within countries' (*Toronto Star*, 2 Feb. 2004: A14). A strong sense of inevitability permeates these reports and, more often than not, globalization is presented as not a choice but a dictate, as the following headline demonstrates: 'There's No Realistic Alternative to Globalization' (*Chronicle-Herald* [Halifax], 5 Mar. 2004: E2). On a rare visit to Vancouver, British Columbia, former Prime Minister Chrétien echoed that sentiment when he surmised that 'We cannot stop globalization. We need to ... adjust to it' (*Georgia Straight*, 26 Mar. – 2 Apr. 1998: 22). Taken at face value, these comments make globalization out to be a formidable force indeed. But to what extent are these observations valid? This is the central question driving this inquiry, which seeks to better understand the process of globalization and to assess whether the theoretical ideas packaged within globalization are reflective of real-life events or are simply rhetoric used to achieve certain political ends.

'Globalization' eludes easy definition, and I will spend some time examining this problem, but for the moment I will simply use it to mean 'society without borders' or a 'borderless world,' a definition that captures both the physical and the political aspects of the term. Related to the theme of a borderless society is the common perception that corporations are increasingly mobile entities, searching for profits outside the industrial world and expediting the movement of jobs from the First World to the Third (e.g., Teeple 2000). This newfound power of capital is said to have occurred at the expense of the state, prompting many observers to predict the latter's eventual demise. This variant, often referred to as corporate globalization, provided the target for the anti-globalization demonstrators who marched in the streets of Seattle, Quebec City, and Genoa.

To what degree such a scenario is accurate is seldom documented, and when it is, only partially; 'partially' meaning that figures are presented for only the post-Second World War period. This is most often the case for trade, arguably the most important strand of the globalization argument. Following the simple logic that as trade goes up economic independence goes down, governments often use international competition as a justification to cut social programs, lower labour standards, and privatize state industries. Escalating imports are provided as evidence that products from abroad, particularly those originating in the Third World, are rendering the Canadian economy uncompetitive. Labour and market conditions in poor countries are increasingly attractive to investors and, in order to compete, Western countries have to match these standards. An effective way of dismantling the globalization argument, then, is to focus on this most politicized aspect of globalization, namely production and trade. Extensive data will be used to provide a historical context for the Canadian economy in order to appraise whether it is indeed becoming more globalized.

Globalization as Ideology

Globalization is the natural end-point of a free-market ideology that celebrates self-initiative and places the burden of responsibility on the individual. It pits each individual in competition not only with everyone else but also with the world. In this sense globalization is the great equalizer, as it treats everyone equally whether that person is the CEO of a large corporation, a migrant worker in India, or a single mother in Elbow, Saskatchewan, or Finger, Manitoba. In its most extreme and pessimistic version, a globalized society is one without borders, states, or regulation, the final realization of Hobbes's state of nature, a dreaded world of a perpetual 'war of one against all.'

But we are a long way from this extreme manifestation of a globalized world, and therein lies the crux of the argument of this book. Globalization is not a unidirectional force that annihilates everything in its way; nor does it cause havoc around the world. For every trend isolated that supports the globalization thesis, an equally powerful counter-trend can be identified that casts doubt on that thesis. In the final analysis, globalization is not something that can easily be quantified (globalization 150; anti-globalization 148?). As a relatively new phenomenon it is a force that is neither uncontested nor unidirectional. The weakest feature of the globalization literature is that it is marred by a hasty tendency to generalize from selective examples and to focus on developments that support the thesis while completely ignoring trends that counter it. Furthermore, it makes the assumption that the flow of goods, ideas, and so on, serves only to undermine national borders not strengthen them. But the flows that globalize and flatten borders can at the same time reinforce them. CNN is often used as an example of technology that transcends national borders, but television is never mentioned as a tool that can be used by government to foster nationalism, thereby strengthening borders (which is what happened in Quebec). The question of whether international flows are matched or even superseded by national flows is seldom considered (except for Helliwell 2002). Yet national flows are the natural counterforce to the threat that globalization is supposed to present. Once this question is posed – whether it concerns the flow of goods, people, information, culture, money, or capital – the threat of transnational movements that constitute globalization becomes immediately less intimidating.

One of the primary tasks of this book is to present the other side of the story and bring to light some less explored counter-trends. This will consist of a history of Canadian trade, an analysis of the continuing and immense role of the state, and an examination of the changing role of foreign direct and international investments. The other objective is to undermine the political rhetoric that surrounds globalization, a point that will be briefly discussed next.

Globalization and Language

'Globalization' is not merely an unbiased description of where the world is headed but a theory that embodies many assumptions about where the world should go and what must be done in order to get there. These assumptions – sometimes explicit, most often not – are mostly about the free market and how it relates to the efficient allocation of resources. Based on the expectation that government interference can only distort market mechanisms, social programs are viewed with suspicion. It is precisely this message that is intended to be conveyed by the business community, revealing the considerable social power that can hide behind a seemingly innocuous word like 'globalization.'

Raymond Williams (1983) has convincingly argued that words – what he calls key words – can play an important role in constructing our social lives. These words are not only reflective of the world, but can also play a role in shaping it; rather than describing reality, they take part in actively structuring social relations (Dehli 1993: 87). Such key words are often full of assumptions, often left unsaid because they appear too commonsensical to require further explanation (Fraser and Gordon 1997). Precisely because they are left unquestioned, these words become all the more powerful in their impact. Thus they are adopted into common discourse, leaving underlying social relations invisible (Smith 1990: 93). This makes social agency invisible – it just happens; it is immutable; nothing can be done about it; no one is to blame. 'Globalization' easily qualifies as a key word, and one of my primary tasks will be, besides challenging the concept itself, to examine the assumptions and social relations that underlie it, as well as to expose who will benefit if the concept is left uncontested, and – equally important – who is likely to lose.

'Globalization' can, even more accurately, be described as a 'code word' – the phrase 'family values' is often recognized as such and can serve as an instructive analogy. This pithy and seemingly innocent phrase, used particularly by the political right in the United States, underpins a political agenda that makes a multitude of assumptions about the gender composition of parents, proper roles for males and females, and, probably most important, the relationship between the family and the state. Although experiencing nowhere near the same success in Canada as south of the border, this phrase has recently been adopted by Canadians who oppose same-sex marriage. While the political rhetoric of family values successfully put a positive spin on this, the movement, at least in the United States, is essentially about severing state responsibility. This has translated into cuts to government funding for single mothers, the mentally ill, the sick, the disabled, and the unemployed. Even a seemingly unrelated problem such as drug addiction is left to the family, with 'family values' providing adequate justification to cut government-initiated drug-rehabilitation programs. In short, a code phrase such as 'family values' is rife with assumptions about proper social relations and has as its target anyone who depends on 'government hand-outs.' This, of course, does not affect everyone equally and can be interpreted as an indirect attack on women (who are forced to take up the slack when the government no longer funds programs that care for the sick or elderly) and African-Americans (in whose communities unemployment and single motherhood are particularly high).

In a similar fashion, 'globalization' makes all kinds of assumptions about the role of workers, the market, and the political process in general. As a code word, 'globalization' has been used successfully to convince people that market forces are not only powerful but also the best way to manage social and political reform. In the contemporary political climate, the state, in both normative and practical terms, can no longer be counted on to intervene. 'Globalization' thus provides a justification for economic setbacks such as high unemployment, government cutbacks, and wage restraints. As with 'family values,' 'globalization' also has specific targets: workers, who are forced to contend with lower wages and fewer benefits, the state, and social programs.

This objective was quite explicit in a labour dispute that took place in British Columbia a few years ago. In a newspaper advertisement placed by Starbucks, the coffee giant rationalized its anti-union stand by claiming that there was no place for the inflexible ways of such an institution in 'the new global economy' (*Vancouver Sun*, 17 May 1997: A7). Of course, there is nothing new about business opposition to union involvement; however, the justification for this opposition now tends to be different in that responsibility is pinned on globalization. The Starbucks advertisement clearly illustrates the larger point made in this book: that the balance of power between capital and labour and the state has not fundamentally changed over the past few decades. Business has always been powerful; the state continues to be so, too; and both are more powerful than labour, especially when business and the state join forces. What has changed is that many people have become convinced that the global economy has rendered national politics ineffective and, furthermore, that any demands for fair treatment for workers or minorities must remain unanswered.

There is, however, one notable difference between 'family values' and 'globalization' that requires further elucidation. Most politically astute observers become immediately suspicious when they hear the phrase 'family values' and rightfully question the political agenda that hides behind its use. Of course, family values in themselves are not a bad thing – nobody rallies against family values *per se*, only against their implicit political agenda. In a similar way, it is not so much my intent to deny that globalization exists as to strip it of its political authority. In some instances, 'globalization' – for example, in reference to communications or travel – may be a perfectly useful term. Neither am I arguing that large corporations or the attack on the welfare state do not constitute a threat or that they should be ignored. What I am arguing is that behind the word 'globalization' lurks a political agenda that, as with 'family values,' is loaded with a myriad of political and social assumptions, many of which are highly questionable. The purpose of this book is to examine these claims and assumptions.

The Globalization of the Economy

An always protean world economy has affected each country differently. If anything, these differences point towards continued divergence within the global economy. There are instances where the globalization argument does hold true: the manufacturing of textiles and clothing, the assembly of computer hardware, tele-learning, and free trade zones such as the Maquiladoras in Mexico. But these examples are, as will become evident throughout this book, the exceptions. As we shall learn in some detail, most of what Canadians consume is produced within Canada's borders, and this will likely continue for some time. The reason is simple. An economy is the combined commercial activity that takes place within a politically defined area, usually a country, and not some abstract entity that can be separated from the people who work and live there. Without people there is no economy.

As was mentioned earlier, globalization has been implicated in almost every activity imaginable, and for that reason it may be prudent to talk about the limitations of this study. This book is primarily, as the title makes explicit, about how globalization – and in particular the globalization of the economy – has affected Canadian society. This study does not examine in any detail the movement and migration of people, the monopolization of capital, the impact of technology and mass communications, or the convergences of cultures. These are all, no doubt, important and worthwhile topics to write about, but space just does not permit a discussion of the 'globalization of everything.' I briefly discuss some of these topics throughout the book wherever relevant, but they are not the focus.

In short, this book is about Canada and how it has been affected by, or alternatively remained independent of, the process of economic globalization. Why Canada? As Canada has historically been dependent on other economies, it provides a good case study of globalization. If Canada, a relatively open economy, can retain its political sovereignty in the context of what is usually referred to as globalization, than less open economies, such as the United States or Germany, should be able to weather the consequences of globalization even better.

Organization of the Book

Now for a short road map to how this book is organized. Chapter 1 examines some of the problems associated with the definition of globalization. Globalization is often ill-defined, and I attempt to untangle the various strands and interpretations of what the concept means to different authors; whether it is a good thing or a bad thing, cause or effect, something to be embraced or something to be shunned. Is globalization new wine in old bottles, a process previously understood within the rhetoric of imperialism, colony and empire, world systems, or capitalism? The chapter first summarizes some of the more popular definitions and then explores the differences and commonalities between popular and academic definitions. The argument that globalization has strong political overtones provides the theme for the chapter.

Chapter 2 further examines the historical roots of 'globalization.' Although the word 'globalization' is of relatively recent vintage, the idea that capitalism uses the globe as its stage comes with a long and illustrious pedigree. The fact is that present-day conservatives are making observations that are remarkably similar to those made by communists more than a century and a half ago, a point not without its irony. Marx and Engels wrote about the globalizing tendencies of capitalism extensively in the middle of the past century, and it will be argued that the general tone of the contemporary literature on globalization is very similar to that of the *Manifesto,* forcing one to ask 'What's new?'

Chapter 3, building on the historical precedent of the world economy, examines literature, primarily from economics but also from sociology, that traces the origins of the 'global economy.' In one important sense, 'global' is a matter of degree, and from that perspective the world economy has never and will likely never be altogether global until the dynamics of the international political economy change. Large portions of the world, such as Africa and most of Latin America, continue to lie outside of the 'global' economy. But in so far as the world economy can be said to be global, it has been this way for at least 180 years, its patterns of trade forged at least another three centuries earlier (Maddison 2001; Wallerstein 1974).

Canada, particularly when compared to the United States, has always been an international trading power with a relatively open economy, first as a key colony to Britain and then as an economic satellite to the United States (Clement 1988: 76; G. Williams 1986). This suggests that globalization is not a new development for Canada. Globaphobes are concerned primarily about imports from the low-wage countries, prompting us to ask whom Canada primarily trades with. Sorting out these international flows is the primary task of chapter 4. In a ground-breaking study critical of globalization, the late American economist David M. Gordon (1988) presents convincing evidence that the world economy, at least in terms of production and trade, has not changed that dramatically in the past few decades. Similar to the approach taken by Gordon, I examine trading (exports and imports) for Canada from 1870 onwards. This entails tracing Canada's trade over the past 133 years, identifying both the origin and destination of these products.

The increasing amount of foreign direct investment (FDI) flowing around the world is also frequently presented as evidence that borders are coming down and that the world is becoming increasingly more globalized. The logic behind this argument is that corporations in the First World are moving to the Third World and taking advantage of lower costs, primarily for labour. FDI is also considered an appropriate indicator of globalization because it usually involves a long-term commitment, especially in contrast to stocks and bonds, which may only stay in a country for days or even hours. Canada occupies an interesting place when it comes to foreign capital in that it has traditionally been the number-one recipient of FDI in the world. Where does this FDI originate, and how much does Canada invest in other parts of the world? In other words, is Canada a destination as well as an originator of FDI? Chapter 5 also examines patterns and changes of FDI on a world basis: where it is going, and in what areas it tends to be concentrated (e.g., manufacturing, real estate, etc.).

Many writers have commented on the distinction between the financial and the productive economies. The argument is that the financial economy (stock and bond prices, currencies, credit) is no longer reflective of the productive or industrial economy. Chapter 6 examines how these two economies have diverged and what lies at the bottom of this divergence. Currency speculation is one of the more obvious threats associated with globalization, and this topic is discussed in some detail. As an alternative, it is argued that debt has increased to such a degree that it has put a drag on the whole economy.

The overall emphasis of economic globalization points to the political fallout that is supposed to follow in its wake, primarily its effect on the state. This conclusion has been reached by commentators from various vantage points: left, right, business, political, and academic. Much of the globalization argument is based on the observation that, as corporations are no longer constrained by borders, national borders will become meaningless. But have governments indeed become less powerful over the past few decades? Chapter 7 takes a sober look at the role of the state and examines expenditures dating back to 1933. Governments around the world started to intervene in the market in a dramatic fashion following the Second World War in order to stabilize the economy in an attempt to avoid another depression. The argument in this section is that the state continues to play this role and that, while this role is always changing and may at times be threatened, these threats originate primarily from within the country.

It is difficult to sustain an argument that the world economy has not undergone any changes since the Second World War. If globalization is not the cause then what is? Chapter 8 provides an overview of the political economy over the past half-century and examines various trends such as the profit squeeze, the lack of aggregate demand, and the switch from Keynesianism to monetarism. The argument is that the economy is going through the very mundane processes of a contraction, and the chapter assesses how this one both differs from and resembles recessions in the past.

The conclusion ties the evidence together and looks at the consistencies, or contradictions, that emerge. We then revisit a typical definition of 'globalization' and examine this in light of what we have learned in the preceding chapters.

Chapter 1

The Life and Times of Globalization: An Unauthorized Biography

'When I use a word,' Humpty-Dumpty said in rather a scornful tone, 'it means just what I choose it to mean – neither more nor less.'

'The question is,' said Alice, 'whether you *can* make words mean so many different things.'

'The question is,' said Humpty-Dumpty, 'which is to be master – that's all.'

Lewis Carroll, *Through the Looking-glass*

In the above quotation, Alice, in a conversation with the most famous egg in history, could well be discussing globalization. The question we shall concern ourselves with in this chapter is whether the word 'globalization' can indeed 'mean so many different things' and which definition of globalization, if any, emerges as master. Globalization theories have become popular in academia as well as among the general public, and I argue that sociological theories have contributed to the political rhetoric in the public realm. The fact that 'globalization' has gained currency in both academia and politics is likely more than just coincidence, a point requiring some elaboration. Scott (1997) has accurately distinguished between these two arenas as the political project and diagnostic analysis. The latter, based on the German *Zeitdiagnose*, refers to social science debates that focus on culture rather than economics (I hereafter refer to this school as the cultural school). Furthermore, Scott raises very important questions about the connection between the two and about whether the cultural debate has inadvertently bought into the political rhetoric of globalization, thereby bolstering the legitimation of 'global talk.' I argue that there has been enough bleeding between the two that a 'pure' theory of globalization is now untenable. Over its relatively short history, the term has become so ideologically sticky that it is no longer possible to use the word without invoking its political imperatives of increased competitiveness and lean states. To put it bluntly, the amount of confusion and ideology surrounding the term 'globalization' has rendered it useless as an analytical tool. It has been killed by its own success.

To set the stage for this argument, I first delineate contemporary definitions of globalization and highlight their similarities and differences. I then show how the cultural and political debates diverge as well as converge, and illustrate how the cultural arguments contribute to the political project of globalization as a whole. Throughout, the idea of globalization as something novel should be kept in mind. Scott's observation that globalization serves as a *Zeitdiagnose*, an analysis of our times, remains important because it cuts to the heart of whether globalization distinguishes contemporary times from the past.

Introduction

The word 'globalization' is of relatively recent vintage, a fact that has led to a constant redrawing of the semantic map. The introduction of new definitions, qualifications, limitations, and provisos has made the task of containing what globalization means (and – just as important – what it does not mean) an arduous one. While some authors are very specific about what globalization means, others use it in a generalized way. Still others may be critical of the concept yet resort to using it anyway. The most dissuading element is that examples from various strands are fused together in an overwhelming flood of evidence. Like a spilled bag of marbles, this onslaught is difficult to contain. As soon as one reaches for an errant marble, others roll away. It is not enough to cast doubt on a particular strand of globalization, such as production, because then questions about other forms of globalization arise – about communication, for example. In order to effectively defuse the globalization argument, a counter-argument is needed that refutes all its strands, a futile endeavour indeed. The fact is that the concept of globalization is more appropriate to a discussion of some processes (e.g., communication) than others (e.g., movement of labour). Nevertheless, the premises and conclusions of the various strands of globalization are often conflated, leading to the conclusion that globalization is indeed a fact. Given these factors, the globalization argument often appears unstoppable, for conceding the legitimacy of one aspect of globalization opens the door to a flood of other claims.

This book is specifically concerned about the globalization of production and financial services and its implications for the nation-state, and for Canada in particular. One cannot, however, ignore the theories about the globalization of culture that have gained popularity over the years in both sociology and cultural studies. Cultural theories of globalization are of course related in some ways to those of economics, but they diverge in many and important ways. First, we will examine popular definitions and then compare these to the cultural definitions.

Definitions

Nederveen Pieterse (1995: 45) observes that in the social sciences there are as many definitions of globalization as there are disciplines. I would even judge this assessment as too optimistic and contend that there are as many definitions as there are authors, indicating that even in a global world there is little consensus. Since the word is relatively new it has provided theorists, journalists, writers, and commentators with the opportunity to forge their own definitions. However, while the reasons for globalization vary widely – they commonly encompass technology, communications, trade, production, financial services, and popular culture – the conclusion is consistently the same, and that is that globalization leads to the dismantling of borders and the decline of the nation-state. As Giddens writes: 'The debates about globalisation ... have concentrated mainly upon its implications for the nation state' (2002: 18).

The vast majority of definitions of globalization are about economic globalization, and these will be discussed first. It is also here that the political imperatives of globalization are most explicit. This literature includes contributions from many sources: governments, supranational organizations such as the World Bank and the International Monetary Fund (IMF), think tanks (both left and right), magazines, journals, and newspapers. Other aspects of globalization are sometimes discussed in the public sphere, the Internet being a particularly popular one, but the overall emphasis is on the economic aspect of globalization and its associated political fallout – primarily, the impotence of the state.

Often, these analyses are quite pessimistic. A common perception of globalization is that corporations are becoming increasingly mobile and searching for profits outside the industrial world, resulting in the movement of jobs from the First World to the Third (see, for example, Teeple

2000). The view that globalization threatens national sovereignty is also popular among the anti-globalization movement, a stance endorsed by Jack Layton, the leader of the New Democratic Party (NDP), who during the 2004 election campaign asserted that 'global corporate powers are taking over our country and threatening our independence' (*Globe and Mail*, 25 May 2004: A23). This newfound power of capital has prompted many observers to predict the state's demise, particularly with respect to the provision of welfare-state services (a topic discussed in more detail in chapter 7). Most criticisms originating from the left, both academic and political, are primarily concerned with the unchecked power of global corporations, a power that is purported to present a threat to democracy and lead to the end of the nation-state:

> At the start of the twenty-first century the inadequacy of the nation-state as the sovereign unit of political organization and economic regulation is increasingly clear ... The era of globalization captures an awareness that at a certain point in the last third of the twentieth century large corporations became more single-mindedly transnational in focus, seeing their home country as only one among many profit centers and reorganizing their operations to coincide with this vision of a globalized world economy. (Tabb 2002: 1, 2)

This position is quite common and constitutes one of the major premises of the globalization thesis. McMurtry (2003: 24) writes that '[t]ransnational trade and investment regulations fashioned by corporate trade lawyers now override national economic sovereignty across continents ...' A similar view is shared by newspaper columnist Ian Urquhart, who fears that 'Globalization means real power has shifted to transnational agencies and corporations; national governments don't matter any more' (*Toronto Star*, 28 June 2004: A25).

More recent debates – particularly in economics, but also spilling into the mainstream media – have meant to highlight the integration of national economies. The definition put forward by Joseph Stiglitz, winner of the 2001 Nobel Prize in economics, defines globalization as 'the removal of barriers to free trade and the closer integration of national economies' (2002: ix). The IMF has defined globalization as 'The post-World War II phenomenon ... of increasingly close international integration of markets both for goods and services, and for capital' (Bordo and Krajnyak 1997: 112). In some circles of academia, however, attempts have been made to distinguish between globalization and internationalization of the economy. Weiss writes that a truly globalized economy would weaken the state while an international one would merely change its role (Weiss 1997: 6). Hirst and Thompson (1996) have made a similar argument. They provide two models or ideal types, one of increased internationalization, which results in a changing role for the state, and one of increased globalization, which would indeed endanger the autonomy of the state.

The important point to note here is that the definition provided by Stiglitz and other economists for what globalization *is* (increased integration) is identical to the one used by some political economists to show what globalization *is not*. This distinction – between increased interdependence orchestrated by nation-states and globalization, where supranational organizations (transnational corporations, the United Nations) have usurped the sovereignty of the nation-state – is crucial. Unfortunately, this same distinction is glossed over in most accounts, leaving globalization a much stronger force.

It should come as no surprise that business observers see the weakening of the state as a favourable development, one in which the market rules and the consumer becomes king. In this scenario, the nation-state is being squeezed out by global powers, and its demise is predicted in unequivocal terms. The best-known proponent of this school is Kenichi Ohmae, who wrote extensively about the topic in the mid- to late 1990s. The title of one of Ohmae's books, *The End of the Nation State* (1995), displays the confidence of this argument. In academia, these accounts are sometimes referred to as 'hyperglobalization' in order to illustrate their exaggerated viewpoint. Sociologists often dismiss these accounts, and especially the oversimplified version provided by Ohmae, as too sensationalistic and lacking in subtlety (Robertson and Khondker 1998).

Be that as it may, this version, which understands globalizing markets as undermining the power of the state, is, for better or worse, also the version people are most familiar with. To downplay this account of globalization as misinformed and inaccurate ignores what 'globalization' means to the average person in the street, to business people, to demonstrators, and to politicians. Humpty-Dumpty's interpretation of language notwithstanding, the meaning of a word is not something that is negotiated or decided upon by academics, but is derived from popular usage, a measure of what most people take the word to mean. Using this criterion, based on the sheer amount of exposure, this definition of globalization wins out.

The Death of the Nation-state

The end-of-the-nation-state conclusion is critical and for this reason requires further discussion. While left and right evaluate these developments differently, both delineate the same sequence of events and reach similar conclusions. The left laments the state's demise as the 'end of social reform,' while the right celebrates the ascendency of the market, only too happy to bid adieu to regulation. Again, there is a strong sense of inevitability permeating these accounts. According to business professor James Tiessen, '[There is a lack of] alternatives. Citizens [everywhere] can only expect more open markets, deregulation, privatization, lower taxes ... and reduced support for their disadvantaged. This policy set is required of all players in the global economy' (*Globe and Mail*, 13 July 2000: B10). Regulation, it should be pointed out, usually concerns progressive legislation such as social programs and minimum-wage laws, and not the kind of regulation that benefits business. Growing legislation, such as the myriad of agreements under the World Trade Organization (WTO), that attempts to regulate trade and protect intellectual property and investors' rights is wilfully ignored in these scenarios.

What becomes apparent when examining various accounts of globalization is that its popularity among both left and right can be explained by the fact that it aligns perfectly with already existing ideologies. For the right, free markets are identified as the saviour from government meddling, particularly social programs. For the left, on the other hand, free-market solutions and a perceived growth of multinational corporations are identified as the enemy. Both are positions long held by their respective parties. The moment that free markets emerged, opposition developed alongside, with socialists and anarchists of all stripes exposing their negative side. Fear of large corporations has a long history as well. Writing in 1776, Adam Smith refused to treat private corporations as a potential threat because he believed that self-interest in these institutions would become too diluted, an observation that was soon proved to be wrong. Starting in the mid-eighteen hundreds, Marx and Engels wrote extensively about the power of multinational corporations. Continuing in this tradition, Lenin (1939) identified monopoly capitalism as a final stage of capitalism. Writing in the 1930s, Berle and Means (1967) predicted a relapse into feudalism, where large corporations would rule instead of lords. In *The Modern Corporation and Private Property*, the authors estimated this would transpire within fifty years of the publication of their book.

Writing almost four decades later, Baran and Sweezy's (1966) *Monopoly Capital*, popular among the left in the 1960s, was an equally pessimistic analysis of the future of capitalism. Current accounts critical of multinationals adhere to a similar line of argumentation, the only difference being that they are now conducted within the theoretical framework of globalization.

What is true for the left is equally true for the right. The contemporary position taken by the right has been around for centuries: support for free markets and opposition to government interference. Starting more than two and a quarter centuries ago with Adam Smith's eloquent *Wealth of Nations* and his powerful metaphor of the invisible hand, any type of state intervention is anathema to the right. This baton was later carried by von Mises, Hayek, and Popper and continues to find expression in the extensive literature published by think-tanks such as the Fraser Institute in Canada and the Kiel Institute in Germany. Interestingly, in *Road to Serfdom*, Hayek wields the same threat as Berle and Means, the crucial difference being that it is not monopoly capitalism but socialism that is responsible for the regression to a feudal order.

For the left in particular, 'globalization' can be considered a euphemism for 'capitalism.' With the collapse of the Soviet Empire, political ideals associated with socialism have become increasingly less palpable. As a consequence of this failure, the left has been less willing to propose socialism as an alternative to capitalism. Critiques of capitalism have traditionally rested on the assumption that socialism would not share capitalism's shortcoming of allowing large wealth and income inequalities. Socialism, as such, has always existed as an alternative, if not explicitly then implicitly. But with the implosion of the Soviet Empire, socialism has become a less viable option. Globalization has provided a way out: consistent with a Marxist critique of capitalism, corporations and unfettered capitalism continue to be identified as the enemy; however, socialism is no longer the implicit alternative. This lack of an alternative has also played an important, if not central, role in the development of globalization. Teeple's (2000) work is a case in point. In his analysis of globalization, the option of a socialist or even social democratic regime is dismissed outright, and the only choices offered are, to quote Woody Allen, 'between despair and utter hopelessness ... and total extinction' (Allen 1981: 81).

The story is diametrically different for the right in that globalization is something to be celebrated rather than dreaded. In many ways the components of globalization constitute a wish list for business: Less government, or even no government, and fewer regulations, lower taxes and fewer social programs, and no borders to impede the movement of goods, services, or capital. The threat of mobility has come to serve as the perfect weapon against regulation, and against taxes in particular. Corporations and capital, it is said, based on market signals, naturally gravitate to where returns are highest. High wages and taxes are considered disincentives to capital because they cut into profits, while low wages and taxes are, well, good for business. While such nostrums are as old as the market itself, the globalization 'imperative' has provided fresh legitimacy for these arguments and further enhanced the bargaining power of capital. Whether the threat of mobility is real or imagined is another question altogether, one that is discussed in some detail in the following chapters; the point is that it is used as a threat, and sometimes effectively so.

But even the role of business is often considered as merely reactive, its actions understood to be necessary to survive in the global economy. On a national basis, globalization rhetoric has enabled business and government to transfer responsibility for their policies to a mysterious force called globalization. When Chrétien commented that we 'can't stop globalization we can only adapt to it,' he expressed a pervasive fatalism that has allowed the abdication of responsibility by business as well as government. In short, demands by labour or voters can no longer be taken seriously in an age of globalization.

One should not fail to notice the irony of the position taken by both business and government. Commentators on the right have long criticized Marxists for being rigid and deterministic, yet their arguments are now remarkably alike. In this sense, business rhetoric has taken on a Marxist cast. Diane Francis (*Maclean's*, 27 Apr. 1992) has likened free trade to gravity – both are inevitable, she writes. This is not to say that those on the left have abandoned their fatalistic stance, as the preceding examples given earlier well illustrate. The theme that emerges from these versions is that globalization is a structure that unfolds and has a logic of its own, leaving little room for agency.

To summarize: under its political guise, globalization is a mere adjunct to the larger debates about the appropriateness of government interference, the threat of unfettered markets, and hostility towards large corporations. Next we examine theories that are currently popular in academia and look for similarities to the more popular accounts just discussed.

The Multifaceted Approach: The Globalization of Everything

Globalization is, of course, not exclusively about the economy but encompasses other developments as well. As a matter of fact, economic approaches are considered reductionist by many, Robertson (1992) in particular. Albrow (1996: 4) outlines five ways in which the world is becoming more globalized: in addition to the economy, he enumerates the environment (the destruction of which is a global threat); the military (ditto on the destruction); communications; and the phenomenology of globalization – the increased realization that we are living on a globe (particularly popular among sociologists). Albrow (1996: 130) defines economic globalization as 'the growth of economic activity which functions beyond national economies and is organized with reference to the world as a whole.' His work is a good example of the common themes that link academic and popular accounts, as he perpetuates some of the more popular myths about globalization. He is of the opinion that the world economy presents many obstacles to the nation-state, some insurmountable (128), and urges that 'transnational corporations cannot ignore any potential source of advantage or threat anywhere on the globe' (130). In addition to Albrow's five points, two other strands of globalization are commonly highlighted: the globalization of culture, as outlined by Robertson (1992), and the globalization of travel in the form of tourism, migration, and labour markets (Waters 2001).

The multifaceted approach, or the globalization of everything, has become particularly popular. Lash and Urry (1994: 280) sum this position up well when they write that globalization is the 'immense flows of capital, money, goods, services, people, information, technologies, policies, ideas, images, and regulations.' This sentiment is echoed by an editorial in the *Globe and Mail* (9 Oct. 1998: A22), a long-time champion of globalization, further revealing the similarities between popular and academic accounts: 'Globalization ... is a dizzying increase in cross-border exchanges of all kinds – information, travel and culture as well as goods, services and capital.' In other words, the harsh winds of globalization are like a hurricane that moves everything that isn't nailed down. And like a hurricane, this force does not respect national borders.

As we shall soon see, generalizations about even one of these strands are difficult to sustain. The appropriateness of this criticism increases as additional strands of globalization are introduced. This problem is further exacerbated by the conflation of premises of the various strands of globalization, premises that are then used to support the same conclusion: the coming down of borders. Thus premises about telecommunications are used to justify the coming down of borders with respect to the economy, although the two are different processes. Giddens writes that 'globalization is not a single process but a complex mixture of processes, which often act in contradictory ways' (1990: 15), a statement that makes one wonder whether general observations can be made about this mixture of processes at all, the aim of globalization. The point is that borders do not present themselves as equally permeable to the various strands of globalization. While the telephone has effectively made distance meaningless, it has become increasingly difficult for people to migrate across borders. With the increase of surveillance in the wake of the terrorist attacks in the United States in 2001, it could easily be argued that it is now more difficult to cross national borders than ever before. As Massey (1994) has argued, movement across borders also greatly depends on one's class, gender, and ethnicity.

The association between globalization and the eradication of borders no doubt finds its origins in the work of Marshall McLuhan. The ubiquitous metaphor of McLuhan's 'global village,' originally conceived for television, has been grafted on to all other aspects of globalization – production and trade, for example. Arguments are usually structured in such a way that the powerful imagery of the global village comes first, and the facts are then selectively presented to support that conclusion. As we shall see, products, services, and corporations are a lot less mobile than is commonly believed. These differences are mostly glossed over, allowing the overall conclusion to stand (the coming down of borders). In other words, the evidence for globalization is typically treated as though there is no difference between its various strands:

> Globalization refers to a set of processes – many economic, others political and cultural – that involves the rapid increase of cross-border movements of goods, capital, ideas, and people that has characterized the late twentieth century. This increased intensity of trade has raised concerns here in Canada and elsewhere about the implications of globalization for sovereignty, policy autonomy of governments, and thus democracy. (Smythe 2003: 326)

In this example, as with previous ones, we find economics, politics, culture, goods, capital, ideas, and people all lumped together, as though they were identical in their ability to leap borders. But as we shall soon see, how well goods and services trade across borders, to say nothing of people and culture, varies significantly. Furthermore, the connection between these various strands and the changing role and influence of government is presented as a natural progression, one that is seldom argued for. This approach, best described as a theoretical leap, is common in the literature. As mentioned above, attitudes towards government intervention have changed little over time; the only difference is that, in globalization discussions, arguments about the state tend to be more descriptive than normative. In the past, the question that has traditionally been asked is whether government interference was morally justified (see, for example, Nozick 1974). This question is now completely sidestepped, and accounts are becoming more descriptive in that they claim to report how the world works. That is, globalization is subverting the power of the state, and there is no need to argue further about the morality of the situation.

One needs to keep in mind that there exists a division of labour between government and business in capitalist societies. Production and trade have always been in private hands, and this has never posed a threat to nation-states. The question then arises, Why would it now? And to what degree has the ability of states to govern really changed? As is argued in the chapter on the nation-state, claims with respect to the diminution or elimination of the state have been greatly exaggerated.

The problem with the 'globalization-of-everything' position is that while some processes may be highly globalized (e.g., communications and television, in particular), others are less so (e.g., the movement of people). And where one process could potentially be harmful to governments (e.g., the unfettered movement of people),[1] others are likely to be only minor in their impact (e.g., the Internet). Unfortunately, the globalization argument does not allow for such distinctions. We should also note that, with the elision of these distinctions, any increase in cross-national activity, such as the trade of goods, is automatically taken to be a measure of the decline of national sovereignty. But why trade, for example, should compromise national sovereignty is never explained. Moreover, if trade does weaken states, why would governments around the world pursue so many free-trade agreements, and with such enthusiasm?

The essence of the problem is that the imagery of globalization is powerful and that sober analysis is a poor counterweight to highly impressionistic examples such as the World Wide Web, Coca-Cola, and CNN. Yet on its own, 'globalization' is an exceedingly vague term.

The tendency to speak about globalization devoid of any content – that is, without some elaboration about what is being globalized – lies at the root of this problem. In order to avoid this confusion, it is important always to be very specific about what particular strand of globalization is being discussed, be it production, financial services, culture, entertainment, or whatever.

Grand Theory: Sociological and Cultural Debates

The globalization debate is atypical among contemporary intellectual debates in that it is also widely discussed in the public sphere, something that cannot be said for either modernism, postmodernism, or post-Fordism. The central question to be considered in this section is whether the academic and public debates are separate or, as Scott (1997: 2) asks, whether the social science debate contributes to the interpretation that globalization is 'historically inevitable and unstoppable?'

The postmodernism debate of the 1980s was built on the shaky foundation of modernism, but there continues to be little agreement about both concepts (see Berman 1982; Therborn 1995). As if this weren't enough, the concept of globalization, equally vague and cumbersome, was plunked clumsily atop the already teetering structure of the other two. That the result is often confusion should not be surprising. In theoretical terms globalization can be seen as a reaction to the one-sidedness of modernization theories, and as an attempt to bring other cultures back into the debate (Mandalios 1996: 290; Robertson 1992: 15).[2] In another sense, the globalization thesis can also be viewed as a continuation of the postmodernism debate popular in the 1980s that, like its predecessor, addresses all sorts of issues such as the end of modernism (of which the nation-state is deemed to be a primary feature), the ushering in of a new era, and the role of identity. However, others position globalization, along with Americanization, and McDonaldization, under the larger rubric of modernism (Ritzer and Stillman 2003: 31). As we saw with politics, in the cultural debate we also find considerable disagreement about what globalization means and when it first began.

Roland Robertson and Anthony Giddens are the two most important theorists of globalization in sociology – Robertson self-admittedly so, with Giddens being a more recent convert. Rosenberg (2000), Albrow (2004; 1994), and Waters (2001) all identify Giddens as a key theorist in the globalization debate. At first, Giddens's approach to globalization was one of cautious scepticism. As he himself noted, the topic of globalization has been 'much bandied about but ... only poorly understood' (1994: 4). In his earlier work, Giddens writes that 'modernism is inherently globalizing' and traces its origins to the beginning of the modern age.[3] In that sense, globalization is not new and can merely be thought of as an adjunct to his already established views on modernity. Giddens's initial *Zeitdiagnose* was specifically about modernity and 'high modernity,' in which globalization played a relatively minor role. But over time Giddens became more enamoured of the concept, as indicated by one of his more recent titles, *Runaway World: How Globalisation Is Reshaping Our Lives* (2002). Giddens offers the kind of comprehensive and far-reaching definition of globalization criticized above, writing that it would be a mistake to describe it in economic terms only, as it is 'political, technological and cultural, as well ...' (Giddens 2002: 10).

Robertson is primarily concerned with the increase of global consciousness, the idea that the world is becoming one place. His major statement on this topic, one that still stands as a definitive work in the field, is *Globalization: Social Theory and Global Culture* (1992). Overall, Robertson considers the process of globalization to be unstoppable. His statement that 'trends towards the unicity of the world are ... inexorable' (1992: 26) answers the question of whether cultural theories contribute to the more popular idea that globalization is inevitable. Scott has criticized the cultural school for lacking a definition for what globalization is and merely relying on definitions about what it is not. This charge could well be directed at Robertson, who vehemently tries to dissociate himself from 'economic-historical perspectives of the world as a whole' (1992: 135), primarily in reference to Wallerstein's work. Yet he offers no alternative. How successful he is at dissociating himself from the economic perspective is another question. Robertson's argument is relevant for our purposes in that he draws conclusions about the end-of-the-nation-state argument similar to those of political accounts. It is also here that he raises issues about the economy: 'With the rapid growth of various supra-national and transnational organizations, movements and institutions (such as global capitalism and the global media system) the boundaries between societies have become more porous because they are much more subject to "interference and constraint" from the outside' (Robertson 1992: 5).' In this passage, Robertson uses a logic and line of argumentation similar to those found in more popular debates. Although he does qualify his observation by maintaining that the nation-state continues to be a powerful institution, the difference is only one of degree. His conflation of various strands, in this case global capitalism and media, and his assumption that in combination they are responsible for the weakening of the state are akin to those of more popular accounts. That these are vastly different activities with vastly different political consequences is ignored.

In an interesting twist, Robertson contends that globalization preceded modernity and therefore provided the conditions necessary for the nation-state, thus laying responsibility for both the introduction and the decline of the nation-state at the feet of globalization. This line of reasoning has subsequently been adopted by other theorists. Rather than questioning the assumptions that underlie this logic, other authors have taken Robertson's lead and elaborated on it. As Nederveen Pieterse writes (1995: 49), 'It is by now a familiar argument that nation-state formation is an expression and function of globalization and not a process contrary to it [he sources Robertson 1992]. At the same time it is apparent that the present phase of globalization involves the relative weakening of nation-states – as in the weakening of the "national economy" in the context of economic globalism and, culturally, the decline of patriotism.'

It is worthwhile noting the casual introduction of the 'now familiar argument' as (the only) evidence of how globalization is responsible for both the introduction *and* the demise of the nation-state. As is typical of much sociological writing, the language here is more tentative than in popular accounts (for a criticism of this type of writing see Becker 1986). Rather than predicting the outright demise of the nation-state, these theorists allude to the 'relative weakening of the nation-state.' But the message is essentially the same. Those who still attribute some power to the nation-state are dismissed in a somewhat patronizing fashion or, worse, referred to pejoratively as xenophobes.

> By seeing their security and prosperity as the result of national policies, national interests or national decision-makers, contemporary consumers and producers often mistake thoroughly transnational or largely local forces as the working of their nation-state. Similarly, xenophobic political appeals, stressing exclusively nationalistic benefits or costs, occlude how closely coupled most present-day core economies and societies have become. Borders today are highly porous, and the pressure of global flows of goods and services [is] continuously eroding them even more every day. (Luke 1995: 101)

Here again the emphasis is on structure. Agency, even on the level of national government, is casually dismissed. Luke attributes the grinding down of borders to 'global flows of goods and services,' as though these events happened outside the control of national governments. As well, he assumes that this erosion will continue to increase, something that we shall question in the section on trade.

The two preceding passages are both taken from separate readings in a collection entitled *Global Modernities*. In the introduction, Featherstone and Lash (1995: 1–2) write that one of the two organizing themes of globalization is the 'sociocultural processes [that] are emerging as the global begins to replace the nation-state as the decisive framework for social life.' The similarities between cultural and popular accounts on the issue of the nation-state are undeniable. In response to Scott's question, then, we are forced to conclude that the academic debate does indeed feed into some of the same assumptions of the more popular accounts. In a special issue on globalization published by *International Sociology*, Robertson and Khondker (1998) address some of the problems associated with the term 'globalization.' The authors are particularly dismayed with the type of economistic accounts of globalization that have become popular among the general public and in political economy, as discussed above. Theirs is an attempt to resurrect a more holistic and comprehensive definition of globalization. Interestingly, two articles in the same issue display the same economistic account that Robertson and Khondker are so critical of. Writing from the political economy perspective, these authors fail even to allude to the cultural aspect of the term that Robertson and Khondker champion. This is indicative of an ongoing trend where cultural and political economy theorists are for the most part talking past one another. While some works have attempted to marry the political economy and cultural aspects (e.g., Waters 2001; Albrow 1996), these are the exception, and the bulk of the literature, particularly that emanating from political economy, is written as though the cultural version of globalization did not exist. No matter how loudly Robertson and his colleagues insist that we need to consider the convenience of a concept like globalization, they are being ignored. In many ways, then, this is a one-sided debate.

Robertson's approach can be criticized on the grounds that it ignores the power of language. As we saw in the introduction, Williams points out that some words come loaded with all kinds of assumptions about social relations. In this sense, the word 'globalization' is so tainted with ideological baggage about the relationship between capital and labour, the role of the nation-state, and the power of the market, that any attempt to resurrect a purified sociological version would likely be futile.[4] Meanwhile, most academics in political economy completely ignore the cultural definition of globalization – and for good reason. In political economy, globalization is generally seen as a recent phenomenon, and evidence is marshalled to show historical precedent. In cultural accounts, globalization is considered to go back for millennia. The two debates are separate, yet what they have in common, especially observations about the coming down of borders and the dwindling of the nation-state, cannot be ignored.

As we have seen, the cultural and popular debates are not completely dissimilar, particularly in their view of the role of the state. In response to Scott's question, then, we must say that cultural theories contribute to the rhetoric of globalization, given that their conclusions are strikingly similar. Theorists such as Robertson provide much of the groundwork for the current debate about globalization in sociology, whether it is about culture, communications, or religion, and their contribution is critical to the understanding of the current era. In this sense, Robertson's take on globalization as a *Zeitdiagnose* cannot be separated from an account of globalization as political project. Conclusions about the nation-state are shared with the political project, and this brings to the fore all kinds of imperatives about markets, the welfare state, and the ability to manage these processes.

What has not become clear in this discussion is the time line of globalization. If Robertson's account is a *Zeitdiagnose*, it raises the very important issue of a break with the past, an issue that represents an especially vague component of the already vague topic of globalization.

A New Age?

The crux of the globalization argument ultimately turns on whether there has been a fundamental change in the way the world is organized over the past few years or decades. As with definitions, we find that the date at which globalization is said to begin varies from author to author. Teeple (2000) traces the beginning of globalization to only the 1980s. Hobsbawm (1994), like many economic historians, claims it originated alongside the Industrial Revolution in Great Britain in the eighteenth century, only to be interrupted by the two world wars. Many historical accounts equate globalization with capitalism or modernity – as, for example, Giddens, who sees globalization as accompanying modernism and as originating in the late fifteenth century (Giddens 2002; 1990).

Robertson identifies globalization as a process that is more than two millennia old; at the same time, he distinguishes a rise of global consciousness that dates to only this century (1992). Similarly, Waters (2001) traces globalization back centuries, but identifies an acceleration that started in the 1960s.

In general, one can say that in popular and political economy debates, the beginning, or acceleration, date is usually given as somewhere between the Second World War and the 1980s. In these accounts, globalization serves as a contrast term, similar to post-Fordism and post-modernism but without the prefix which aims to distinguish the contemporary age from the past (Kumar 1995). In cultural debates, it is sometimes difficult to say whether globalization is meant to be a contrast term, as the date often spans centuries. This raises the issue of how far a *Zeitdiagnose* can be stretched and still be appropriate as a characterization of our times. The farther back one goes, the more doubts are raised, and at two thousand years one indeed begins to wonder about what ties this age together. The question then becomes whether globalization is a disjuncture from the past (i.e., a new age) or not. Equally important, in cultural debates the question arises whether and how the process is separate from modernity.

There is a crucial distinction, then, between those who see globalization as something that developed at some point following the Second World War and those who see it as having deeper historical roots. The post-Second World War view is usually adopted by the political project and political economy accounts, while the long-term historical perspective is taken by the cultural theorists and economic historians. As a matter of fact, many political economy accounts fail even to provide a date. Globalization is just one of many explanations for the world economic slump that began in the early 1970s with the closing of the gold window and the first oil shock. In political economy debates, proponents of globalization argue that there is something fundamentally different about the world economy, while detractors disagree. Much the same is true for popular and business accounts.

Things are somewhat more complicated in cultural theory. Both Robertson and Giddens identify globalization as a process that harks back centuries. Robertson dates globalization to before the birth of Christ, two thousand years ago. Giddens understands modernity (and therefore globalization) as emerging in the fifteen hundreds. In short, he denies a recent disjuncture with the past. The only break Giddens identifies is one with traditional societies; that is, modernity is central and serves as the contrast term. To Giddens, globalization is primarily about time-space distanciation and telecommunications. He tends to downplay arguments about the power of corporations (1994: 89), and draws attention to the fact, based on Weber, that states continue to be the only organizations that can legitimately exercise violence. Giddens ties contemporary society solidly to the past and exposes much of what we consider new today as a faithful companion of modernity. In short, Giddens's observations reveal that contemporary changes are part and parcel of the 'juggernaut of modernity.' This raises the question 'What's new?' about globalization, a question that will be investigated further in the following chapter.

While I have some sympathy for Giddens's view, and relatedly Hobsbawm's (who sees it as a result of the Industrial Revolution), these conceptualizations of globalization are not really about anything that is new but merely resurrect old arguments – about modernity and industrialization, respectively. In some sense, these theories are just tacked onto a position already taken, often as a way of incorporating globalization. As is well known in sociological and economic circles, the globalizing tendencies of industrialism and modernism were central tenets of theories put forward by Comte, St Simon, Adam Smith, and Marx. As an adjunct to one of these theories, globalization fails to illuminate anything new about the world. Worse, it tends to further complicate already complicated theoretical issues.

Robertson, on the other hand, who himself takes credit for the naming of the concept (1992: 3), does identify a break, although exactly where this break occurs is difficult to pinpoint. Robertson tries to have it both ways by acknowledging the past as well as isolating the new. His argument becomes most vulnerable when he simultaneously delineates globalization as a process that goes back millennia and that also has the markings of a new age in which we think more globally (the phenomenological aspect). By proclaiming that globalization is both new and old, Robertson's theory fits well both with accounts of globalization that emphasize its novelty and with those that see it as a continuation of an ongoing historical process. Essentially, he declares that globalization is both old and new, a vagueness that may well border on contradiction. In summary: Giddens, in addition to being at times more critical of the concept of globalization, is also more consistent in that he discerns modernity (and therefore globalization) as a disjuncture from traditional society. By focusing on the continuation of modernity, he avoids the need to explain this confusing old-new contradiction that Robertson and Waters are forced to grapple with.

This view of globalization as both new and old is echoed by other globalists. Waters (2001: 46–7) explains the current interest in globalization by the fact that it 'is a predominant pattern in contemporary social change [and it should therefore] not come as a surprise that several sociologists should hit on the concept at the same time.' But this contradicts statements that globalization goes back 'at least ... to the sixteenth century' (Waters 2001: 62). This raises the very important question of why a process that has been going on for centuries has only been identified in the past two decades or so, and then by politicians, sociologists, business people, and journalists alike. More than anything this reveals that cultural and political theories of globalization have similar roots. The fact that the end of the nation-state is predicted in both the political project and cultural theories hints at their common origins and thereby rules out coincidence.

Albrow (1996; 2004) is more forthright than most theorists and unequivocally affirms that the modern age has been replaced by a global one. Albrow sees the global age as a rejection of the institutions of modernity: rationality, growth, control of nature, and so forth. This has been brought on by the realization of the finitude of the planet (1996: 106). For him, three events frame the global age, starting with the dropping of atom bombs on Hiroshima and Nagasaki in 1945, followed by the falling of the Berlin Wall in 1989, and culminating in the recognition of the potential consequences of global warming (Albrow 1996; 2004). To him modernity, with its ideology of expansion, and the end of the nation-state are intimately linked (1996: 4). Once expansion is curtailed, so is modernism. The glass is full, so to speak, and the rules change, ushering in a new era. In Albrow's thesis, as in Beck's theory of risk, the recognition of environmental deterioration plays a central role, but Albrow breaks with Beck, who is a proponent of reflexive modernity, with his insistence on the inauguration of a new age. Be that as it may, Albrow firmly situates globalization in the postwar period.

The debate about the starting date is crucial. If one takes the position that globalization is new (as do, for example, Teeple, Albrow, or the IMF [see Bordo and Krajnyak 1997]), then one could plausibly argue that changes such as the decline of the nation-state are occurring. If, however, one argues that globalization is part of a longer historical process, then one must explain how a process that gave birth to the nation-state now serves to destroy it. More importantly, given that the 'new' and 'long historical process' positions appear to exist comfortably side by side, it is difficult to argue against globalization. Globalists have successfully used this tactic as a defence. When attempts are made to undermine the short-term globalization argument by providing evidence that it is part of a long historical process, cultural globalists respond by invoking someone like Wallerstein, whose world-system theory dates back to the fifteenth century.

By acknowledging this past, globalists have attempted to appropriate the economic-historical debate and present it as their own. (I see this debate as including economic historians such as Wallerstein and Maddison; see chapter 3.) Yet writers like Wallerstein are neutral towards globalization in that they fail to acknowledge the political imperatives that go along with this concept and that are part of the present debate. Wallerstein himself has referred to globalization as a misleading concept (2002: 249). As a matter of fact, as we shall soon see, economic historians see nothing unusual about the present phase of the economy. Globalists, however, use the economic debate as evidence that globalization has been an ongoing historical process and thereby, intentionally or not, brand the economic historians as globalists. Wallerstein is lauded by many as the first sociologist to have written about the world economy. Nederveen Pieterse (1995: 47) misrepresents Wallerstein's position by imposing a beginning date of 'globalization' for Wallerstein's history of world capitalism. Labelling these theorists as globalists automatically pushes them into the debate, whether they want to participate or not. This tactic is somewhat disingenuous, as many of these writers see little value in the concept and try to distance themselves from it. It also shifts the focus of the debate from whether globalization exists to when it first started. In the latter case, globalization is presented as a given that requires no further confirmation.

The point is that globalization reveals itself to be a rather useless term if the issue of the date is not settled. Even more to the point, if it is a contrast term, what is it in contrast to? If globalization does hark back centuries, one must wonder about the similarities between CNN and the rise of world religions two thousand years ago. Without a specific date, the beginning of globalization can be moved arbitrarily to suit one's objectives. A lack of consensus surrounding the date means that no effective counter-position can be taken. For example, the argument that Canada's economy has long been globalized can easily be accommodated by Robertson's theory, as can the syndication of TV shows such as *Dallas, Friends*, or *Bay Watch*. Robertson casts his net widely, and his definitional boundaries for globalization include nothing less than the globe going back two millennia. As long as it happened within that time period and on this planet, his theory can comfortably accommodate it. Obviously, this is too far-reaching to qualify as a *Zeit-diagnose*. Such definitional messiness would not be possible with a theory that identifies a break, as is the case with some popular accounts and political economy accounts.

The pinpointing of a break raises further issues with respect to Robertson's work. As we saw, dates range from two millennia ago to the 1980s. Interestingly, Robertson first set the date for globalization as originating a hundred years ago. But as evidence critical of globalization poured in and showed that the process was not new to either industrial, modern, or capitalistic society, Robertson was forced to move the date. This he did, to two thousand years ago (Robertson 1992; Friedman 1995: 70). As the organization of our daily lives (wage labour, urban living) has very little resemblance to that of two thousand years ago, this could be considered somewhat of an overreaction. If one uses the criterion of extra-national developments, as Robertson does, one may just as well move the date back to the very beginning of human history. This is precisely what Daniels and Hyslop (2003: 326) do when they define globalization as a process that 'began with early humans as they migrated out of Africa before recorded history.' This serves as convincing evidence that the human race has been 'globalized' from its very beginning, the presence of humans on every continent (with the exception of Antarctica) serving as irrefutable evidence. The subsequent 'discovery' of these continents shows how much we rely on written documents as history and tend to dismiss events for which we lack direct or written evidence (Garraty and Gay 1972: 49). The dearth of knowledge about how our ancestors were able to vault across continents does not take away from the fact that political and geographical constraints meant little back then. If a global community is one without borders then the world was arguably more global 100,000 years ago than it is now. Throughout the past one hundred millennia, the free movement of people has been a constant, and probably to a greater extent in earler times than now. It helps to remember that the English are not native to Great Britain, nor the Turks to Turkey, nor the Malay to Malaysia (Sowell 1996).

Robertson arguably has the most invested in globalization and has understandably been one of its staunchest proponents. In an article by Robertson and Khondker, the authors attempt to rescue the term 'globalization' from ambiguity, arguing that its omission would leave us without a term that includes issues of global reach such as the environment, human rights, and the economy (1998: 33). The authors lament the popular adoption of the term 'globalization,' as it 'endangers [the] analytic and interpretive viability and usefulness' of the term (1998: 26), and seek to bring it back to sociology where they claim it originated, only to be appropriated by the popular press. However, evidence shows that the term first originated in the business sector, not in academia, confirming Harvey's suspicion that globalization is a plot by the banking sector (Harvey 1995: 8). Robertson maintains that he was the first to use the word 'globalization' in print, in 1985 (Robertson 1985). But *The American Banker* had already used the term in 1978. In 1983, two years before Robertson's article first appeared, a book about globalization written by management guru Theodore Levitt (1983) caused much discussion in the media across North America. In other words, by the time Robertson 'introduced' the concept to the academic world, it was already in wide use in the business press.[5]

It is curious that Robertson should hold so tenaciously to this term, especially since his field is cultural studies, a discipline notorious for its neologisms. Despite Robertson's protestations, at this point it is no longer possible to use the word without invoking all the political overtones that it has collected over the years. The crucial point here is that the globalization thesis in cultural studies is not able to free itself from the ideological baggage that spills over from the political realm. The overwhelming predominance of ideas associated with economic globalization, as well as allusions to global economics in cultural theory, strongly indicate that the course of the meaning of 'globalization' is now as fixed as that of words such as 'fascism' and 'dictator.' The fact that sociologists, journalists, politicians, and the public hit on the term at the same time strongly indicates similar beginnings. In other words, there is more at play here than coincidence. Whether cultural theories arose independently of political theories is really a moot point, as the two are so inextricably tied now that it is impossible to separate them.

Self-fulfilling Prophecy

Somewhat tangential to the debate about definitions but central to that about globalization in general is the issue of self-fulfilling prophecy. To be precise, this argument posits that the *idea* of globalization is so powerful that it will eventually shape the world in its own image. This argument has strong echoes of the social constructionist school. Here the starting point for analysis is political philosophy (Scott 1997: 10). As people believe that globalization is a reality they will construct the world that way, or (as Robertson might say) structure the world as one place, and thus it will become so. Writing about globalization, Piven states that the 'explanation itself has become a political force, helping to create the institutional realities it purportedly merely describes' (1995: 108). Waters (2001) projects that the nation-state will crumble once we act as though the nation-state were powerless. To some degree, this is exactly what the political right has been practising; pretend the state does not exist and eventually it will go away. While there is some merit to this argument, it has definite limitations. Thinking, wishing, or theorizing the state away works only to a point. As we shall see in the chapter on the nation-state (chapter 7), governments have taken on enormous responsibilities over the past few decades, and to shed these obligations requires considerably more effort than mere wishing. In the real world, the state's responsibilities are complex and involve bureaucrats, voters, interest groups, and even other states. For example, business often acts in contradictory fashions: it both rejects government intervention and cannot survive without it. While business routinely toes the free-market/globalization line, it also depends on government to enforce rules (e.g., patent laws) and provide services.

No matter how much one opposes government intervention, sooner or later conditions arise where that intervention is needed. As individuals and institutions, we often fail to notice how much we depend on government (e.g., for free education and use of infrastructure). In this sense, it is governments that often act like the invisible hand, a fact often overlooked by pro-globalists. As Heilbroner has so astutely noted, history does not take corners, and the disappearance of the state would be a sharp corner indeed, self-fulfilling prophecy notwithstanding. Seen through the lens of a political project, we can see that this is mostly a normative debate – that is, a debate about whether we should support state intervention – and not a debate about whether the nation-state will actually endure. This question will be discussed in detail in chapter 7.

Conclusion

There is no doubt that 'global talk' is a relatively recent development, while the time line for the process of globalization itself is much more nebulous. In popular and political economy accounts, globalization is intended to describe something new and is often used to contrast the uncertainties of contemporary times to the more stable period of the 'Golden Age.' Most historical accounts see nothing unusual about the present phase of capitalism and refrain from using the term 'globalization.' In cultural studies, attempts have been made to move the date back in order to save the theory by acknowledging a historical context. This has created problems of definition, as globalization has become a process that is considered new by some and old by others.

The admission by cultural theorists that globalization is a historical process makes the theory unfalsifiable. The question of the date also switches the terrain of the debate from whether globalization exists to whether it is old or new. The argument then becomes imprisoned, in the sense that the conclusion is predetermined; globalization itself is not questioned but presented as fact. Whether one identifies the process as old or new, globalization is a given. The only way out of this conundrum is to be very specific about a date or, better yet, to avoid using the term altogether.

In general, then, 'globalization' appears to be an exceedingly troublesome term. First, and this is particularly true for cultural studies, the time line of globalization is vague, making it difficult to ascertain whether this process is an old or a new one. Lack of commitment regarding whether it is a contrast term lies at the root of this ambiguity. Second, globalization can apply to almost everything – religion, capital, communication, people, democracy – at which point it becomes almost meaningless. As Eagleton writes, 'Any word which covers everything loses its cutting edge and dwindles to an empty sound' (1991: 7). Robertson (1995) – reminiscent of Humpty-Dumpty's assertion that a word can mean anything he wants – contends that people are at liberty to define globalization as they please. Humpty-Dumpty's and Robertson's tolerance is admirable, and they are right insofar as there are no laws governing what a word should mean. Language is, after all, remarkably fluid, and meanings do change. But on a more practical level this kind of attitude makes little sense, for it effectively subverts meaningful communication.

Agreed-on definitions allow us to communicate, and for this reason it may be useful, rather than focusing on differences, to close this chapter by examining the similarities that the various definitions of globalization share. This is not to say that these are an accurate reflection of events, only to attempt to arrive at a working definition. As we have seen, people's interpretations of what globalization means may diverge, but there is usually a common core that holds these meanings together. When someone utters the word 'globalization' he or she does not mean to describe a tree or a new dance, but the unification of the world. It is these common elements of the concept that I wish to highlight. These can be summarized, as follows, in three points:

- One pertains to the frequently made observation about increased cross-border movement. Steger (2003: 7) summarizes globalization as follows: '[G]lobal economic, political, cultural, and environmental interconnections and flows ... make many of the currently existing borders and boundaries irrelevant.' This is similar to the numerous definitions given above.
- While there is much dispute about when globalization first started, there is at least agreement that even if it did start centuries ago, this process accelerated some time following the Second World War (be it in the 1960s or the 1980s).
- The conclusion consistently points to how globalization has undermined the nation-state's ability to effectively govern affairs within its borders. Predictions range from a tentative 'weakening' of the state to its outright disappearance, but the gist is always that the nation-state is becoming an antiquated institution.

In the more popular versions, the globalization argument is impregnated with the political rhetoric of powerful corporations and feckless states. As I have argued, some of this rhetoric has leaked into and contaminated the academic debate. Hence the academic debate cannot be thought of as entirely separate from the more popular ones.

In short, globalization can be defined as *the rapid acceleration of the flows of goods, services, and capital in the past half-century, which, in turn, has led to the weakening of the state.* This definition should stand whether one is sceptical about the process or believes it to be fact. From this it follows that one can either argue for globalization or against it. As should be obvious by this point, I will argue against it.

Whether changes in recent years amount to a realization of the fears or the hopes of globalists is an empirical question and will be answered in the following chapters. But first, much has been written about an apparent unease that we have been experiencing in recent years, an uncertainty often traced to globalization. By closely examining Marx and Engels's *Manifesto of the Communist Party*, I will attempt to show that 'globalization' is merely a new word for an old process and that the only novelty is that the political agenda has shifted from left to right.

Chapter 2

Marx, Globalization, and Modernity: What Is Old Becomes New Again

Everything has been thought of before, but the problem is to think of it again.

Johann W. von Goethe

Hegel remarks somewhere that all great world-historic facts and personages appear, so to speak, twice. He forgot to add: the first time as tragedy, the second time as farce.

Karl Marx

What's New?

Is it true, as Hegel and then Marx observed, that everything happens twice? With respect to globalization, then, are we living amid tragedy or farce? Or as Goethe would suggest, has the idea of globalization been thought of before? In this chapter I argue that globalization has been thought of before and that it was identified in everything but name by Marx and Engels more than 150 years ago in their *Manifesto of the Communist Party*. At the time of writing, 1848, the ideas embraced by communists were disseminated in the *Manifesto* to warn of the drastic consequences of capitalism, a mode of production that the authors predicted would eventually collapse under its own weight and open the way to socialism. More than a century and a half later, socialism has come and gone while capitalism reigns (notwithstanding exceptions such as North Korea, Cuba, and China). In an ironic twist, in what could only be described as farce, the political right has now appropriated some of the ideas from the *Manifesto* and used a similar kind of logic to predict not the collapse of capitalism but its final triumph.

First, I take a close look at the language of the *Manifesto* to highlight the similarities between it and current accounts of globalization.[1] The section following again uses the *Manifesto* for comparative purposes, this time as a *Zeitdiagnose* originating in cultural studies that attempts to capture the mood of the current age. Here it is argued that we've had this feeling before.

Globalization, *der Weltmarkt, le Monde*

Many authors have tried to link the novelty of the process of globalization to the newness of the word itself. Albrow (1996) has traced the genealogy of 'globalization' to the postwar period. In this respect, we can be reasonably sure that the word 'globalization' is new. *Merriam Webster's Dictionary* traces the first use of 'globalize' to 1944, and the *Oxford English Dictionary* dates the first use of 'globalization' to only 1962. The novelty of the word, however, should not be overemphasized, as this equates the process to the word, and even some staunch advocates of globalization insist that the process has been unfolding for centuries. Since the globalization perspective is proudly anti-Westerncentric, it should pay heed to the fact that other languages or cultures may have incorporated this concept, a fact automatically precluded by an approach focusing on the brief history of its use since the Second World War.

In other words, presenting the word's etymology as equivalent to its history constitutes too literal an interpretation, as it ignores the fact that the concept of global markets has existed for a long time. Using selected passages from the *Manifesto*, I am going to argue that Marx and Engels painted a picture of society that is remarkably similar to that presented by globalists today. It is essential to keep in mind that Marx and Engels wrote primarily in German, and that the word 'globalization' is, after all, English. In fact a case can be made that had the word 'globalization' existed in the mid-eighteen hundreds, Marx and Engels would have used it. The *Manifesto* provides many examples of how capitalism uses the globe as its stage, revealing that this idea can lay claim to an ancestry that goes back at least a century and a half. The following passage might well be found in a contemporary account of globalization:

> The need of a constantly expanding market for its products chases the bourgeoisie over the whole surface of the globe. It must nestle every-

where, settle everywhere, establish connexion everywhere. (Marx and Engels 1986: 37)

Compare this to a definition of globalization offered by the *Fortune Encyclopaedia of Economics*: 'The owners of these mobile production factors ... are increasingly "shopping around" the world for the labor and the style of government administration that promise them a high rate of return (and low risks) ... Internationally, this has led to the phenomenon of globalization ...' (Kasper 1993: 84). The general thrust of the two arguments is strikingly similar, although the terminology is not. In contemporary discussions about globalization, 'bourgeoisie' is replaced by 'capital' or 'multinational corporations.' Reference in the *Manifesto* to an 'expanding market' leaves little doubt not only that unfettered capitalism has long been recognized, but that it has invited criticism as well. The frequent use of the word 'globe' itself brings into sharp focus the long-term historical awareness (the phenomenological aspect) of the process of globalization that Robertson (1992) and Waters (2001) contend differentiates our age from those past.

The use of the word 'globe' is not the only reference to this worldly consciousness. Allusions to the 'world as one place' set the tone for much of the *Manifesto*: 'The bourgeoisie has through its exploitation of the world market given a cosmopolitan character to production and consumption in every country' (Marx and Engels 1986: 37). The emphasis here is on a process that is greater than any individual country. The word 'cosmopolitan' (*kosmopolitisch* in German), derived from the Greek *cosmo*, meaning 'world,' could easily serve as a synonym for 'global.' The word 'world' is used nine times throughout the *Manifesto* and is indicative of the inclusive and expansive world-view adopted by the authors. In German the word for 'world' is *Welt*, where it can mean many things, not only the world, but also the universe or the globe (Marx and Engels 1989). Recognition of a 'world market' (Marx and Engels 1986: 36, 37) serves as strong evidence that the consciousness of the 'globe' as a single society has been with us for some time.

Even some of the geographical regions highlighted in the *Manifesto*, such as China, are identical to those identified as major players in today's global economy. The references to distant locales around the globe, their connection to technology, and the rise of the bourgeoisie are strikingly similar to current observations about 'globalization.'

The discovery of America, the rounding of the Cape, opened up fresh ground for the rising bourgeoisie. The East-Indian and Chinese markets, the colonisation of America, trade with the colonies, the increase in the means of exchange and in commodities generally, gave to commerce, to navigation, to industry, an impulse never before known, and thereby, to the revolutionary element in the tottering feudal society, a rapid development. (Marx and Engels 1986: 33)

The fact that Marx and Engels attributed this 'impulse' to the forces of capitalism is less critical than their consciousness of the process, and of the general climate of instability and insecurity it created.

Marx and Engels's diagnosis of their time includes recognition not only of the diminishing role of the nation-state and the exploitation of remote regions, but also of the establishment of a world culture.

> To the great chagrin of Reactionists, it has drawn from under the feet of industry the national ground on which it stood. All old-established national industries have been destroyed or are daily being destroyed. They are dislodged by new industries, whose introduction becomes a life and death question for all civilised nations, by industries that no longer work up indigenous raw material, but raw material drawn from the remotest zones; industries whose products are consumed, not only at home, but in every quarter of the globe. In place of the old wants, satisfied by the productions of the country, we find new wants requiring for their satisfaction the products of distant lands and climes. In place of the old local and national seclusion and self-sufficiency, we have intercourse in every direction, universal inter-dependence of nations. And as in material, so also in intellectual production. The intellectual creations of individual nations become common property. National one-sidedness and narrow-mindedness become more and more impossible, and from the numerous national and local literatures, there arises a world literature. (Marx and Engels 1986: 37–8)

Berman (1982: 123) has interpreted the rise of 'world literature' to mean that 'bourgeois society was bringing a world culture into being,' an idea remarkably similar to claims about a global culture made by the likes of Robertson.

Another concept that pertains to globalization and that may well have lost meaning in translation is signalled by use of the word *Geist*, meaning 'spirit.' Marx's interest in this topic is the subject of a book by Derrida (1994) in which he argues that Marx was obsessed with all sorts of issues spiritual. Relevant to our discussion is the multiple meanings associated with this word. 'Und wie in der materiellen, so auch in der geistigen Produktion' has been translated as 'And as in material, so also in intellectual production.' Although this is an accurate translation, *'geistige Produktion'* can mean not only mere 'intellectual production' but also the production of ideas as such. In light of Marx's theory of history, which sees ideas as epiphenomenal to material production (see for example the *German Ideology* [Marx and Engels 1968]), this can be interpreted to mean that the rise of the bourgeoisie and the 'new industries' are responsible for the ideology of globalization. Ideologies, including that of globalization, have definite class origins. Then, as now, 'The ruling ideas of each age have ever been the ideas of its ruling class' (Marx and Engels 1986: 52). It is important to note that, from a Marxist perspective, the word 'ideology' is meant to be pejorative and signifies that ideas associated with it are false. In the current frenzy over globalization, the idea that corporations can roam the world with impunity should therefore be viewed with suspicion.

The preceding points indicate that the *Manifesto* could well have been subtitled 'Globalization I: Tragedy.' One does not necessarily have to read the German edition to arrive at this conclusion, but knowing about its language of origin can throw some fresh light on the topic. The German language has long had a much more expansive and inclusive view of the world, as anglicized words such as *Weltanschauung* and *Weltschmerz* indicate. The use of the French word *mondial*, essentially meaning 'global,' suggests that other languages have long incorporated the idea of the global into their language and therefore their consciousness. The fact that English has adopted these words from other languages shows an inability to express such thoughts. Linguists and sociologist have long recognized that language can both expand and limit our world. The recent proliferation of the word 'globalization' and the new consciousness of global phenomena should thus be considered no more than the overdue recognition of a process that has long been identified by people of non-English-speaking countries. The *Manifesto*, originally written in German, stands as a historical testament to this.

Marx, Modernity, and the New

The *Manifesto*, however, is significant not only as a harbinger of contemporary accounts of globalization but also as a snapshot of modernity. Here I argue that globalization is neither new nor distinct from modernism but is merely modernism by another name. The *Manifesto* has been identified as 'the first major sociopolitical affirmation of modernity'

(Therborn 1995: 125), and in this sense it has proved to be an enduring document. In their overall tenor, contemporary accounts of globalization are strangely similar to the *Zeitdiagnose* identified by Marx and Engels 150 years ago, a climate of change that the two German expatriates attributed to 'Modern Industry' and the 'Modern State.' Use of the word 'modern' is key here; it appears thirty-two times in the approximately thirty-page document.[2] The argument that follows makes the case that observations about globalization in contemporary society are not distinct enough from observations about modernism to qualify as a new theory.

The critical question that needs to be asked is whether globalization is a useful concept or theory. In order for a concept to meet such criteria, a *new* concept should correspondingly explain something *new* about the world. Most importantly, to be valuable, the concept of globalization should refer to processes that are clearly different from those that fall under the rubric of 'modernity,' a concept to which 'globalization' ostensibly stands in contrast. The impact of technology, the increased interconnection of different peoples, and the phenomenon of time-space compression have all been commented on by a multitude of observers and are often recognized as hallmarks of modernity. The emphasis of modernity has long been to differentiate our society from those of a preceding age, to identify the new (Kumar 1994: 392). Ideally a useful theory of globalization would identify new institutions and processes that separate it from modernity without relying on modernist conceptual tools (e.g., time-space compression, technology). At a minimum, a theory of globalization should make a convincing case for why an acceleration in this process amounts to a qualitative transformation. In short, a new theory should be more than simply anti-modern in sentiment and should provide evidence of how the rejection of modernism is manifested in the social world.

Further analysis of the *Manifesto* shows that the globalization theory fails on both counts: (1) it fails to isolate new institutions, and (2) it fails to provide convincing evidence of how this process has qualitatively changed. Similarities between contemporary accounts of globalization and modernism are not confined to the political project but spill over and incorporate the *Zeitdiagnose*. One resemblance between early modernist and the current literature on globalization is an ambivalent attitude towards technology. Throughout the globalization literature there exists an awe towards, even reverence for, technology. In much the same way that Marx and Engels saw the spread of capitalism and technology beyond the reach of 'national one-sidedness and narrow-mind-edness,' technology is implicated in today's events.

> [The] *flows* of ideas, commodities, symbols, people, images and money on a global scale ... are disjunctive and fragmenting, anarchical and disordered ... unbounded by spatial borders ... Many institutions of existing nation-states are now a fetter upon the emerging glocal modes of productions ... Borders today are highly porous, and the pressure of glocal flows of goods and services are continuously eroding them even more every day. (Luke 1995: 99; italics in original)

Compare this to the following passage from the *Manifesto*.

> The bourgeoisie, during its rule of scarce one hundred years, has created more massive and more colossal productive forces than have all preceding generations together. Subjection of Nature's forces to man, machinery, application of chemistry to industry and agriculture, steam-navigation, railways, electric telegraphs, clearing of whole continents for cultivation, canalisation of rivers, whole populations conjured out of the ground – what earlier century had even a presentiment that such productive forces slumbered in the lap of social labour? (Marx and Engels 1986: 38, 39)

The global consequences of this process are also noted by Marx and Engels: 'The bourgeoisie, by the rapid improvement of all instruments of production, by the immensely facilitated means of communication, draw all, even the most barbarian, nations into civilisation ... It compels all nations, on pain of extinction, to adopt the bourgeois mode of production ... In one word, it creates a world after its own image' (Marx and Engels 1986: 38). This passage was written more than 150 years ago. As we have seen in the preceding chapter, the phenomena it describes have been incorporated into contemporary theories of globalization, but with the important proviso that these changes are now qualitatively different.

> Plainly, a 'transnational' flow of goods, capital, people and ideas has existed for centuries; it antedates even the rise of nation-states. However, this historical flow, at least until the 1950s and 1960s, tended to move more slowly, move less and more narrowly than the rush of products, ideas, persons and money that develops with jet transportation, electronic telecommunications, massive decolonization and extensive computerization after 1960. It is these greater intensities, rates, densities, levels and

velocities of the post-historical flows, which have transmuted it quantitatively into something qualitatively new, complex and different. (Luke 1995: 99)

Here again we encounter an emphasis on technology as a primary impetus for globalization. Most interesting is how adamant the author is about the novelty of this process. Jet engines, computerization, and electronic telecommunications, all of which are relatively recent inventions, are introduced to stress just how far technology has advanced, an advance that, in the eyes of the author, serves as a justification to announce the advent of a new age. But as Harvey (1995: 9) points out, 'the newness of the railroad and the telegraph, the automobile, the radio, and the telephone in their day impressed equally.' To put it in everyday language, if it's not one thing, it's another.

Two further comments can be made with respect to contemporary observations about technology and globalization. First, in light of Marx and Engels's work, the emphasis on technology and how it is implicated in the acceleration of globalization borders on the hackneyed. Only a fool would argue that technology is less advanced now than it was around Marx's time, but this misses the bigger point. The more important observation is that this relentless accumulation of technology, commonly called progress, is a constant by-product of modernity. It is far from new, and it differs merely in degree.

Second, as is only too common in cultural accounts, there is scant evidence presented for these increased flows. The overall thrust of the passage is a combination of enthusiasm for and unease about contemporary changes, yet there is no evidence of the degree to which these flows have increased, despite a claim of a transformation from the quantitative to the qualitative. Furthermore, as mentioned in the introduction, a focus on international flows completely ignores national flows, which may well counteract the denationalizing effects of international flows. And finally, these flows are far from unrestricted, as the movement of goods, services, ideas, and people continues to be tightly controlled by states. Massey has properly noted that globalization is primarily written about by people who are able to enjoy intercontinental travel: academics and journalists. Such an approach ignores how 'differential mobility can weaken the leverage of the already weak' (Massey 1994: 150).[3]

A theory that attempts to distinguish itself from modernity, as globalization does, would have to spell out how the world is moving away from its reverence for technology. In other words, in order to eclipse modernism, such a theory would have to successfully escape the strait-jacket of technology and reject the allure of the new. Postmodernism spelled out what some of these conditions might be – a rejection of the institutions of modernism (see Giddens 1990) – but postmodernism remains primarily a vision about how society *ought* to be and not about what it is. Similar charges can be made against visions of globalization. And when it comes to how contemporary society *is*, it continues to be very much modern.

Similarities between the *Manifesto* and contemporary writings indicate that globalists continue the old modernist admiration for the new. Often this new world is simultaneously revered and feared. Moreover, control over new technology is perceived to be out of our hands. Flows of money, people, goods, and so on, are so chaotic and uncontrollable that they cause us to experience a general sense of unease or 'ontological insecurity' (Giddens 1990). This admiration of the new and at the same time the anxiety it engenders are hallmarks of the 'juggernaut of modernity,' an analogy used by Giddens. In powerful language, Marx and Engels write about the turbulent times that accompany modernism, their account sounding strangely similar to present-day observations about the novel characteristics of globalization.

> Constant revolutionising of production, uninterrupted disturbance of all social conditions, everlasting uncertainty and agitation distinguish the bourgeois epoch from earlier ones. All fixed, fast-frozen relations, with their train of ancient and venerable prejudices and opinions, are swept away, all new-formed ones become antiquated before they can ossify. All that is solid melts into air, all that is holy is profaned, and man is at last compelled to face, with sober senses, his real conditions of life, and his relations with his kind. (Marx and Engels 1986: 37)

In his incisive account of modernism, Berman puts contemporary observations that echo these sentiments into perspective: 'People who find themselves in the midst of this maelstrom are apt to feel that they are the first ones, and maybe the only ones, that are going through it ... In fact, however, great and ever-increasing numbers of people have been going through it for close to five hundred years' (Berman 1982: 16). This suggests that the subjective component of globalization, the increased consciousness of the new, may not be all that good an indicator of a new age. The excitement generated by the perceived novelty of our world is a faithful, often silent, companion of modernism. According to Therborn (1995) modernism is, more than anything, an experience, and this experience is remarkably similar to that described by globalists. For that reason, we cannot rely on general impressions as evidence of globalization. In the end, evidence of globalization amounts to no more than impressions, impressions that appear to be not particularly original. To perceive these observations as new is no more than a globalist's conceit; these characteristics are already emblematic of another age: modernism.

Optimally we might expect similar features from a theory of globalization to what we find with modernity. That is, a theory that identifies, and preferably explains, a break similar to the break from traditional society that characterizes modernity. A theory of globalization should set itself apart from modernity not only by being anti-modern, that is, by rejecting ideas of modernism (as do the Club of Rome and many environmental movements, for example), but also by presenting evidence of how the world has made concrete changes in an anti-modern direction. The fact is that people and governments are still very much bound by the principles and beliefs of modernity. The continual attention paid to growth, the persistence of a consumer culture, and the unwillingness to change in the face of potential environmental disaster indicate that anti-modernism exists only in spirit and is not manifested in action.

It is easy to see why the *Manifesto* continues to inspire so many people. Its language is uncompromising, concise, and forceful – its observations timeless. A reading of the *Manifesto* reveals that the ideas associated with globalization – ideas about its power, inevitability, and intractability – are already more than a century and a half old and may be as old as capitalism itself. It is no small irony that those on the right, who in the past have derided Marx as deterministic and rigid, have now adopted a similar approach when they portray contemporary markets. Marx regarded what he identified as the tumultuous circumstances surrounding capitalism as tragedy. One hundred and fifty-seven years later, the same ideas are used to celebrate the victory of capitalism. As Marx said, first there was tragedy, then there was farce.

Chapter 3

The World Economy

As the previous chapters have shown, recognition of a world economy is not new; use of the word 'globalization,' however, is. In the social sciences the debate about the origins of the world economy has been going on for some time, long before any discussions about globalization. These debates have been ongoing in economics, political economy, and sociology for decades, with various attempts to identify the point at which national economies first started to grow, trade, and interact on a substantial basis. The underlying question driving these inquiries is When did a world economy first begin? This starting point is often referred to as the 'take-off' period. It is generally agreed that the inchoate stirrings of a world economy can first be identified beginning in the fifteenth century, while it is also acknowledged that a full-fledged world economy did not come into being until somewhere in the early eighteen hundreds. These developments are commonly measured by way of a combination of trade and output (GDP).

From this perspective, economic and sociological accounts are quite similar. Both identify a 'proto-capitalist' period that lasted from the middle of the second millennium to somewhere in the early nineteenth century and that was followed by a full-blown world capitalist economy. The economic and sociological accounts complement each other well, as the numbers from the more empirical economic versions substantiate claims made by sociologists. What distinguishes the two disciplines is that in economics the accounts are primarily descriptive and seldom go beyond simple theorizing (for example, economies going through a series of stages from traditional to high consumption; see Rostow 1990). In sociology, theories focus on social relations between societies, with Marxist accounts, it should come as no surprise, stressing the unequal power relations characteristic of the capitalist mode of production.

By far the best-known account of the world economy in sociology is Immanuel Wallerstein's (1974) conception of the world system. According to this theory, the economic world can be divided into three regions: The core composed of the wealthy countries – primarily Western Europe and North America – which dominates the world economy; the periphery, which includes most of the poor countries in Asia and Africa, Central and South America, and the Caribbean; and the semi-periphery – countries that do not solidly fit into either the core or the periphery, countries that are neither rich nor poor – which consists of a handful of countries in Southeast Asia and South America. The central point of Wallerstein's thesis is that an unequal relationship exists between core and periphery that tends to work to the advantage of the former. Another feature of the world system is that this hierarchical structure remains relatively intact over time. For the most part, core countries remain part of the core, and periphery countries remain part of the periphery, with only a few countries experiencing significant mobility. History substantiates this model, as only a small number of countries have been displaced from the core. Portugal and Spain were the first to colonize the Americas in the fifteenth century and gained considerable wealth because of it. However, they squandered much of this wealth and experienced rapid downward mobility as a consequence. Portugal is now one of the poorest countries in Western Europe, with Spain not far behind. The Netherlands, France, and Great Britain soon followed and built their own empires through colonization, and all are still firmly situated within the core. In the seventeenth century, the United States and Canada were both part of the periphery but were soon catapulted through the semi-periphery on their way to the core, based on the very same resources that initially made them attractive to economic exploitation. Japan is the only country in the twentieth century that took the rarely travelled road from semi-periphery to core, although this did not occur until after the Second World War. In comparison, the United States and Canada were already part of the core by the nineteenth century. Most mobility, however, involves countries that drift in and out of the semi-periphery, and even here movement takes decades and appears to be relatively infrequent. Contemporary developments in East Asia are all examples of countries (Taiwan, South Korea, Singapore) moving from the periphery into the semi-periphery.

One characteristic that distinguishes the world capitalist system from past empires is that, once a core state collapses, the system moves on and continues to thrive elsewhere. Hence the collapse of the Spanish/Portuguese Empire did not spell the end of merchant capitalism but allowed the Netherlands and later on the United Kingdom to take the helm. The power vacuum left by the decline of the British Empire, in turn, was assumed by the United States (although a weakened United Kingdom remains part of the core). Wallerstein has predicted that the next candidate for the core could well be in Asia, a combination of China and Japan.

The essential point to take note of here is that the core, periphery, and semi-periphery may change while the integrity of the system remains. This detail differentiates world-system theory from modernization theory; the latter assumes that all countries will eventually evolve into fully modern and industrial economies. The world-system perspective recognizes that there is always some mobility among countries and regions, but alerts our attention to the fact that the structure of the system itself – defined by a hierarchical interrelationship of core, periphery, and semi-periphery – remains. A quick overview of the world economy indicates that the general contours of the world economy, and the ways in which economic power is distributed around the globe, remain firmly cemented in place. The lone entrant to the core in the past half-century was Japan, and only a handful of countries in Southeast Asia have experienced enough upward mobility to qualify them as entrants to the semi-periphery. Much has been made of this by supporters of globalization, but one country or region does not globalization make. Africa, most of South America, and large parts of Asia (including the ex-Soviet Empire), continue to remain shut out of the world economy, with all these regions having experienced a decline in living standards over the past two decades.

The World Economy: A Brief History

Now that we have sketched the outlines of the world-system theory, we need to examine how the empirical evidence provided by economists fits this theory. Trade has been with us for thousands of years, but this activity did not occur on a substantial basis until the neolithic revolution; that is, when people abandoned their nomadic lifestyles and began to practise horticulture. Agriculture and the domestication of animals first occurred around 8000 BCE in the Middle East. Higher productivity and an increased division of labour allowed for surpluses to accumulate that could then be traded for other products. Once the nomadic lifestyle was abandoned, it also became more practical to store wealth. Trade, however, was geographically contained, as the technology needed to transport goods over large distances, both land and water, had not yet been developed. In the absence of mass communication and a monetary system, most trade also depended on face-to-face interaction, as there needed to be a coincidence of what one person wanted and another person produced and vice versa.

Economic activity and the accumulation of surpluses eventually led to urbanization and the founding of the first city states in approximately 3500 BCE. Trade further increased with the rise of the early empires. The first empires, such as Akkad and Babylonia, were geographically contained, but empires had a tendency to grow and soon encroached on neighbouring territories. The Roman Empire incorporated parts of several continents – Europe, Asia, and Africa – and united them under one rule. From the sixth century onwards, the Islamic world, spanning North Africa and Central Asia, served as an intermediary that facilitated trade between China and Europe (Cameron and Neal 2003: 79). China and India also had extensive trade ties that included most of Southeast Asia, and the Mongolian Empire of the thirteenth and fourteenth centuries united much of Asia. By 1400, trading centres dotted the coasts of Asia, the Mediterranean, and Europe, and overland routes existed to unite the whole of the Eurasian continent (Robbins 2002: 62–6). This meant that a skeleton for the world economy was already well in place by the time of the European voyages that led to the colonization of the Americas and other parts of the world.

Eventually economic activity and interaction reached the critical mass necessary to constitute a world economy. When exactly this happened is a topic of extensive academic debate, but it is generally agreed that the world economy did not grow significantly until the beginning of the nineteenth century. This period, from 1820 to the present, is often referred to as the take-off stage, and describes, as the name implies, the point at which the world economy first began to expand at an accelerated pace (Maddison 2001). But it took centuries of economic activity to reach the level of economic integration necessary for the take-off stage. This period is known by a variety of names, and is referred to as the 'proto-capitalist' stage by Maddison (1995).

According to Wallerstein, the roots of the world economy coincide with the European expansion in the late fifteenth century. It was also around this time that states began to become interdependent economically; that is, individual economies were no longer self-sufficient but gradually came to depend on products imported from other countries for their economic well-being. While there is general agreement that the world economy originated around that time, Maddison (2001) has recently moved this date back another five centuries to the beginning of the second millennium. He points to the absence of a discernible break in the middle of the second millennium that would allow historians to declare the inauguration of a new age. As his evidence illustrates, economic developments around the turn of the fifteenth century were part of a much longer trend that began nearly five centuries earlier, in the year 1000.

Furthermore, trading empires such as that of the Venetian Republic were already well established long before the turn of the fifteenth century. By the thirteenth century Venice was the richest republic in Europe and administered several colonies in the Mediterranean. It had also forged trade routes with what are now Germany, Austria, and the Baltic countries, and imported products from as far away as China and India. Venice also laid claim to an advanced banking and accounting system that included foreign-exchange and credit markets. Equally important, the arts and intellectual activities such as book publishing flourished. Portugal was another centre that was commercially active before 1492, the usual date given for the beginning of the proto-capitalist period. Between 1420 and 1460, Prince Henrique explored the Atlantic Ocean off Portugal. His explorations led to the colonization of Madeira and the Azores and took him down the west coast of Africa as far as Cape Verde. His goal of circumnavigating Africa was not realized within his lifetime, but his expeditions led to the necessary advances in naval technology needed for such a journey. Thirty-eight years after Prince Henrique's death, Vasco da Gama successfully reached the Indian Ocean by the sea route (Maddison 2001: 52–9).

i) The Proto-capitalist Period

Whether one pegs the beginning of the proto-capitalist period as early as the year 1000 or as late as the late fifteenth century is not critical for our present purposes. Whatever the century, growth up until 1820 was generally slow. But at least, in contrast to the previous millennium, it was positive. Throughout the first 1000 years of the Common Era, particularly in the years following the fall of the Roman Empire, Europe underwent a steady downward trend with respect to economic growth, so that by the year 1000 average income was below that found in Asia and North Africa. However, at the turn of the second millennium fortunes turned, and over the next few centuries economic growth in Europe, and most noticeably in Northern Europe, exceeded that of all other regions. By 1400, European GDP was already the highest in the world, even surpassing that of China (Maddison 2001). Yet growth throughout the proto-capitalist period was typically stagnant and sporadic. Between 1000 and 1820, world income per capita increased by approximately 50 per cent, in stark contrast to the robust growth experienced in the much shorter take-off phase between 1820 and 1998, when growth increased by 850 per cent.

By the time the world economy entered the take-off phase in 1820, trading patterns were already firmly established, as was the hierarchal relationship between core and periphery. The reasons why the economy entered the take-off stage in Europe are many: political organization, a sophisticated credit system, as well as an increased division of labour, which, in combination with rapid advances in technology, led to massive increases in productivity. However, one should not lose sight of the fact that Europe's economic ascendancy depended on colonization that entailed the expropriation of vast tracts of land and natural resources, political and economic domination, the use of forced labour, and, at times, even genocide. In the sixteenth century, for example, Spain and Portugal exploited South America, using its indigenous population as slave labour to mine metals. Once this labour force was exhausted, the colonizing powers instituted the forced migration of millions of slaves from Africa. By 1820, most countries of the world – all of the Americas, as well as most of Asia, Oceania, and Africa – were, or had been at some point, under the control of one of the major European powers: Spain, Portugal, the Netherlands, France, and Great Britain. Notable exceptions were China, which was militarily strong enough to keep Europeans at bay and elude full colonization, and Japan, which engaged in some colonization of its own. There were also internal reasons why economies diverged – why some countries grew richer and others poorer. Wallerstein places much emphasis on how the landed aristocracy of Eastern Europe exploited their own serfs to supply Western Europe with grain, and in turn bought manufactured products made in Great Britain. This meant that technological advances and craft manufacturing remained comparatively undeveloped in the regions outside the core, a circumstance that served to further reinforce the division of labour among regions.

Through the process of colonization the world system was already well established by the time the Industrial Revolution began, so it was not technological superiority, as is often believed, that allowed Europe to dominate the world economy. Advances in industry accentuated rather than mitigated inequality among countries. This was not a natural consequence of the technology itself but an outcome that was carefully nurtured by the Europeans (Stearns 1993: 35) and was achieved by the colonizing powers' tactic of stipulating what industries the colonies could compete in. The European powers also created demand for their products in the colonies through the practice of mercantilism, whereby the colonizing powers were able to enforce a virtual monopoly of production and trade within their empires. For example, Britain imported raw materials from its colonies and in turn exported manufactured products to be sold there, transported on ships built within the empire and operated by British crews. Europe had other advantages as well. Great Britain had ready access to a free labour force available for work in the manufacturing sector, the result of a population explosion and the displacement of agricultural workers through the enclosure movement. In contrast, countries that were still primarily engaged in agriculture lacked both the surplus labour and the technology to compete with the economically advanced countries. Continued reliance on income from agricultural products meant that resources, especially in terms of labour, had to be directed towards that activity in order to survive. The end result was that these countries came to depend on manufactured products from outside, further securing their relationship of dependence.

This power relationship between core and periphery exists even today. There is convincing evidence that countries like Taiwan and South Korea were 'allowed' to industrialize in an effort by the United States to contain communism in Asia. American involvement in this region, with the Korean and Vietnam wars in particular, made it necessary for the Americans to establish strong allies in East Asia (Stubbs 1994). The transfer of technology and capital, amounting to billions of dollars in the form of subsidies by the United States in pursuit of military dominance, facilitated industrialization in this region. In the absence of these wars, the Asian miracle might never have happened. Similar financial assistance has not been available to Indonesia or Vietnam, and there is no guarantee that these countries will continue to prosper and reach the levels of wealth attained in the West.

ii) The Take-off Phase

Despite the European expansion that accelerated throughout the seventeenth and eighteenth centuries, the world economy continued to grow slowly. The precise dating of when the economy made the qualitative leap to a full-blown 'world economy' is a point of contention among economists, although the range of dates is by no means extensive. Wallerstein estimates that this break took place around 1815. Kuznets (1966) puts the transition closer to 1750, with the most recent evidence suggesting a date around 1820 (Maddison 1995; Rostow 1990). Maddison (1995) calculates that the average gross world product (GWP) per-capita growth between 1820 to 1992 was thirty times that found between 1500 to 1820. As was noted earlier, some economies were already thriving by that point, but in general world growth was relatively slow, sporadic, and restricted to isolated regions. Between 1500 and 1820 world output did not even triple, and what little growth did occur was basically a function of population growth; consequently, gross world product per capita increased only slightly. In marked contrast, world output grew fortyfold between 1820 and 1992, resulting in an eightfold increase in GWP per capita (Maddison 1995). The reasons Maddison gives for the explosive growth in the early to mid-eighteen hundreds are rapid developments in transportation and communications technology, an increase in capital stock (mostly machinery), and the spread of education, a combination of changes that resulted in vast increases in productivity.

Between the years 1820 and 1913 growth was especially robust, the fastest in history up to that point. Moreover, economic integration increased substantially throughout this period, and for that reason it is often referred to as the first wave of globalization. Trade and investment, as well as people, moved freely across borders, primarily as a result of a precipitous drop in transportation costs. Writing in 2003, Estevadeordal and colleagues conclude that, 'As for the present, by many measures, the process of global integration has not surpassed the marks set by the world economy in 1913 ...' (2003: 397). This economic integration was most apparent when it came to trade and investment. By 1913, merchandise exports accounted for 7.9 per cent of world GWP, a level that would not be matched until the 1970s (Findlay and O'Rourke 2003: 41, table 1.3). Furthermore, the movement of cross-border capital was by all accounts as great in 1913 as it is currently, if not more so (Obstfeld and Taylor 2003).

However, the current and past waves of globalization differ significantly with respect to the movement of people. Throughout the first wave, mass emigration from Europe to North America and other European offshoots such as Australia was significantly less restricted than it is in the current era. Migration levels during the first wave were unprecedented, have not been matched since, and will likely not be repeated in the near future. These migrations had a momentous impact on both the Old World and New. In Europe wages rose as the availability of labour became scarcer. In the United States, the resulting glut of labour had precisely the opposite effect and put downward pressure on wages, the overall effect being that wages in the New World and the Old converged (O'Rourke and Williamson 1999). European workers had the option of pursuing economic opportunities in other parts of the world, and this assured that unemployment remained low and did not lead to further social problems. In contrast, migration is drastically restricted today, and the safety valve of emigration is no longer available. This means that workers who currently find themselves displaced or unemployed in China, the Middle East, Brazil, or Argentina have nowhere to go if they seek to improve their lot in life.

As is well known, this first wave of globalization did not last and was interrupted by two world wars and a depression, with the second wave not emerging until the 1950s. O'Rourke and Williamson (1999) relate that the primary causes for this interruption were an increase in transportation costs and a backlash against immigration in North America, rather than, as is often believed, the rise of protectionism that culminated in the Smoot Hawley Tariff Act of 1930. Similarly, Estevadeordal and colleagues (2003: 397) warn that the experiences of the interwar years serve to illustrate that there is no reason to believe that the second wave of globalization is going to last forever. A sharp increase in the price of oil, an environmental disaster, an escalation in the war against terrorism, or some other unforeseen event could well impede this current wave of economic interaction.

All this evidence and how it relates to the growth of the global economy appears convincing enough, but let us step back for moment and, keeping with the theme of this book, critically assess the use of the term 'globalization.' The first wave of globalization as isolated by O'Rourke and Williamson (1999) occurred in what the authors describe as the Atlantic economy; that is, Western Europe and North America – essentially the OECD world of today. With the exception of Southeast Asia, Brazil, and maybe Argentina, the current phase of economic integration is also limited geographically and, in fact, excludes the majority of countries in the world. The question then arises whether the term 'globalization' amounts, as is the case with the 'world' series in baseball, to little more than self-aggrandizement.

Furthermore, the unprecedented explosion of growth that began in the early to mid-eighteen hundreds was and continues to be undertaken in the context of an economically divided world. As noted at the outset of this chapter, the world economy found its origin in Western Europe, and it is also there, in addition to its offshoots of North America, Australia, and New Zealand, that the majority of its benefits continue to be reaped. From this vantage point, the gulf between rich and poor has consistently widened, a divergence of living standards that has been relentless and without break. In 1820, the ratio of economic output between the richest region and the poorest was 3:1 (Western Europe and offshoots, Eastern Europe, Southern Europe, Latin America, Asia, and Africa). The monumental growth of the world economy affected each region differently, and by 1998 this ratio had grown to 17:1 (Maddison 2001: 27). In terms of countries rather than regions, this ratio is even more dramatic, diverging from 3:1 in 1820 to 72:1 in 1992 (Maddison 1995). Nowhere throughout this period did this process of polarization let up, let alone reverse.

Robert Wade reports similar findings. First, although it only represents a snapshot of global inequality and is not indicative of a trend, it is worthwhile knowing that the richest 20 per cent of the world's population earns a startling 82.7 per cent of world income, leaving the remaining 17.3 per cent to be shared by the other 80 per cent of the world's population (Wade 2001: 37). However, Wade also presents longitudinal data showing that income inequalities have recently widened. Two studies, both based on the most comprehensive data currently available and provided by the World Bank, show that inequality throughout the world increased rapidly throughout the late 1980s and early 1990s. While overall incomes may be rising in China and India, inequality in both countries is becoming more polarized between urban and rural areas, contributing to a worldwide trend of diverging incomes. Between 1988 and 1993 the distribution of world income, according to the Gini coefficient (where 0 is perfect equality and 100 is perfect inequality), increased by 6 per cent, from 63.1 to 66.9 (*The Economist*, 28 Apr. 2001: 72). (As a point of comparison, the Gini coefficient in Canada in the mid-1990s was 28.7 [Harris 2003: 62]). In terms of income distribution, then, the world was a much more homogeneous place in the 1820s than at the closing of the twentieth century, a fact that casts considerable doubt on theories of convergence and modernization that continue to be popular to this day.

These figures give support to Wallerstein's world-system theory. Not only have the countries that were part of the core in the early days of the world economy been able to hold onto their position of dominance, they have been able to entrench it. The West strategically laid the groundwork for the political and economic dynamics of the world system over the centuries that made up the proto-capitalist period. The rise of Southeast Asia notwithstanding, Europe and the United States continue to wield most of the economic power in the global economy. If anything, the core has become more powerful and has done so at the expense of the periphery. The numbers above corroborate this concentration of power. Contrary to the theory of convergence, where all countries are destined to go through a similar economic evolution, core countries are holding onto their wealth, and the gap between rich and poor continues to be a persistent feature of the world economy. Even throughout the period of purported globalization this trend has remained unchanged. In this sense, world-system theory is much better at explaining current events than are theories of modernization or globalization. Rather than focus on isolated developments such as the industrialization of a few countries in Southeast Asia and extrapolating a theory of globalization from there, world-system theory focuses on the overall structure and history of the world economy and explains mobility among countries as a long-standing characteristic of the system.

iii) World Trade

Although, as we have just seen, economic expansion accelerated after 1820, world trade continued to be negligible in the early part of the nineteenth century. Most 'international trade' occurred between Europe and its colonies. As a portion of GWP, trade made up only 1 per cent of the world economy in 1820 (Maddison 1995). From the perspective of trade, then, most economies were still relatively self-sufficient at the beginning of the take-off stage. But that changed quickly as trade grew to 5 per cent of GWP in 1870, 8.7 per cent in 1913, 13.2 per cent in 1992, and 17.2 per cent in 1998. It should be noted that in the past, as now, trade varied considerably among regions; moreover, not surprisingly, trade volume initially followed the colonization routes laid down by Western Europeans.

In summary, the world economy has been global for close to two centuries now, and the groundwork for this, the proto-capitalist state, can be traced back at least another three. Given the power imbalances proposed by Wallerstein's world system, Canada, for example, is unlikely to be economically threatened by countries from the periphery. The degree to which economic competition from the periphery is a potential threat to Canada will be examined in detail in the next chapter on trade. For now, suffice it to say that from a theoretical perspective the privileged position that Canada enjoys as a core country is not under siege. Being part of the core brings with it a certain amount of economic momentum, which, if anything, appears to be responsible for putting ever more distance between the core and the periphery. In short, living standards are diverging, not converging.

Capitalism and the World Economy

When Maddison writes about his findings on the origins of the world economy, he explicitly uses the term 'capitalist' (as in his writings on the proto-capitalist stage). For evidence he primarily relies on demographics, including population growth, GDP growth, and the rate of urbanization. But the world economy is more than the accretion of goods produced or goods traded. A defining characteristic of the world economy is, after all, as Maddison himself admits, the fact that it is capitalist. But this has not always been the case, and the onset of the world economy must be explained in more than quantitative terms. This raises one of the central questions surrounding the debate about the origins of the world economy: When did capitalism first emerge, or, to be even more precise, become dominant? It is well known that merchants and traders have long existed comfortably alongside the monarchy, aristocracy, and other forms of ruling elites. But the fifteenth century constitutes a qualitative break, in that capitalist activities started to dominate economically and politically, or, as Heilbroner (1980) puts it, it was the first time in history that power followed money instead of the other way around.

Along these lines, historian Robert Brenner assails writers such as Wallerstein, Sweezy, and Frank because they 'equate capitalism with a trade-based division of labour' (Brenner 1977: 38; see also Wood 2002). As Brenner points out, trade itself does not automatically translate into capitalist relations. As was mentioned earlier, trade long preceded capitalism; furthermore, it was relatively slow up until 1820. Brenner also convincingly argues that trade does not necessarily involve exploitation, and puts forward that it was a change in social relations that inaugurated capitalism. Brenner's thesis is that the economy evolved from feudalism to capitalism when English landlords first leased land to farmers, who in turn employed wage labour. This effectively meant that

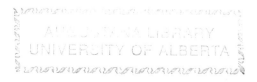

farmers became capitalists who extracted surplus labour from the workers they hired. Slowly capitalism spread across the English countryside,
and eventually this social arrangement was exported to other regions
around the world. What is of importance here are the social relations
that constitute a capitalist mode of production, for in many ways there
is considerable overlap between Brenner's and Wallerstein's theses, in
that both trace the origins of capitalism to fifteenth-century England
and agree that it radiated from there. In that sense, then, this charge
does not present an obstacle to the thesis that globalization is not new
and first started more than 500 years ago.

Brenner's second charge is more salient for our purposes and concerns the exploitive relationship purported to exist between core and
periphery. Again, Brenner singles out Wallerstein and Frank because
they presuppose an exploitive relationship between the developed and
the underdeveloped world, an assumption that in Brenner's eyes is
unjustified. He is highly critical of Frank's observation that 'economic
development and underdevelopment are the opposite faces of the same
coin' (Brenner 1977: 28) or a position that is often referred to, as Frank
writes elsewhere, as 'the development of underdevelopment.' The
belief that the wealthy countries do *not* depend on poor countries for
their economic success can be traced back to Adam Smith, who had
already suggested in 1776 that Great Britain should divest itself of its
colonies, for he felt that they were a relatively unprofitable proposition.
While colonization was responsible for charting important trade routes,
this is not enough to establish that exploitation occurred. Whether colonization actually enriched the core countries – or, relatedly, whether
there continues to be relationship of exploitation between core and
periphery today – is a question that continues to be hotly debated. Supporters of open markets tend to believe that free trade is beneficial to all
parties involved, and put forth that there is no coercion or exploitation
involved when individuals or countries participate in trade. This argument rests on the premise that people enter trade relationships voluntarily, which does indeed raise important questions about the exploitive
nature of transections between core and periphery, a crucial component
of the world-system theory.

In order to establish exploitation one would have to trace how economic conditions in the Third World have changed over the past
decades. Somewhat surprisingly, research in this area is far from definitive. First, there exists the problem of definition. The World Bank has
long argued that absolute poverty, measured in terms of caloric intake

and life expectancy, has decreased over the past few decades, meaning that material conditions are improving even in the poorest parts of the world. However, even this proposition has come under attack. Chossudovsky (2003: 27–34) claims that figures on global poverty are manipulated by the World Bank and like institutions, and suggests that worldwide poverty is significantly underestimated. Wade is similarly suspicious of World Bank figures and concludes that the income of the poorest 10 per cent of the world population has 'probably fallen absolutely since the 1980s' (2001: 39). Furthermore, countries are differently assessed by institutions like the World Bank when it comes to economic inequality, and this results in comparisons that show, for example, that Canada has a higher percentage of people living in poverty than Mexico (Chossudovsky 2003: 27–34).

As we have seen above, figures that focus on the relative distribution of income also indicate a widening of inequality between rich and poor countries. But even if the poor are getting poorer in both an absolute and a relative sense, it would be a logical leap to conclude that this was because of exploitation. The core countries could well be getting richer because their wealth is internally produced and because they take advantage of technology and education, which increase productivity and wealth, while the poor countries may not be getting any farther ahead because of a lack of technology, political instability, or climatic turmoil. In other words, the core could be getting richer on its own merit, with a similar argument applying to the periphery. According to this line of argument, all that poor countries have to do is emulate wealthy ones. This view, that Third World countries will prosper through globalization, previously known as modernization theory, is widely held by the World Bank, the IMF, and the business community in general. Jagdish Bhagwati (2004) in his *In Defense of Globalization*, argues that free trade itself is enough to raise living standards wherever it is allowed to flourish. The underlying thrust of this perspective is that liberalized markets will pave the way for economic prosperity for all countries, with Third World countries having the most to gain. According to economic liberals, then, the quickest way to alleviate global inequality is for poor countries to open up their borders and welcome the free market.

On the other hand, just because trade relationships are voluntary does not automatically mean that exploitation does not exist on some other level. Much has been made of the Doha Round of the World Trade Organization (WTO), often referred to as the Development Round.

With this comes the implicit realization that poor countries have been held back from fully participating in the world economy. The biggest obstacles to Third World producers are the immense agricultural subsidies, amounting to more than U.S. $300 billion in the West. Unfair trade practices are evident in other areas as well. Competition to attract automobile manufacturers has resulted in a bidding war between the United States and Canada, and compelled the federal government in 2004 to promise subsidies of $1 billion to the manufacturing sector in Canada. Of this amount, $300 million went directly to General Motors and Ford in order to update existing plants in southern Ontario. Poor countries are hardly in a position to offer such extravagant subsidies. At the same time, Third World countries are often faced with quotas when they attempt to sell their products in the West, a hurdle most apparent in the clothing and textile industries. As well, the costs of purchasing technology are often unattainably high in the Third World because of patent protection and intellectual property rights. While none of this may amount to exploitation, it plainly makes it more difficult for poor countries to compete.

Besides trade and subsidies, there are other signs that the First World has a distinct advantage in the world economy. Through organizations like the World Bank and the IMF, both of which are part of the 'Washington Consensus,' a free-market model is promoted throughout the Third World. In the past, poor countries were encouraged to borrow money to industrialize so that they ran up huge debts and sent billions of dollars in interest payments back to the First World. Through Structural Adjustment Policies, the IMF and the World Bank impose free-market measures that include small government, elimination of subsidies (often for food and cooking fuel), and a strict monetary policy. Moreover, continual military interference in the periphery by the core suggests an unequal power relationship. For example, the Middle East has been under the control of core countries, first Great Britain and then the United States, for close to a century. The most recent manifestation of this is the American invasion of Iraq, which has led David Harvey (2003) and Gore Vidal (2004) to observe that we are witnessing a new kind of imperialism. All this serves as evidence that the global capitalist class relationship that has constituted the world system for centuries endures to this day.

The question of whether trade lies at the basis of capitalist relations or whether the core actually benefits from the global economy at the expense of the periphery is beyond the scope of this work, and may indeed be tangential. Brenner and Wallerstein both agree that the global economy has a history that stretches back at least 500 years and that it first began in England and from there was gradually exported to the rest of the world. In other words, what is popularly known as globalization is far from new.

Economic Cycles

The growth of the world economy has not been smooth and linear, but rather cyclical in nature, littered with an endless string of booms and busts. A number of prominent economic historians have identified a series of cycles to which they have generously given their names. One of the first to do so was the Russian economist Nikolai Kondratieff, who wrote a series of papers on this topic between 1922 and 1928. Kondratieff (1984: 25), who was careful to point out that these cycles applied only to capitalist economies, identified cycles of bust and boom in the world economy that lasted approximately between fifty to fifty-five years from start to finish. At the basis of these cycles are changes in technology, such as developments in the use of water power, coal, internal combustion engines, and microelectronics.

Simon Kuznets identified a similar series of cycles, appropriately named Kuznets cycles, which incorporate a shorter time span of twenty-two to thirty years. These cycles are a combination of approximately eleven to fifteen years of acceleration matched by an equivalent period of deceleration. More important for our purposes is the observation that each of these cycles can be attributed to the dynamic of a capitalist economy. At the trough of a cycle, demand increases and suppliers compete in order to meet that demand. Eventually that demand is not only met but exceeded, resulting in a collapse of the cycle that is manifested in idle factories, high unemployment, and low investment. Wallerstein has emphasized the cyclical nature of the capitalist world economy (see, for example, Wallerstein 2003) as has Arrighi (1994). According to the Kondratieff perspective, we are currently in a period of contraction that started in the late 1960s and that followed the boom of 1945 to 1967 (Shannon 1996: 132). These cycles represent a persistent problem for capitalism, which by its very nature is oriented towards growth and fails to perform well in its absence. It is important to keep in mind that we are presently in a period of slowed growth, and while the severity of this downturn has been managed to some degree, a downturn cannot be reversed. Of course, all contractions are different, including the current one. The details of this will be discussed in chapter 7, where we will examine the world economy from the Second World War to the present.

Conclusion

To economic historians the world economy is not a recent development but one that stretches back more than 500 years. Further evidence suggests that a full-blown world economy has been established for close to two centuries. Modern Canada and other colonies were the direct result of the European expansion that laid the foundations for the current world economy. During this expansion, Europe's outlook was indeed outward. At other times, as in the period that spanned the beginning of the First World War and the close of the Second, countries become relatively inward looking.

> One of the persisting themes of the history of the modern world is the seesaw between 'nationalism' and 'internationalism.' I do not refer to the ideological seesaw, though it of course exists, but to the organizational one. At some points in time the major economic and political institutions are geared to operating in the international arena and feel that local interests are tied in some immediate way to developments elsewhere in the world. At other points of time, the social actors tend to engage their efforts locally, tend to see the reinforcement of state boundaries as primary, and move toward a relative indifference about events beyond them. (Wallerstein 1974: 225)

Since the Second World War, and particularly since the mid-1980s, the outlook has again become internationalized. Many commentators have understood this latest phase as something novel and described it as globalization. But this process in neither new nor, if history is any indication, unidirectional.

In the following chapters, we will see whether Canada's economy has indeed been catapulted beyond the bounds of Wallerstein's seesaw or whether it still operates within its confines. In other words, we are going to examine this last phase of internationalism to determine whether it is unusual in degree. We will start by taking a detailed look at Canada's trading patterns.

Chapter 4

Trade

Introduction

The impact of globalization is most commonly illustrated by way of trade statistics. This 'dizzying increase in cross-border exchanges,' as the *Globe and Mail* has put it, shows an impressive increase in international trade over the past few decades. For the most part, figures presented usually go back to the 1950s or 1960s, but seldom farther. One reason for this lack of data may well be that most organizations that track this sort of activity did not come into existence until after the Second World War. The United Nations (UN) and associated organizations such as the World Bank, the International Monetary Fund (IMF), and the United Nations Conference on Trade and Development (UNCTAD) were not formed until 1945.[1] And the Organization for Economic Cooperation and Development (OECD) did not come into existence until 1960. Figures for individual countries do exist, of course, but bringing them together is time consuming and riddled with methodological obstacles. There are statistical compendia in existence, such as Rostow's excellent *The World Economy: History and Prospect* (1978), that do investigate economic indicators extensively, but they are esoteric in the sense that they are not widely available, and insufficient in that they are often incomplete. But, as we saw in chapter 3, a lack of statistics does not mean that the countries of the world only started to trade extensively following the Second World War. This paucity of data makes one wonder whether we are turning a deaf ear to history. It is this longer history that we focus on in this chapter. But first a few methodological details.

GDP and GNP in Canada

To track trade statistics in current dollars as they are published by Statistics Canada would be essentially meaningless. Inflation and a
steadily growing population provide a constantly changing context in
which this trade takes place. For this reason, the best and most common
way to present such data is as a proportion of the economy; that is, trade
as a percentage of the Gross Domestic Product (GDP). Given the ongoing and current obsession with the GDP, it is somewhat surprising that
this statistic did not come into common use until after the Second World
War (Block and Burns 1986). Canada, along with the Soviet Union, was
one of the first countries to track this indicator, starting in 1926, with
other nations following suit throughout the Second World War (Hobsbawm 1994). Given the shortage of Canadian data before that time, I
relied on estimates provided by M.C. Urquhart (1993) for the years
1870–1925. Trade figures for the years 1868 and 1869 are available, as are
Gross National Product (GNP) figures (Firestone 1958), but in light of
Urquhart's work, the GNP estimates must be treated with caution, and
consequently the data are presented only from 1870 onwards.

Canada in Comparative Perspective

It is no coincidence that the bulk of the globalization literature originates
in the United States, a country that has historically been self-reliant and
that has only recently adopted a more open approach to trade. Having
emerged as the undisputed economic power following the Second
World War, the United States has since had its economic dominance
challenged by Japan and Europe. These developments have prompted
many economists to look for an explanation. Globalization is one theory
that seems to fit the facts and provides a plausible explanation for the relative decline of the American Empire.

   Canada, on the other hand, particularly when compared to the United
States, has always been an international trading power with a relatively
open economy (Clement 1988: 76), first as a key colony of Britain and
then as an economic satellite of the United States (G. Williams 1986).
Support for open borders first gathered momentum when the British
adopted free trade in the mid-1840s. This meant that Canada lost pref-
erential treatment within the empire, the next logical step being a free-
trade agreement with the United States. Canada has attempted to nego-
tiate such a deal at least a dozen times since, most notably in 1854 (an

Table 4.1
Exports as a percentage of GDP, selected OECD countries, OECD total, and as a percentage of GWP

	Canada	U.S.	U.K.	Australia	Sweden	OECD	World
1960	18.4	4.4	22.3	20.1	20.1	10.9	9.6
1970	20.1	5.5	22.2	24.3	24.3	12.7	
1980	26.6	10.9	25.0	17.6	31.4	20.1	
1990	25.8	11.4	27.1	17.7	29.5	18.7	20.0
2001	43.8	10.3	27.1	21.4	45.2	23.7	29.0

Source: OECD (1997, 2003b), Brown et al. (1996), Human Development Report (2003)

agreement that lasted for twelve years), 1911 (Canada rejected free trade in an election), and 1989 (the present agreement that was expanded into NAFTA in 1994).

This urge to trade is reflective of smaller developed countries, which have always been more international in their outlook than larger ones (Helliwell 2002: 17). In other words, smaller industrial economies are more dependent on trade. Table 4.1 shows that Canada's exports are close to triple those of the United States and approximately double the OECD average. Canadian trading figures are also considerably higher than those for Australia, which is also largely dependent on resource extraction and exports. The only country that matches Canada's exports is Sweden, which has a much smaller economy and population (9 million people) than Canada (31 million), but is also more industrialized. In the OECD as a whole, exports have more than doubled between 1960 and 2001, meaning that Canada is not an atypical case. The United States now ships fewer exports as a percentage of GDP than Canada did in 1960. This does not, however, mean that U.S. trade is insignificant. Given that the U.S. economy is so large, the relatively small percentage devoted to trade still constitutes the largest amount in the world in terms of dollar value. Table 4.2, which tracks imports for the same period, tells much the same story as for exports – a doubling of imports for the majority of countries as well as increased trade dependence for the smaller countries.

The Canadian Data

The following data trace Canada's trading patterns back to 1870, three years after Confederation, first with all countries, and then according

Table 4.2
Imports as a percentage of GDP, selected OECD countries, and OECD total

	Canada	U.S.	U.K.	Australia	Sweden	OECD
1960	17.2	5.2	20.9	13.6	22.7	11.3
1970	22.7	5.8	23.1	14.9	23.8	13.1
1980	28.5	10.2	27.3	17.0	29.5	19.3
1990	25.5	9.9	24.4	16.9	29.9	18.5
2001	38.6	13.8	29.5	21.6	39.4	24.3

Source: OECD (1997, 2003b)

to its major trading partners in the various regions or continents (for details, please see the appendix). It should be kept in mind that these figures are for goods only (merchandise trade) and therefore lower than the OECD figures presented above, which are for both goods and services. This distinction is important because, as we shall learn later, services do not trade as well as goods.

Figure 4.1 depicts foreign trade from 1960 through 2003 as a percentage of GDP. As was noted earlier, this is the sort of graph usually presented when the globalization argument is invoked. The graph does indeed show a considerable rise in trade, in terms of both exports and imports (which are almost always identical and more indicative of a barter system than of a truly internationalized trade system). That rise in trade is especially apparent from 1990 onwards, with the introduction of the Canada–U.S. Free Trade Agreement (FTA). In the decade spanning 1990 to 1999, trade rose from 20 per cent of GDP to 30 per cent, a 50 per cent increase. However, it started to fall again by the year 2000. But the graph is biased in that it includes only a short segment of Canada's history and obscures two-thirds of Canada's economy (that is, if the scale on the left were to include 100 per cent of the economy, the lines would obviously be much less impressive).

Figure 4.2 presents Canada's international trade in terms of exports and imports from 1870 to 2003. The first observation that can be made is that the sharp increase in trade that occurred in the 1990s is much less impressive when put into the historical context of the past 133 years. Exports reached 30 per cent of GDP during both world wars, and import figures in the 1870s and up to and including the early part of the twentieth century were not matched again until the 1990s. Trade figures, especially for exports, experienced a trough in the early 1960s

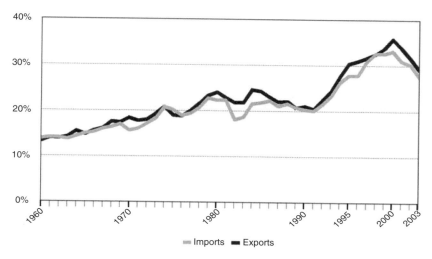

Figure 4.1. Canadian exports and imports as a percentage of GDP, 1960–2003

and were considerably lower than in the era preceding the First World War. This is also true for the rest of the world, as world trade figures did not match the pre-First World War figures until well into the 1970s (Findlay and O'Rourke 2003). One of the assumptions that globalists make is that the increase in trade we have experienced since the 1960s will continue; if the past is any indication, however, trade patterns are cyclical and there is no guarantee that this trend will continue. As can be seen, trade started to decline in the early twenty-first century. This probably occurred for a variety of reasons, the rise of the Canadian dollar being one of the more important.

Figure 4.2 also reveals that trade has always been an important aspect of Canada's economy. But who is this trade with? This is a key question because a central tenet of the globalization argument is concerned with increased competition, and hence imports, from Third World countries, which are perceived to be a threat to the Canadian economy because of their lower wages and labour standards. The most accurate way to answer this question is to examine exports[2] and imports according to continent or region: Europe, Asia, Africa, Oceania (which economically consists primarily of Australia and New Zealand), the United States, and Other Americas (which includes Mexico, South America, Central America, and the Caribbean), and, starting in 1954, the Middle East

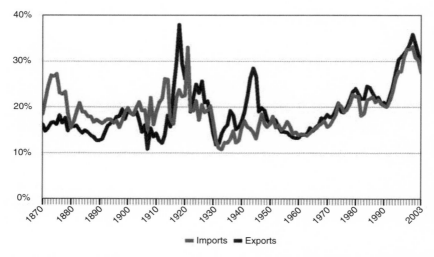

Figure 4.2. Canadian exports and imports as a percentage of GDP, 1870–2003

(which is included in Asia and Africa statistics prior to that date). We first examine exports, because world trade figures are usually presented that way, and then move on to imports.

Exports

Once Canada's three most important trading regions are examined, the growing importance of the U.S. market since the Second World War becomes abundantly clear (see figure 4.3). Exports to the United States were relatively even at around 5 per cent of GDP in the nineteenth century and only started to increase shortly before the First World War. They settled back to 5 per cent in the depth of the Depression but from that time on pursued an upward trend that has seen few setbacks. This upward rally started to accelerate in the mid-1960s and again in 1990 with the signing of the FTA (officially signed in 1988 and implemented in 1989). In all, exports to the United States constituted 87 per cent of Canada's total exports in 2002 compared to an average of just below 60 per cent in the 1960s.

Also notable is the doubling of exports to Asia. At just over 3 per cent of GDP, however, their importance appears to be exaggerated in globalization accounts. Asia is less important to Canada's economy

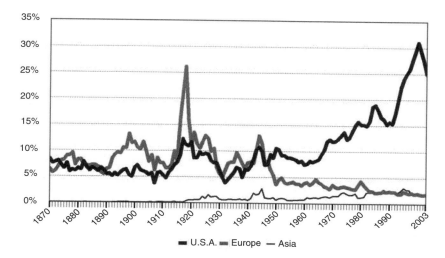

Figure 4.3. Canadian exports as a percentage of GDP, various continents, 1870–2003

now than Europe was in the nineteenth century or most of the twentieth. As can clearly be seen, exports to Europe shot up during the First World War and again during the Second World War. Overall, it may be observed that the importance of the European market has declined since Confederation while that of the Asian market has increased. The magnitude of these fluctuations, however, cannot compare with the overwhelming importance of the U.S. market. Another way of looking at this is to view this as a battle for economic dominance between the United States and Europe for the first eighty years following Confederation, a battle that was clearly won by the United States following the Second World War. After that point, Canadian trade ties with Europe progressively weakened, perhaps as a result of an increase in insularity among the countries of the European Union.

What about the other regions of the world: Africa, Australia, the Middle East, and Latin America? It should be noted that the scale used for figure 4.4 is one-tenth (0–3 per cent) of the previous figure (0–30 per cent), which should give some indication of just how peripheral these areas are to the Canadian economy (with a few exceptions such as Africa during the Second World War and, as we shall soon see in the section on imports, the Middle East during the oil shocks of the mid-

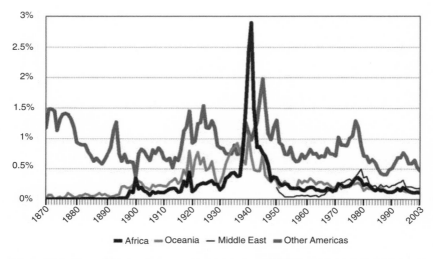

Figure 4.4. Canadian exports as a percentage of GDP, various continents, 1870–2003

1970s). The largest export market for Canada among these regions is the Other Americas. Current export figures to this area are relatively low by historical standards, even with the entry of Mexico into NAFTA in 1994. These figures reached their zenith around the turn of the twentieth century, when Canada's trade with this region focused on the West Indies.

International data show that during the Second World War indications were that South America was going to successfully join the world economy, although such predictions were never fulfilled (Gordon 1988: 34, 35). Canada's exports to this region fell following the Second World War, and this trend continued right into the 1960s, mirroring a larger global trend. Canadian exports to the region did pick up slowly during the 1970s but fell again with the beginning of the debt crisis in the 1980s. Trade with the Other Americas increased marginally after the introduction of NAFTA, but declined again at the beginning of the new millennium. Still, exports to this region are, historically speaking, low. As a matter of fact, exports as a percentage of GDP to the Other Americas throughout the 1870s were at their highest, except for the period of the Second World War. Africa is essentially shut out of Canada's economy, and this is true for the world economy as a whole, suggesting that globalization is at best a relative term. Oceania and the

Middle East are also only marginal to Canada's economy, although for different reasons. While Africa is shut out for political reasons, Oceania and the Middle East have relatively small populations and therefore markets. Combined exports to Africa, Oceania, and the Middle East have been below 1.5 per cent of Canada's GDP since the close of the Second World War. Given the distance of these regions from Canada, this paucity of trade is understandable, although globalization theory, with its emphasis on the collapse of time and space, would have a tendency to diminish this explanation.

With the exception of the importance of the U.S. market, world trade is generally consistent with Canada's trade patterns. Asia's share has risen, but in global terms it is far from astounding. The four Asian newly industrial economies (NICs) more than doubled their share of world trade from 2.2 per cent in 1970 to 5.5 per cent in 1990. During the same period, the share of the Latin American NICs (Mexico, Brazil, and Argentina) shrank from 2.6 per cent to 2.1 per cent. Another way to look at these figures is in terms of industrial output. While the share of industrial output of the Asian and Latin American NICs (minus Argentina) has increased considerably, from 2.7 per cent in 1970 to 5.8 per cent in 1989, this share remains only a small portion of the world economy (Wade 1996: 69).[3] Interestingly, it is usually these regions on which attention is focused. Given the experiences of Latin America of late, Southeast Asia is really the only region in the world that has experienced a protracted boom since the mid-1970s. Everywhere else, economies have stagnated or slumped. And one region does not globalization make.

Imports

As expected, imports tell a story remarkably similar to that of exports. Figure 4.5 shows a secular decrease of imports from Europe into Canada and the increasing importance of those originating south of the border. Here the divergence between Europe and the United States is even more apparent than with exports. This trend also begins much earlier for imports – in 1900, compared to 1945 for exports. The only period in which European imports were higher than those from the United States was in the 1870s. From then on European imports became increasingly less important to the Canadian economy. American imports follow exactly the opposite trend. Throughout the twentieth century, U.S. imports dominated Canada's economy, a dominance that was further buttressed by the two free-trade agreements signed

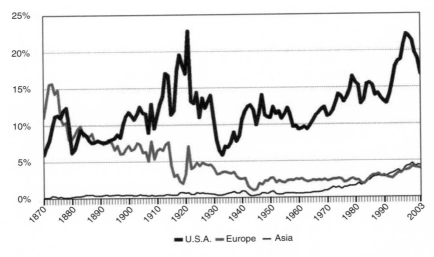

Figure 4.5. Canadian imports as a percentage of GDP, various continents, 1870–2003

since 1988. Asian imports have also increased, but again, not in comparison with those from Canada's southern neighbour. Current imports from Asia are also lower than imports from Europe have been at any time during the past century. As with exports, imports from Asia at present make up only about 4 per cent of Canada's GDP, a trend that has been slow but steady in the making.

Noting again the difference in scale (2 per cent versus 25 per cent), figure 4.6 shows that imports from the Other Americas have waxed and waned considerably since Confederation and are currently only slightly above average. With the exception of Middle Eastern imports around the time of the oil shocks, the value of goods shipped from Oceania, Africa, and the Middle East amounts to approximately 0.25 per cent each, totalling less than 1 per cent of Canada's GDP. Again, these regions are virtually shut out of Canada's economy. Imports from the Other Americas are marginally higher, but only once did they even reach 2 per cent of Canada's GDP. In the nineteenth century, sugar cane played an important role, and in the twentieth the Second World War provided economic opportunities for that region. These opportunities seem to have been on the decline in the postwar years, only to be resurrected in the 1990s.

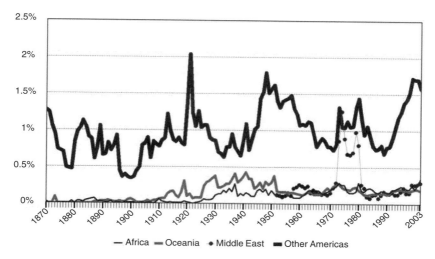

Figure 4.6. Canadian imports as a percentage of GDP, various continents, 1870–2003

The graphs we have seen so far illustrate the overwhelming importance of the U.S. market for the Canadian economy in terms of both exports and imports, and, with the exception of Asia, the declining significance of other regions. We now take a closer look at this trend by aggregating some of the above findings.

A Summary

The preceding trade figures show an ever-increasing reliance on the American economy, a reliance that has escalated consistently and with few breaks since Confederation. This development is well illustrated in figure 4.7 where Canada's global trade (exports plus imports) is presented both with and without the U.S. data. Viewed from this perspective, Canada's trade with the rest of the world has stayed relatively flat since 1950. In fact, world trade has generally been lower in the past half-century than in the half-century following Confederation.

In other words, Canada's economy is *less globalized* now than at any time before the 1920s. The reason global trade was high in the nineteenth century was primarily because of vigorous trade with Great Britain, a reliance that has waned considerably since. This economic

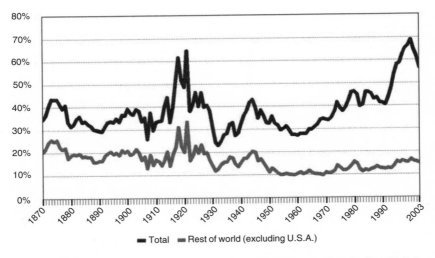

Figure 4.7. Canadian trade as a percentage of GDP, total and excluding U.S.A.,
1870–2003

vacuum was taken up by the United States, which has increasingly come to dominate Canadian trade, despite the decreasing costs of transportation so much celebrated by globalists. As a share of its economy, Canada's overseas trade (or trans-oceanic trade, to be more precise) was greater at any time in the nineteenth century than it has been in the past fifty years. This is despite the relatively unsophisticated transportation technologies available then. Data such as these demonstrate that politics mattered immensely in the last century, much more than geographical constraints. The same can, no doubt, be said for today.

Yet another way of examining aggregate trade data is to put them into the context of Canada's entire economy. This shows that, once the exports and imports of goods are accounted for, Canada's economy is still close to 70 per cent domestic. Figure 4.8 shows that when 100 per cent of the economy is taken into consideration, the importance of trade appears to be significantly diminished. Furthermore, the vast majority of these imports come from Canada's only contiguous neighbour, the United States. Figure 4.9 shows that once only newly industrializing and non-industrial countries are considered (that is, when the advanced industrial countries of Japan, the United States, Europe, and Oceania are excluded), imports amounted to only 5.5 per cent of Canada's economy

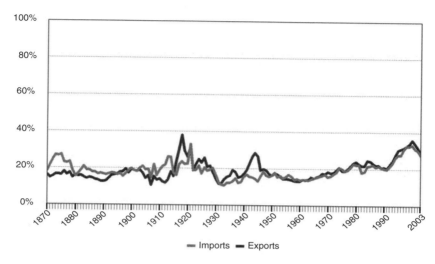

Figure 4.8. Canadian exports and imports as a percentage of GDP, 1870–2003

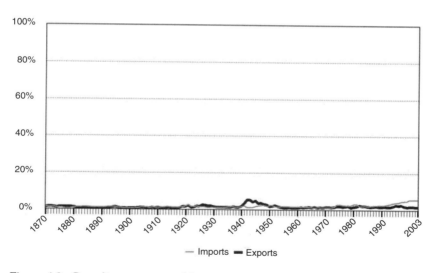

Figure 4.9. Canadian exports and imports, non-industrial world only, as a percentage of GDP, 1870–2003

in 2003. At $70 billion this is considerable, but not enough to endanger Canada's $1.2 trillion economy. These figures show the harsh winds of globalization to be nothing more than a draft.

The preceding data demonstrate that seven-tenths of Canada's economic activity is conducted within its own borders and that many problems, including high unemployment, are not likely to be caused by outside events such as competition from low-wage countries. Nor are Canada's economic shortcomings likely to be solved by more trade. Trade has acted as a kind of diversion, and pressures for increased competitiveness have only served as an excuse to cut social programs or keep wages low. Such debates are, of course, important, but they should be more comprehensive and explore how social programs can help make Canada more competitive rather than just focusing on their imagined negative impact.

Goods and Services

The preceding data refer only to exchanges of goods and are vulnerable to criticism on the grounds that modern economies are becoming increasingly service-oriented or postindustrial. Also, it is often believed that products associated with a service economy can be produced anywhere and are not subject to the same constraints as material products (Lash and Urry 1994; Waters 2001). Others, however, have taken exactly the opposite tack and argued that, as economies become more reliant on services, they also become less trade-intensive (Wade 1996). Figure 4.10 clearly shows that, as economies become more service oriented, they are not likely to experience increased trade. In Canada, as a percentage of GDP, trade in services has consistently hovered around the 5 to 6 per cent mark since 1926 (with the exception of the Second World War, when imports of services briefly rose to 14 per cent).

A service-oriented economy means less trade for a number of reasons. First, in a service society the emphasis is on education, which is not easily traded. In Canada, education expenditures amount to between 7 and 8 per cent of Canada's GDP. Second, as the population ages, it consumes more health services, which, with few exceptions, are provided domestically. In Canada, this currently amounts to more than 10 per cent of the economy. Real estate, financial services, and food services are also products not amenable to trade. Add to that private and public consumption that is also unlikely to move (for example, construction), and the result is an economy that is firmly planted within Canada's borders.

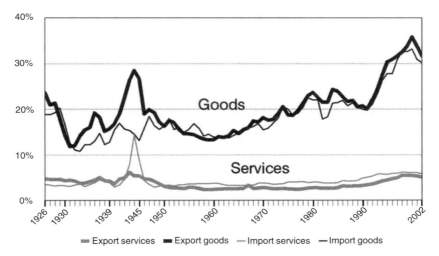

Figure 4.10. Exports and imports of goods and services as a percentage of GDP, Canada, 1926–2002

Services such as tourism and entertainment may indeed be globalizing, but they account for only a small proportion of the average consumer's budget.

The degree to which the Canadian economy has become more service-oriented is best illustrated by labour-market trends. Almost three-quarters of the Canadian labour force (74 per cent, to be precise) work in the service sector (*The Daily*, 12 Feb. 2003). Once construction is included, this proportion rises to 80 per cent. This is not to dismiss the importance of the manufacturing and resource sectors to Canada's economy, only to point out that the threat of footloose corporations is an idle one to most Canadian workers. The majority of Canadian workers (e.g., teachers, nurses, sales clerks, knowledge workers) are employed in the service industry and do not compete with workers from abroad.

It is commonly believed that manufacturing provides the backbone for the economy, and that its absence would lead to economic collapse. This kind of thinking, sometimes referred to as a 'manufacturing fetish' (Howlett et al. 1999: 37), is implicit in the globalization thesis, which laments the de-industrialization of the First World and identifies industrial growth in the Third World. The best response to this position is to compare our contemporary debate to debates that took place during the transition from an agrarian to an industrial society. This view is mostly associated with a group of French economists known as the physiocrats, who believed that agriculture was the only source of real prosperity and that the manufacturing industry was nothing short of parasitic (Heilbroner 1980). In short, now as then, people believe there to be a 'noble sector' of the economy, a belief which, now as then, is completely unfounded (Maddison 1995: 39).

Discussion

One of the claims of this book is that the globalization thesis is biased in that it focuses on selected parts of the economy while ignoring others. The focus on consumer goods produced outside of the country is a case in point. While a TV or a VCR may be a sizeable investment, purchases of this type make up only a small portion of the average consumer's annual income. The same is true for clothes. Compared to rent, food, transportation, education, and health (with the last two funded primarily by taxes), we spend relatively little on electronic products or clothes. Even after a foreign-made product arrives in Canada, much of the profit stays within the country (in terms of sales and handling profits). Only a minority of goods and services consumed in Canada are produced outside the country, and those that are come primarily from the industrial world. The visibility of the small number of goods coming from low-wage countries may be unduly exploited by globalists. The fact that a shirt comes with a label identifying its country of origin ('made in China'), while an education or a building does not, only serves to strengthen the globalization argument. But as we have seen, this rather selective approach leaves out an important part of the story.

Of course, this may change, and imports from Asia, South America, or Africa may increase while American imports decrease. But such a scenario is unlikely for a number of reasons. Although many Third World countries do pay lower wages and have lower labour standards than are found in Canada, they still are not necessarily a threat. For one thing, productivity and wages are highly correlated (*The Economist*, 20–26 Sept. 1997: 38), meaning that corporations that do relocate to low-wage areas are in turn stuck with low productivity. Moreover, labour costs are not the only variable that companies consider. The European Commission has concluded that unit wage costs mean little without factors such as existing skills of the workforce and the ability of that workforce to adapt to new technology (*European Industrial Relations Review* 241, Feb. 1994: 15). In other words, one of the major components firms look for is a well-educated workforce. Another is political stability. In the United States, for example, trade with low-wage countries (defined as countries with less than 50 per cent of U.S. wages) is only about 3 per cent of its GDP and has not increased significantly since 1960 (Wade 1996: 67).

In general, Canada has done well when it comes to attracting industries and has experienced the exact opposite of what the globalization thesis would lead one to expect. Between the years 1995 and 2002, the number of industrial jobs has been shrinking worldwide, even in newly industrializing countries such as China, South Korea, and Brazil. Interestingly, throughout that same period, Spain and Canada, in that order, were the only two countries that were able to substantially increase their manufacturing employment (*Left Business Observer*, 24 Jan. 2004: 1, 8). This increase in industrial jobs in Canada in an era of de-industrialization can probably be linked to the automobile industry. In the four decades between 1960 and 2000, world production of passenger cars tripled (Dicken 2003: 357). Of this world production, Canada's share increased from 2.5 per cent in 1960 to 4.1 per cent in 2000 (Dicken 2003: table 11.1). Canada has also been able to grab a larger share of the North American market. Of the total number of cars built in North America, Canada's share rose consistently between 1961 and 1991, from 5.8 per cent to 17.5 per cent (Holmes 1996).

Politics

Trade agreements such as the FTA and NAFTA underscore the ongoing importance of politics. In 2003, around 80 per cent of Canada's trade took place on this continent, and 90 per cent within the OECD world. In other words, Canadian trade occurs primarily within the industrial and developed world. This flies directly in the face of globalization theory, which identifies a diminished importance for politics and geography. Canada's situation is not unique and is indicative of a larger trend towards the geographic concentration of trade within trade blocs. In single-unit Europe, Japan, and North America, trade amounts to less than 12 per cent of GDP, and the percentage is even lower for Asia and South America. This highly regionalized trade has led Wade to conclude that '*90 percent or more of these economies consists of production for the domestic market and ... 90 percent of consumption is produced at home'* (1996: 66; italics in original). From that perspective, the North American economies are becoming increasingly integrated, and Canada's economy is not so much becoming internationalized as it is continentalized. Canada's trade continues to be primarily North American (see figure 4.7). Or, to put it slightly differently, trade among the three NAFTA countries increased from 68 per cent of total trade in 1980 to 79 per cent in 1992, meaning that the rest of the world is shut out (Weiss 1997: 11). This is indicative of a larger trend of a world economy that is becoming more concentrated in the North. Between 1970 and 1989 the North's share of world trade increased from 81 to 84 per cent (Weiss 1997).

Canadian trade has long been dominated by the United States and, with the introduction of the FTA and NAFTA, this trend has only become more pronounced, which means that other countries (i.e., the rest of the globe) are becoming less important. The dramatic increase in trade with the United States is no accident but was carefully planned and reveals a vision that is anything but global. In 1976, duty-free imports to Canada from the United States and the rest of the world were identical and amounted to 61 per cent for each. By 1987 (one year before the signing of the FTA) the proportion of U.S. duty-free imports had increased to 73 per cent, while those from the rest of the world had decreased to 47 per cent (Norcliffe 1996: 41). Such developments have forced Wade (1996: 79) to conclude that *'national borders continue to be control points where governments can affect the quantity and price of cross-border merchandise transactions,* nowadays less through tariffs than through a whole panoply of nontariff barriers' (italics in original). In this sense, regional trade agreements such as NAFTA and the EU are a direct contradiction of a globalization trend and, legally speaking, are contrary to the international spirit embodied in the string of trade agreements governed by the WTO.

The increased dominance of the U.S. economy has made Canada's economy increasingly vulnerable to external shocks from the United States, and may even magnify them in the future; that is, the effect of an economic recession might be worse here in Canada than in the United States (Barnes 1996: 48). As several commentators have observed, Canada is hitching its fortunes to one star, and this dependence may turn out to be an imprudent strategy. Despite all the rhetoric about globalization, Canada's economy is becoming *not* more global but more insular and confined to this continent. Essentially, all of the increase in Canada's trade in the past four decades can be attributed to trade with the United States. It would, no doubt, be in the best interests of Canadians to diversify and pursue other opportunities in order to spread economic risk.

The left in Canada has long criticized the government for its dependence on the export of resources, often without adding value. This has resulted in a lack of an industrial base in Canada. In recent decades, this resource dependence has continued to play an important role. So, rather than experiencing the transformation of Canada's economy – that is, globalization – we are witnessing the further strengthening of economic ties with a single power, a historical pattern that began with France and continued with Great Britain and, now, the United States. As Norcliffe (1996: 25) writes,

> Since the 1960s several Pacific states have become important trading partners, and Japan and Hong Kong major sources of investment. But in its bare essentials, the mechanism of Canadian development has not changed in 500 years.

It is interesting to note that this development is completely contrary to the globalization thesis.

Conclusion

The data we have just examined indicate that, from a historical perspective, Canada's economy is becoming anything but more globalized. Some changes have occurred over the past half-century, such as an increase in imports from Asia. But even with Japan included, imports from Asia are far from flooding Canada's markets. Japan is a high-wage country, and imports from the Third World are considerably lower than from Japan, with the notable exception of those from China. As the various graphs shown above illustrate, other regions of the world are virtually excluded from Canada's economy.

This allows us to make a few observations that are true for both the global and the Canadian economy. Overall, at between 3 and 4 per cent of GDP, the influx of Third World products into the Canadian economy is relatively insignificant. Based on this, threats of competition from low-wage countries cannot be taken too seriously. The only region in the world that has been able to make inroads into the world economy in the past few decades has been Southeast Asia. And even within that region, growth has been uneven. Japan is the only country that has successfully joined the core; the four tigers (Singapore, Taiwan, South Korea, and Hong Kong) have also done well, but even there growth is slowing, and economic indicators still put them firmly in the semi-periphery. China and India are both posting robust economic growth, but this growth is benefiting only a small proportion of their huge populations, with the majority of people remaining poor. Argentina and Brazil, the economic child prodigies of the past, have experienced considerable setbacks in the past few years. In the end, only a single region has made substantial gains in the world economy over the past forty years, and this hardly justifies the declaration of globalization as the new trend.

Chapter 5

Foreign Direct Investment

Besides trade, the increase in Foreign Direct Investment (FDI) is most frequently trumpeted as evidence of globalization. FDI is rightly considered a better indicator of foreign control than portfolio investments (stocks and bonds), as the latter may stay in the host country for only days, even hours. The rapidity of these transactions has earned this kind of investment the moniker 'hot money.' In contrast, FDI often remains in the host country for years or even decades. Here in Canada, nationalists have long expressed fear about foreign investment because of a perceived loss of national control, a concern that long predates any anxiety associated with globalization.

The basis for the FDI argument with respect to globalization is not always as consistent or straightforward as it is for trade. On the one hand, large volumes of FDI are said to serve as evidence for what is often referred to as 'revolving-door' production. As the name implies, this involves the temporary use of foreign plants (preferably low-wage ones) to produce or assemble goods that are then re-imported to the wealthy countries. If that were the case, it would be reflected in the data, not only in an increase in FDI but also in an increase in imports from that country or region. In short, high FDI and high imports are part of the same equation.

On the other hand, a convincing argument can be made that an increase in FDI is indicative of a deglobalization trend. FDI, particularly here in Canada, often involves the establishment of branch plants in order to avoid restrictions such as non-tariff trade barriers on imports. In theory, in a perfectly globalized world such tactics would not be necessary, as a firm would simply be able to service the world market from a single location. But this is not the case. For example, Japanese car manufacturers are forced to build branch plants in North America in order to avoid import quotas (voluntary restraint agreements or VRAs).

Although both these arguments have some merit, looking solely at aggregate data is not enough to tell us which of these two scenarios fits best. That is, aggregate figures in isolation obscure whether FDI is the result of non-tariff barriers (an anti-globalization trend) or low-wage sites (a globalization trend). In other words, in order for FDI data to be meaningful, they need to be broken down by region in terms of both origin and destination. If FDI is moving to the Third World, then globalization is occurring; if it is primarily staying within the West, then the globalization hypothesis must be called into question.

FDI can be measured in one of two ways: flows and stocks. Flows, the more commonly used statistic, track the amount of money that crosses a border within a given year. Another involves the presentation of FDI stock – that is, the amount of accumulated FDI, including reinvestments by foreign investors. For example, if General Motors makes a $1 billion profit and reinvests half of this in the Canadian operation, its FDI stock will have risen by half a billion dollars, a figure that is ignored by flow figures. For that reason, stock data can be considered to be a more accurate indicator (see Alan D. MacPherson 1996).

FDI data for Canada are not as extensively available as trade data and do not go back farther than 1920 (for details, please see the appendix). This is unfortunate given what economists tell us about the first wave of globalization that ended with the outbreak of the First World War. This paucity of data is also regrettable because Canada has long depended on FDI, especially in its formative years immediately following Confederation, and it would be illuminating to see how figures from the nineteenth century compare to those of the twentieth. The dominance of French and then British foreign investment in the Canadian economy in its early years laid the groundwork for what some political economists have characterized as a relationship of dependency (Naylor 1972; J. Laxer 1973). Near the middle of the twentieth century, this position of domination was assumed by the United States. Of course, a theory of dependency is at odds with one that would situate Canada solidly in the core, as has been argued above. The following data should throw some light on this issue. The fact that most other countries, including the United States, are receiving increasing amounts of incoming FDI is a relatively new development that has led Gordon Laxer to conclude that we are now experiencing the 'Canadianization of the world' (1995). For FDI figures, I continue to use GDP in current dollars as a point of reference, as is commonly done (see, for example, Dicken 2003).

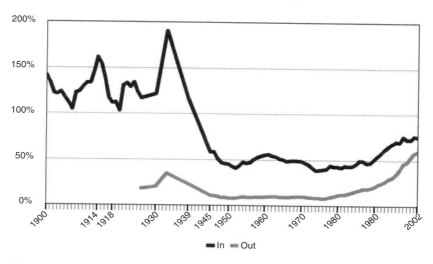

Figure 5.1. Total investment (foreign direct and portfolio), Canada, as a percentage of GDP, 1900–2002

Portfolio Investment and Foreign Direct Investment

Before examining FDI figures in detail let us step back for a moment and look at combined investment figures (FDI plus stocks and bonds) in order to get a comprehensive overview of foreign ownership in the Canadian economy. These numbers, seen in figure 5.1, clearly emphasize three important trends. First, the amount of foreign capital currently invested in Canada pales in comparison to amounts invested in any period before the Second World War. From 1900 until about 1940 this figure consistently surpassed 100 per cent of GDP, reaching almost 200 per cent during the Depression. This is somewhat surprising given the recent hysteria around the debt and deficit, where foreigners were purported to hold an ever-increasing grip on Canada's economy. In historical terms, as illustrated in the graph, this outcry appears to have been somewhat of an overreaction. Since the Second World War, Canada has had less of its economy controlled by foreign interests than at any time before that. This held true even into the 1980s and 1990s when globalization is said to have accelerated.

The second trend, not apparent in the graph, is that British dominance in the early years gradually came to be replaced by American dominance. In 1900, 85 per cent of all foreign investment originated in Great

Britain. By 1922, this plummeted to less than half (47 per cent) of all investment, with the other half coming from the United States (and only 3 per cent from other countries). Following the Second World War, the United States came to dominate foreign investment in Canada and continues to do so today. The graph also shows that the stock of investment held abroad (data are only available starting in 1920) is historically unprecedented, indicating that Canada has recently become a dominant player in the export of capital. The third and related trend is that outgoing and ingoing investments have converged and are now more similar than at any other point in history.

Flows

Much of the discussion about FDI has concentrated on flows. The figures paraded usually show a considerable increase, especially in outgoing investment; for example, from just under $50 million in 1960 to more than $66 billion in the year 2000, a dramatic rise indeed. Even when the size of the economy and inflation are taken into consideration, the pace of growth is impressive: from 0.13 per cent of GDP in 1960 to just over 6 per cent of GDP in 2000. Also interesting is the fact that while Canada was largely on the receiving end of FDI throughout the 1950s, 1960s, and 1970s, this relationship gradually became more equitable in the 1980s, with outgoing investment surpassing incoming flows for several years in the early 1990s (see figure 5.2). From 1950 to 1990, the figures for incoming FDI rarely exceed 2 per cent. But in the late 1990s figures skyrocketed to 9 per cent for incoming FDI and 6 per cent for outgoing, only to settle back to more typical levels in 2003. As a matter of fact, the figure for 2003 plummeted to considerably less than average – less than 1 per cent for incoming and slightly over 2 per cent for outgoing FDI. This is reflective of a worldwide speculative bubble that saw a spate of mergers and takeovers in the late 1990s and all but collapsed in 2003. As with trade, foreign direct investment is also influenced by changes in the value of the dollar. When the Canadian dollar was undervalued in the late 1990s and early 2000s, bargain hunters in the United States took advantage and acquired existing businesses in Canada. This behaviour stopped suddenly with the rise of the dollar in 2003.

Flow figures, however, may not be all that good an indicator of FDI, as they ignore how capital accumulates. In this sense, FDI stock paints a more accurate picture of foreign ownership in Canada, and for that reason stock data will provide the bulk of the analysis.

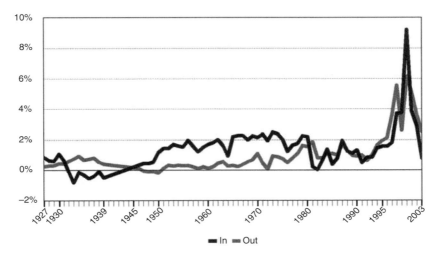

Figure 5.2. Foreign direct investment flows, Canada, as a percentage of GDP, 1927–2003

FDI Stock

In this section we examine FDI stock in more detail. In addition to looking at aggregate figures, we trace the point of origin for FDI stock in Canada and the destinations for Canadian-owned FDI abroad. To quickly review, the logic behind the globalization argument goes something like this: Capital is no longer constrained by geographic boundaries and will naturally gravitate to where returns are highest. Often this entails investing in Third World countries where labour is cheapest. Globalization also means that national governments are less able to dictate policies to investors, as capital that has become dissatisfied with too much regulation can easily move elsewhere.

One problem with direct investment data is that any movement of capital can be variously interpreted. An increase of FDI stock can be read to mean that foreign capital is controlling more of the host country's economy, a circumstance that is often feared to impinge on a nation's sovereignty. On the other hand, a decrease of FDI can be understood to mean that foreign investors are pulling out their money in order to invest in the Third World, where more profits can be realized. The globalization argument is thus unfalsifiable in that both an increase

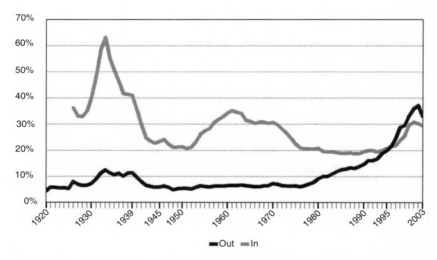

Figure 5.3. FDI stock, in and out, Canada, as a percentage of GDP, 1920–2003

and a decrease in FDI can be used as evidence to support its claims. Once we are able to identify the sources and reasons behind these kinds of investment we can better determine whether FDI undermines or corroborates the globalization thesis. This is the task of the following section, where we take a closer look at incoming and outgoing FDI in turn.

Incoming

As a quick overview, figure 5.3 shows that the foreign-owned stock of FDI in Canada as a percentage of GDP is, by historical standards, relatively unremarkable. It reached a high point during the 1930s, dropped near the beginning of the Second World War, rose again throughout the 1960s and underwent a steady decline between 1975 and 1990. From approximately 1995 onwards, incoming FDI increased and returned to 1960s levels. Outgoing FDI, on the other hand, is at a historic high, having more than tripled since the late 1970s. This is the first time in Canada's history that there is a relative balance between outgoing and incoming FDI. And, since the mid-1990s, Canada's foreign holdings have actually exceeded those held in Canada by investors abroad.

In 2003, Canadian FDI abroad amounted to $429 billion, while FDI in Canada was $358 billion. However, as a proportion of global direct

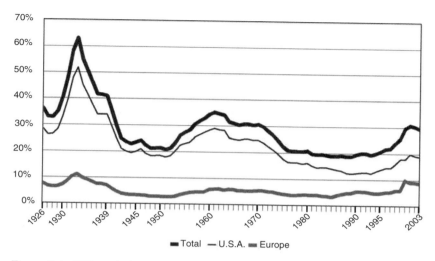

Figure 5.4. FDI stock, in, various continents, Canada, as a percentage of GDP, 1926–2003

investment, Canada's share has been falling. Between 1980 and 2002, Canada's share fell from 7.7 to 3.1 per cent. But this loss 'cannot be blamed on increasing investment flows to India, China and other developing countries, because developed economies such as the United States and the European Union have been able to maintain or increase their share of global investment' (Conference Board of Canada 2004).

A closer examination of incoming FDI shows that the pattern of foreign ownership is very much the result of American investment, which, although somewhat gradually on the wane, continues to dominate (see figure 5.4). Next in order of importance, and this should come as no surprise, is investment originating in Europe. This second-place position has remained relatively consistent since 1926. Before the Second World War, FDI from countries other than the United States and Europe was virtually non-existent. Another way of analysing these data is to combine American and European investments, in which case 94 per cent of all foreign direct investment in Canada is accounted for. As we saw with trade, the United States dominates FDI in Canada. While American investment rose substantially in the late 1990s, it started a downward trend throughout 2002 and 2003, reflecting the rise of the Canadian dollar and the general demise of the investment boom.

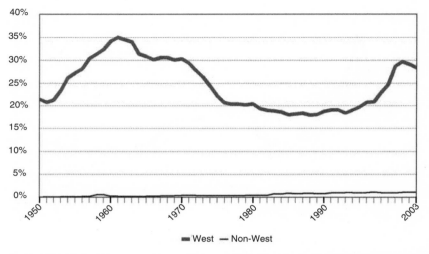

Figure 5.5. FDI stock, in and out, Canada, as a percentage of GDP, 1920–2003

One reason behind the increase in foreign direct investment, other than mergers and takeovers, is good old protectionism. In order to circumvent 'voluntary' trade barriers, foreign firms are forced to establish a presence abroad through branch plants. In Canada, Honda and Toyota have invested billions in car plants in southern Ontario. And Americans continue to invest billions in Canada, taking advantage of a low dollar and generous welfare-state programs. Lately, generous incentives provided by state governments in the southern United States have meant that manufacturing plants are relocating within the United States, rather than moving abroad. However, Canada has recently fought back, with the promise of a billion dollars' worth of subsidies geared towards manufacturing industries.

In sum, the vast majority of FDI in Canada originates within the First World. In order to isolate changes in FDI originating in non-Western countries, we need to make use of a magnifying device they are so small. FDI owned outside of Europe and the United States was essentially non-existent until after the Second World War, and for that reason the time span used in figure 5.5. has been truncated to go back only to 1950. But even from that period onwards, these figures are minuscule, rarely exceeding 1 per cent. The source of this non-Western investment is primarily Southeast Asia.

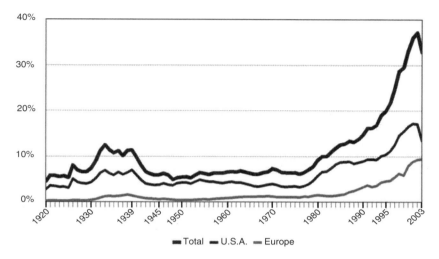

■Total ■U.S.A. ■Europe

Figure 5.6. FDI stock, out, various regions, Canada, as a percentage of GDP, 1920–2003

Outgoing

While Canada has long been a significant recipient of FDI, it has only recently taken on the role of major exporter. This trend first started to become noticeable in the late 1970s, with the major destinations for Canadian FDI, as with incoming investments, being the United States and Europe (see figure 5.6). Investment in Europe did not start to increase appreciably until the mid-1980s, and it still constitutes less than U.S. assets. The reasons for the changes in FDI owned abroad are both different from and similar to those for FDI owned in Canada. Different in the sense that some outgoing FDI, especially that located in the United States, has primarily consisted of mergers and acquisitions. The rapid increase in FDI stock starting in the late 1980s and early 1990s can be traced directly to large-scale corporate mergers. Between 1997 and 2002, the Canadian stock of foreign FDI nearly doubled, from $218 billion to $429 billion, an increase of $211 billion. Of this, $144 billion was accounted for by mergers and acquisitions. During the same time period, incoming stocks increased by $154 billion, $124 billion of which involved corporate takeovers (*The Daily*, 25 May 2004). This situation is not unique to Canada but represents a worldwide trend that has seen

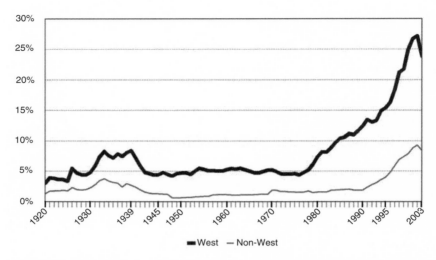

Figure 5.7. FDI stock, out, West and non-West, Canada, as a percentage of GDP, 1920–2003

FDI going towards existing rather than new enterprises. Corporate mergers and acquisitions grew sevenfold throughout the 1990s. In 2000, worldwide cross-border takeovers exceeded the U.S. $1 trillion mark; however, by 2003, these flows plummeted to less than $200 billion (OECD 2003c: 8).

Another reason for the increase of Canadian FDI located in Europe is an attempt to avoid voluntary import restrictions. The upsurge of FDI, beginning in the 1980s, occurred as Canadian companies such as Northern Telecom, Bombardier, and Fleet Aerospace built branch plants inside the European community. The motivation behind these moves was the need to acquire stable access to the European market, which is in danger of being restricted by EU technical standards and discriminatory procurements (Alan D. MacPherson 1996: 78).

As can be seen in figure 5.7, as a percentage of GDP, FDI going to the Third World has increased considerably, from less than 2 per cent of GDP in the 1980s to around 9 per cent in 2002, although it receded somewhat in 2003. While the amount of FDI stock in the Third World has increased, as a proportion of total FDI it has remained relatively stable and continues to range somewhere between 15 and 25 per cent of total foreign assets abroad, as it has for most of the past eighty-three years.

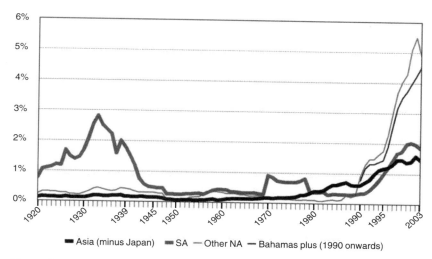

Figure 5.8. FDI stock, out, various regions, Canada, as a percentage of GDP, 1920–2003

But where exactly in the Third World is Canadian FDI located? Figure 5.8 illustrates that, historically, the majority of direct investment went to South America, a pattern most noticeable during the Depression. In the past two decades, investment destined for Asia has also increased substantially, and accumulated assets in that location approximately match those in South America. In South America, Brazil and Argentina are the major recipients of Canadian foreign investment; in Asia, in 2003, it was, in descending order, Indonesia, Singapore, and Hong Kong. It is somewhat surprising that little investment is located in either India or China, two countries that have experienced robust economic growth in recent years.

The largest increase of Canadian investment going abroad, however, is in investment destined for the Caribbean (included in 'Other NA' in the graph). This figure increased rapidly from less than one-third of 1 per cent of GDP in 1989 to over 5 per cent by 2002. However, closer inspection reveals that, throughout that same time period, between 80 and 90 per cent of FDI found its way to only four countries in that region: the Bahamas, Bermuda, Barbados, and the Cayman Islands. The thin line in figure 5.8 that shadows the 'Other NA' figures represents these four Caribbean countries and shows that the increase of FDI going to 'Other NA' can be virtually entirely explained by money going to these four tax havens. As a matter of fact, around half (between 41 and 53 per cent) of the increase in Canadian foreign-owned assets outside of the industrial world (see figure 5.7) can be explained by funds channelled to these four Caribbean countries. This primarily involves Canadian companies that have moved their headquarters abroad for income-tax purposes, a practice condemned by the auditor general. By the year 2000, there were 1,700 such Canadian companies found in Barbados alone, Prime Minister Paul Martin's (now his sons') Canada Steamship Lines being one of them (*National Post*, 15 Jan. 2004: 3).

Figures for other countries in the Caribbean, Central and South America, and Asia, remain low. Looked at from another angle, in 1970, of all the Canadian FDI owned abroad, 25 per cent was located in the non-developing world. For most of the 1980s, this share decreased to around 15 per cent, only to return to its 25 per cent share in the 2000s. This means that Canadian foreign investment remains concentrated in the West and, once the Caribbean countries are taken into account, Canadian FDI is less inclusive of the Third World now than at any time in the past. Furthermore, outgoing investment located in the Third World is not going towards productive enterprises but to avoid domestic taxes, with almost half of Canadian investment in the Third World going to the Caribbean.

Canada is not unusual in having the bulk of its investment in the First World. Eighty per cent of the world's stock of FDI in 2000 was concentrated in the United States, the European Union, and Japan; 88 per cent of it originated in the industrial world, principally in the United States, Great Britain, and France (Dicken 2003: 73, 56). In the Third World, the majority (70.4 per cent) of direct investment is located in already established NICs, Hong Kong, China, and Brazil being the top three. The rest of the world is bypassed. Furthermore, there was more FDI going to the Third World in the first wave of globalization than in the present one. In 1913, 63 per cent of FDI went to the Third World; in 1996 it was only 28 per cent (Ferguson 2003).

Manufacturing

The globalization argument rests on the premise that manufacturing is moving from the First World to the Third. In order to investigate this claim further, it is worthwhile to examine this sector of the economy in more detail. Unfortunately, these figures are available only up until 1991, as Statistics Canada subsequently changed the way it categorized

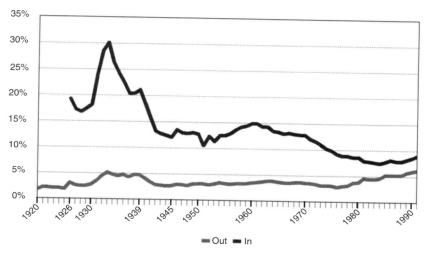

Figure 5.9. Manufacturing FDI, Canada, as a percentage of GDP, 1920–1991

these data. Figure 5.9 shows that outgoing and incoming manufacturing FDI in Canada, as a percentage of GDP, has undergone a gradual convergence, although Canada remains a net winner in that it is able to attract more manufacturing FDI than it exports. Since 1960, manufacturing FDI has averaged about one-third of total FDI for incoming and one-quarter for outgoing assets. As a percentage of GDP, manufacturing FDI made up 6 per cent of GDP for outgoing and 10 per cent for incoming in 1991. While the manufacturing portion of FDI has been shrinking, this cannot be directly linked to globalization as it merely reflects a de-industrialization trend occurring worldwide.

In Canada, outgoing manufacturing FDI (as a percentage of GDP) was remarkably stable between 1920 and 1980, with a slow and steady increase between 1980 and 1991. This FDI, however, is going not to the Third World but to the First. As figure 5.10 illustrates, only about one-half of 1 per cent of GDP is invested in manufacturing outside of the OECD world, a figure that was lower in 1990 than in 1960. As a share of all manufacturing FDI, the portion going to non-OECD countries has also been shrinking. This figure peaked at just over 15 per cent in 1965, averaged around 9 per cent in the 1970s, and dropped to an average of 6 per cent in the 1980s. In short, any increase in manufacturing FDI invested outside of Canada has followed a diverging trend between the OECD and non-OECD world in favour of the already wealthy industrial

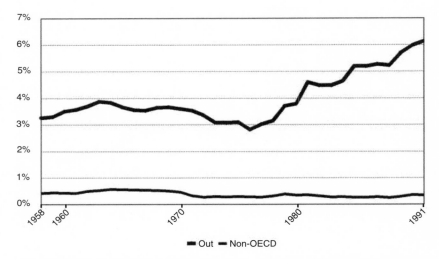

Figure 5.10. Manufacturing FDI, Canada, as a percentage of GDP, total and to non-OECD world, 1958–1991

world. This trend is not unique to Canada and is apparent worldwide:

> [This study shows] developed markets continue to get an ever larger share of [manufacturing] investments – now standing at nearly 84 percent and up from 61 percent in 2000. While investments into developed markets of Western Europe, Canada, and Asia-Pacific have remained steady for the last 4 years, investments into emerging, low-cost locations in developing economies have dropped more than 80 percent. For example, U.S. manufacturing FDI into China fell to just US$500 million in 2002, down nearly 70 percent from US$1.6 billion in 2001. (Deloitte and Touche 2004)

This is the exact opposite of what one would expect to find based on the globalization thesis. Why would this be so? While there is a general downward trend of manufacturing FDI located in Canada (which would support the globalization thesis), this is matched by a decrease of FDI going to the Third World or the non-OECD world (which refutes the same theory). Combined, the overall trend points to less manufacturing investment both within Canada and the rest of the world, suggesting a trend towards de-industrialization rather than globalization. The globalization thesis is further undermined by an increase in Canadian manufacturing FDI going to Europe. These trends are indicative not of borders coming down but of borders that are going up as manufacturers try to establish safe havens within the markets they seek to service.

The United States of America

Given its size, as well as its historical relationship with Canada, the United States deserves special attention. To paraphrase Oscar Wilde, the only thing worse than having American FDI is not having it. The decrease of American investment in Canada is part of a general decline of American economic dominance. In 1960, almost half (47.1 per cent) of worldwide FDI stock was held by the United States, but this amount had dropped to 20.8 per cent by the year 2000 (Dicken 2003: 57). This pattern can be detected in Canada as well. In the early 1960s, the American stock of FDI in Canada reached nearly 30 per cent of GDP but had decreased to 19 per cent by 2003. On the other side of the coin, Canada's share of foreign stock in the United States increased from 4 per cent to 13.5 per cent throughout the same period.

The decrease of FDI from the United States might support the globalization hypothesis, but only if those same funds were finding their way to more profitable Third World locations. However, this is not the case. In 1950, Canada was the number-one destination for American outgoing FDI, accounting for 30.4 per cent of its total. This decreased to 16.1 per cent by 1990, by which point Canada had slipped to second place, with the number-one position assumed not by some emerging economy in the Third World but by the United Kingdom. This is indicative of the larger tendency that has seen American investment concentrating in Europe (most of it going to mergers and acquisitions, some to avoid voluntary trade restrictions). In addition, the reduction of American-owned FDI in Canada is reflective of a larger trend that has seen the United States go from being a major net exporter of FDI to also being an important destination, primarily for European and Japanese firms. By the year 2000, outward and inward stocks of FDI were almost identical (Dicken 2003: 59).

Conclusion

The foreign-owned stock of direct investment in Canada has undergone changes that are quite different from what we saw with trade. Whereas the United States has, over the past half-century, come to dominate Canadian trade, foreign direct investment has become more diversified. This is particularly true of Canadian-owned investment abroad. In 1950, Canadian-owned assets in the United States amounted to 78 per cent of total investment abroad, a figure that declined to 41 per cent by 2003. But rather than investing in countries where labour costs are cheap, Canadians are rerouting their money to Europe. All in all, around three-quarters of Canadian foreign investment stays within the First World, and there exists little evidence that FDI is moving to the Third World in any significant amounts, a fact further corroborated by trade figures that fail to indicate a significant increase in economic interaction with these areas. While most of this investment continues to stay within the industrial world, it is at least leaving the continent. The same cannot be said for trade.

The story varies slightly for American-owned investments in Canada. These amounted to 87 per cent of total direct investment in the early 1950s and remain at close to two-thirds today (64 per cent in 2003) – still a sizeable majority. The increase of imports of merchandise from the United States in combination with the relative decrease of FDI suggests that North America is becoming more of a single market, as U.S. branch plants in Canada are shutting down and this market is being directly serviced from the American manufacturing base.

There is little doubt that there have been impressive increases in the growth of FDI stock throughout the world in the past half-century, and even Canada has seen a substantial increase in its foreign holdings. But, as we saw in the chapter on trade, most of this activity occurs within the First World and, to a smaller extent, in parts of Asia. In the geographic sense, then, globalization is restricted to the First World. However, in terms of mergers and acquisitions – that is, corporate concentration – globalization can be said to be taking place. Most of the explosion of FDI in the 1990s can be directly linked to corporate marriages. But this activity has cooled significantly in the past couple of years, and whether this is a long-term trend or just another investment bubble similar to what occurred in the stock markets is too early to tell. Although we saw export and import figures rise substantially, in terms of foreign-owned capital Canada is becoming less dependent on the United States. At the same time, the ratio of outgoing and incoming investment is more equitable now than at any time in the past. Consequently, any concerns about foreign domination, and especially U.S. domination, need not be taken seriously.

Chapter 6

The Financial Economy

Laissez-faire was planned.

Karl Polyani

Introduction

When discussion drifts towards financial markets, the mix of awe and dread associated with globalization becomes most apparent. This awe is often fuelled by the presentation of gargantuan figures such as a trillion-dollar-a-day currency market or a $23-trillion worldwide bond market. Implicit in these descriptions is that financial markets are out of control.

> In the new global electronic economy, fund managers, banks, corporations, as well as millions of individual investors, can transfer vast amounts of capital from one side of the world to another at the click of a mouse. As they do so, they can destabilise what might have seemed rock-solid economies – as happened in the events in Asia. (Giddens 2002: 9)

As this example demonstrates, the underlying cause usually given for the globalization of finance is computer technology, which is reputed to be so advanced that it can circumvent any type of regulation that states are able to muster. In this and many other ways, finance is the globalization argument writ large: Because of technology, borders have become so porous that governments can no longer claim to be in control.

The 'globalization of finance' argument suffers from the same fatalistic attitude as the globalization literature in general and dismisses any solutions as impractical. And, like most technology arguments, this one flirts with determinism by assuming that, just because nothing is being done, nothing can be done. It also glosses over the power dynamics that underlie the relationship between countries and between classes in domestic politics. Changes are, no doubt, difficult to implement for, as we have seen in Asia, Mexico, and Russia, the financial class wields considerable power both globally and domestically. Bienefeld (1992) argues that the disorganized nature of the financial system is one of the most overlooked aspects of the economy, and this, in his words, 'is a grave mistake ... since [it] has been a central driving force behind the severe social and economic problems currently emerging in Canada.' Unfortunately, this system is not only overlooked but also misunderstood. Few people can make sense of all the talk of puts, futures, swaps, and derivatives; fewer still are able to understand its social impact.[1] These criticisms emanate not only from the left but also from the business community itself. Joel Kurtzman (1993), past executive editor of the *Harvard Business Review,* writes that if the system is not brought under control it is likely to result in mayhem. And every once in a while, the system does show its dysfunctional side. As an example, in the United States, the stock markets lost $8.5 trillion in 2000 and 2001 (Stiglitz 2003: 6), and there have been 'roughly 100 financial collapses' that involved national banking systems and IMF intervention in the past twenty years alone (*Globe and Mail,* 22 July 2004: A15).

Wall Street and Technology

Much has been made of how powerful financiers are able to use technology in order to escape the clutches of governments and the regulations they attempt to impose. As is often the case, these observations have some truth to them. Technology itself is often held responsible for the separation of the financial economy (stocks, bonds, and currencies) and the productive or 'real' economy (the production of goods and services). An example of the uncoupling between the two economies is Black Monday, 19 October 1987. On that day the Dow Jones plunged 508 points, falling proportionally twice as far as during the crash of 1929. The fact that there was little change in the rest of the 'real' economy and that a depression never followed indicates that the two economies no longer parallel one another. Even with the often irrational stock market performance of the past few years, the underlying economy has performed relatively well.

The growth of financial markets has involved a massive increase in the trading of government and corporate bonds, stocks, mutual funds, and currencies, a process that has been greatly aided by technology. Probably the most chaotic, and potentially damaging, of all markets entails the buying and selling of national currencies. With the closing of the gold window, currencies fluctuated wildly, and investors were able to profit by speculating on the rise or fall of the price of a currency. This activity first became legal in 1972, when a licence was granted for trading futures on money in Chicago. According to the Bank for the International Settlements (BIS), worldwide currency speculation amounts to U.S. $1.9 trillion a day (*Economist*, 2 Oct. 2004: 72). Add to this the extensive speculation on stocks, bonds, and treasury bills and the result is an economy worth seventy times that of goods traded, up from a ratio of 2 to 1 in 1973 (Dicken 2003: 438). All this speculation is predicated not on the underlying performance of a particular stock or currency but on the probability that it will go up or down. The industry is now greatly dependent on computers to assess probabilities and make investment decisions. It employs PhDs in physics, mathematics, and computer science to write formulae to ascertain odds and profit from them. This has led to the replacement of investment bankers by scientists on Wall Street.

But this economy only works to the benefit of a few. The myth is that with the introduction of computer technology everyone is able to take advantage of the stock market and profit from the global economy. The reality is otherwise, for playing the markets properly requires considerable resources in terms of both knowledge and money. In general, individual stockholders seldom beat the market. People in the business tend to scoff at people who go it alone. This may be for good reason, as it is estimated that 80 to 90 per cent of ordinary people who play the market lose (Henwood 1997). Technology obviously plays a central role in the recent explosion of speculation, but I argue that it has been a mere catalyst in a process that is the result of a deeper underlying problem associated with capitalist economies. In order to make this argument, I provide some historical background.

Historical Perspective

Speculative bubbles are far from new and have been around as long as capitalism itself. But, as Marx noted, money and credit are needed in order for the productive economy to survive, and finance capital is as 'necessary to accumulation as fixed capital itself' (Harvey 1982: 269). Money lubricates the economy, and capitalists require credit (loans, stocks, bonds) in order to finance their projects. The first responsibility of financial capitalists is to 'facilitate accumulation,' yet financiers also constitute a separate class that tends to look out for its own interests (ibid.: 286). Naturally, financiers endeavour to keep a slice of capitalist profits for themselves, making it necessary for the surplus value to be shared between the industrial and the money classes. This leads to 'intense factional struggles' within the bourgeoisie and a 'constant guerilla warfare between industrialists and financiers [that] plays a similar kind of role to the struggle between capital and labour over the wage rate' (ibid.: 299). The system works best when there is an equilibrium between the two factions – when there is approximately the right amount of capital available to finance industrial projects. But sometimes those in the financial community turn greedy, and speculation can run rampant. Yet here, too, there are structural aspects.

Arrighi (1994) argues that the dominance of finance typically accompanies the downswing of the capitalist cycle. Arguing from the world-system and economic-cycles perspective, he observes that financial speculation consistently occurs in the 'autumn' of an empire and documents how similar developments occurred near the end of the Genoese, Dutch, and British Empires. His thesis is based on Marx's theory of profits, which states that capitalists invest money (M) in commodities (C) in order to make a profit (M'), resulting in a cycle of M→C→M'. Capitalists, of course, have little interest in the commodity itself; they are concerned only with the profit. Optimally, the capitalist would prefer to completely eliminate the commodity from the formulation, resulting in M→M', a purely financial transaction reminiscent of a machine that prints money.

Arrighi further argues that capitalism consists of an up-cycle, the material expansion, when commodities are used for profits, and a down-cycle, when a decline of profits in the productive economy lures many capitalists to opt for speculation in the financial market instead. Keynes, following Marx, noted that in times of shrinking profits investors aim to keep their money liquid and avoid long-term productive investments in favour of more speculative ones. This usually results in a volatile economy where short-term 'take-what-you-can-while-you-can-get-it' behaviour is more rational than investing in long-term projects (Kurtzman 1993: 230). This has aptly been referred to as 'casino capitalism' by Keynes. Predictably, this type of speculation usually results in a bubble and eventually bursts. The stories of Nortel stocks, the Japanese real estate market, and the Asian crisis are only a few recent examples.

The important point to glean from Arrighi's analysis is that contemporary events in the financial economy are simply a manifestation of a deeper and recurring problem associated with capitalism. In other words, the current surge in speculation is not an anomaly. As well, while technology has contributed to making this type of speculation more intense, it is by no means the cause. Arrighi interprets such developments as the natural reaction of capitalists searching for financial gains in an economy where the productive economy has been depleted of profits. Focusing on events of the postwar period, Gordon's analysis fits well into this historical and theoretical framework.

> When economic conditions are prosperous and stable, financial capital flows help support and even foster productive investment. But when the economy has become stagnant and unstable, investors tend to move their capital out of productive investments – because of increasingly cloudy longer-term prospects – and into short-term financial investments. The investment climate becomes increasingly speculative. The past fifteen years appear to have illustrated the latter dynamic. As the rate of return on fixed investment in plant and equipment has declined as global economic conditions have become increasingly volatile, firms and banks have moved toward paper investments ... Far from stimulating productive investment, however, these financial flows are best understood as a symptom of the diminishing attractiveness [of] and increasing uncertainty about prospects for fixed investments. (Gordon 1988: 59)

This scenario has seen funds steered towards the financial sector, where the only motive is profit. Cox asks 'What drives the decision-making of the financial manipulators?' His answer: 'the short-range thinking of immediate financial gain, not the long-range thinking of industrial development.' Rather than blaming globalization, he writes that 'The result of financial power's dominance over the real economy was as often as not the destruction of jobs and productive capital' (Cox 1994: 48). A slower-growing economy is testament to the fact that the problem of the profit squeeze has not been resolved. Financial speculation has only made things worse by providing an attractive alternative to productive investments, further starving the latter for investment.

A deeper understanding of the cycles of a capitalist economy indicates that contemporary speculative tendencies are far from new and can therefore not simply be blamed on technology. With this understanding we can now focus on the political event often pointed to as the watershed of the postwar economy, the abandonment of the Bretton Woods agreement.

The Global System: Bretton Woods

The Bretton Woods system was put in place after the Second World War with the intention of facilitating international trade. One of the objectives of this system was to provide a stable financial climate for investment. It was decided that, rather than having each country's currency pegged to gold, all currencies would be pegged to the U.S. dollar, which in turn would be pegged to gold. Technology is often implicated in the downfall of Bretton Woods, but Helleiner (1994) claims this to be a rather shallow explanation. He puts forward the argument that the collapse of Bretton Woods can be better understood as a desperate attempt by the United States to reassert its hegemonic grip on the world economy. By the early 1970s, the United States had borrowed billions of dollars from abroad in order to finance endeavours such as the Vietnam War. As a result, the dollar ceased to be worth its pegged value. Since the dollar was pegged to gold but increasingly worth less than its advertised amount (a dollar was worth, say, only eighty cents but could still buy a dollar's worth of gold), countries started to trade in their inflated U.S. dollars for American gold en masse. In order to prevent a run on gold, the United States was forced to close the gold window and float the dollar. Abandoning the gold standard undermined the whole Bretton Woods system, since all other currencies were pegged to the U.S. dollar. Kurtzman claims that this could all have been avoided had the United States been willing to raise taxes in order to fund the Vietnam War (1993: 55). Be that as it may, the point is that the events leading to the collapse of Bretton Woods were political in nature and not the result of technology or globalization.

Currency Speculation

Currency speculation is often presented as prima facie evidence of globalization: first, it is claimed to be global in the sense that all countries are forced to participate, and second, technology is supposed to have rendered this activity intractable. But as Harvey (1995) points out, the transition to the floating exchange system has little to do with globalization because the system previous to that, the Bretton Woods system itself, was already global to begin with. Furthermore, currency speculation requires national economies in order to take advantage of relative changes in their currencies. Without nation-states there would be no currency speculation.

The second charge, that technology makes these developments unstoppable, requires further elaboration. There is little doubt that currency speculation has resulted in grave consequences for some economies. During the Asian crisis in 1997, the Thai bhat fell by 25 per cent in less than twenty-four hours, and in the course of 2002 the Argentinian peso lost two-thirds of its value. Even modest changes in the price of a currency can have a powerful impact. A manufacturer producing for the export market working on a profit margin of 10 per cent can see her profits wiped out overnight by a rise in the national currency. Many Canadian industries, for example, lost their competitive edge when the dollar rose over 20 per cent throughout 2003 and 2004.

Still, things are unlikely to change, and currency speculation is not likely to be regulated anytime soon. The case for the status quo is usually based on the perceived advantages of an open market coupled with fears about what the wrong kind of regulation might bring. This perspective is usually based on two assumptions. One is that market intervention should be rejected on the grounds that the price of a currency serves as a signal to investors about where to put their money. This kind of information would be lost if the industry were regulated. The second objection is that technology is so far advanced that any kind of regulation is futile in the first place. Since it is unlikely that all countries would agree to currency regulation, speculators would merely relocate to where such regulation did not apply. We will examine both of these assumptions in turn.

i) The Market

The lack of support for any kind of regulation has less to do with market efficiency than with the interests of financial elites. As is to be expected, currency speculators, like the financial community in general, have a particular view of the world. They gauge government performance and economic credibility by the size of government deficits, budgets, profitability, rate of inflation, and so on. By claiming that these indicators are emblematic of a prosperous economy, currency speculators are engaging in a kind of self-fulfilling prophecy, for it is precisely these indicators that investors subsequently rely on to make decisions. But these indicators are biased in favour of economic liberalism, and there is little evidence that fiscal probity or low inflation is the fastest way to economic growth. As the example of Norway or Sweden shows, there is convincing evidence that universally accessible education and health or high levels of employment are more important to economic growth than, say, low inflation. And if financial advisers were to focus on these indicators instead, no doubt *they* would determine investment flows. In other words, currency speculators wield power not because they play the market but, as Henwood (1997) has so astutely put it, because they *are* the market.

There is a considerable amount of conceit underlying the claim that the market always knows best. A related claim, as often explicit as implicit, is that the market works best when investors are given full access to all relevant information. But these assessments are overly sanguine about the possibilities of our knowledge, as it pertains to investments and otherwise. As economic debates from time immemorial indicate, there exists little consensus about how inflation, free trade, unemployment, or social programs affect economic performance. Each of these examples serves as the basis for endless political debate, and a claim by investors that they know the optimum level of, say, unemployment or inflation, should be looked upon with great suspicion. Furthermore, in the real world, the market works not on information but on 'misinformation, leaked information, guarded information, misplaced information, and noisy information ...' and people working in the industry have little success in differentiating among them (Kurtzman 1993: 194).

As the secular decline of the Canadian dollar in the late 1990s and early 2000s illustrates, investor decisions are often difficult to comprehend. The drop of the Canadian dollar closely followed the drop in worldwide commodity prices, based on the 'knowledge' that our economy is primarily resource based. Yet fewer than one-third of Canadian exports are raw materials and, as a percentage of GDP, the resource industry accounts for less than 5 per cent of the Canadian economy. But this is not the only example where the market is shown to have serious shortcomings when it comes to the gathering of information. In the mid-1990s, Canada turned its deficit into a surplus, posted low inflation, and experienced respectable growth. In other words, Canada's fundamentals were all in good order. Yet the Canadian dollar kept falling. In 2000, the American economy was slowing and economists predicted a recession; by comparison, Canada's economic future looked much brighter, yet the Canadian dollar fell. In the immediate aftermath of the U.S. election in 2000, there was uncertainty about who would be the next president, and again the Canadian dollar fell. In 2001, the United States was the victim of the worst terrorist attack in history; meanwhile, it was the Canadian dollar that fell. Throughout 2003, Canada experienced SARS, mad cow disease, forest fires, and floods, and the Canadian dollar took an unprecedented rise. All this is to say that the value of the dollar does not reflect much of anything, except maybe a penchant for disaster. Most certainly, fundamentals appear to be ignored. So either the market is poor at conveying these signals, or speculators are not apt at reading them. Either way, it is difficult to conclude that the market is the best mechanism for allocating resources.

Nevertheless, economic indicators such as the rate of inflation, the size of government, debt levels, and the openness of the economy serve as the foundation of 'knowledge' for financial institutions such as Wall Street and international institutions such as the IMF and the World Bank. Furthermore, the evidence shows that austerity packages imposed by the IMF often fail to restore economic health, as interventions in Southeast Asia, Russia, or Mexico testify. Such shortcomings are increasingly recognized, and not just by anti-globalization demonstrators. Nobel laureate and former chief economist and senior vice-president of the World Bank Joseph Stiglitz (2002: 55) writes that 'the IMF simply assume[s] that markets arise quickly to meet every need, when in fact, many government activities arise because markets have *failed* to provide essential services' (italics in original). Stiglitz has also admitted that the World Bank's confidence about the right thing to do may not always be justified, and he urges a 'greater degree of humility, the frank acknowledgment that we do not have all the answers' (*CCPA Monitor*, Oct. 1998: 6).

The claim that currency speculators avail themselves of any kind of real-world information may be giving them more credit than they deserve. Currency speculators can insist all they want that they rely on economic fundamentals, but the fact is that their livelihood depends directly on volatility. It is only through fluctuation in currencies and interest rates that profits can be won. As Kurtzman (1993: 66) puts it, 'Without volatile markets there would be no speculation.' A Chicago currency trader commenting on Canada's low dollar in the late 1990s attributed the fall to Canada's stable interest rates. Another speculator revealed that they 'don't care whether [a currency] goes up or down' as long as there is movement (*Vancouver Sun*, 10 Aug. 1998: A1). In other words, stability is shunned. A lack of volatility translates into decreased demand, which in turn undermines the value of the currency. Of course, in the real economy, stability is precisely what one

desires, another instance of how the financial and productive economies often work at cross purposes.

After years of lecturing Canadians that they needed to get their economic fundamentals in order, even the *Globe and Mail* (17 Nov. 2000:
A14) was forced to recognize in an editorial that 'currency traders in
London and New York don't actually give a fig for domestic economic
performance.' New Zealand found this out the hard way. In the mid-
1980s, it pursued the liberal market agenda with particular zeal. Purportedly because of a currency crisis, the government felt it necessary
to cut social programs and privatize public corporations in order to
appease foreign investors, with drastic consequences for the economy
and social inequality (New Zealand's economy actually contracted
between 1985 and 1992 and posted the slowest growth between 1975
and 2001 of all the high human development countries with the exception of ex-communist countries). Yet the only Western country that
suffered more than Canada from the currency storm in the late 1990s
was New Zealand, when its currency dropped 44 per cent against the
U.S. dollar between November 1996 and October 2000.

The fact that currency speculation is condoned is difficult to understand in light of the intolerance towards inflation. The reason commonly given for rationalizing the fight against inflation is investor
confidence. Investors, it is said, are better able to make long-term decisions in an environment of stability where they can feel confident that
their investments will not be eroded by inflation. If this is true, one must
wonder why the financial community has at the same time condoned
volatility in almost every other area of the economy: currencies, stocks,
and bonds. The only logical conclusion is that, for some inexplicable
reason, the market is capable of deciding everything but the rate of
inflation. This inconsistency can, of course, be explained by the fact that
the financial community does not benefit from inflation, but profits
from currency speculation and high interest rates. The lack of support
for most types of regulation may also be explained by the fact that, in its
absence, the market prevails, putting capital in a more favourable position vis-à-vis government. If regulation were to be introduced, the capitalist class could conceivably lose that advantage.

ii) Technology

The fact that Bretton Woods worked successfully for close to three
decades is evidence that an international system of regulation is feasi-

ble. Moreover, as Helleiner argues, its abandonment was political in nature and not technological, suggesting that a return to regulation is also a possibility. After the turmoil in Asia, Brazil, and Russia, currency controls are starting to look appealing once again. The most frequent solution offered is the Tobin tax, as proposed by Nobel laureate James Tobin. This legislation would dissuade speculation by taxing one-quarter of 1 per cent of each currency transaction, making the majority of speculation unprofitable.

Such a tax is often opposed on the grounds that is would be difficult, if not impossible, to enforce. Detractors of the tax also like to argue that it could be circumvented by moving the whole operation to a country that refused to charge the tax, easily done with the far-reaching hand of technology. But this argument glosses over who gains and loses from the present arrangement. Helleiner (1995) is of the opinion that currency speculation is permitted only because two very powerful economies, namely those of the United States and Great Britain, continue to benefit from it. Furthermore, the technology argument makes the assumption that all countries are equally involved when it comes to currency trading, which is not the case. By far the most frequently traded currency is the U.S. dollar, based on its role as a vehicle currency. Say, for example, a currency trader wanted to exchange German marks for Swedish kronor, she would first have to trade German marks for U.S. dollars, which would then be converted to Swedish kronor. The participation of the United States is thus crucial in the establishment of any kind of regulation. Once the United States agreed to charge the tax, another currency would have to act as a vehicle currency in order for speculation to continue. It is unlikely that Europe would support this activity, as the goal of currency stability has been the main impetus behind the formation of the EU. Once the United States and Europe are eliminated, it is unlikely that another currency would have the clout to act as a vehicle currency.

Currency speculators would also encounter difficulties in relocating to a Third World country in that the industry is dependent on the technology and skill available in the West. The reasons for this are identical to the reasons why corporations seldom relocate to the Third World: inadequate power and communications infrastructure and a relatively uneducated workforce. In short, once the United States and Europe are onside, it is unlikely that the industry would locate elsewhere. At this point, however, it is only the United States that 'remains cool' to any kind of regulation (*Globe and Mail*, 22 Jan. 1999: B9)

Money and Trust

How can this go on? First, most people wrongly believe that technology and globalization are to blame and that, in one way or another, the whole process is beyond human intervention. Second, the majority of the population has considerable faith in the market, often more than they have in the ability of politicians to implement effective regulation. Third, people generally believe that the money system works and, in the absence of any kind of financial calamity (particularly in the West), they have no reason to believe otherwise. It is likely no accident that Giddens uses money as an example of a symbolic form of disembedding mechanism (1990). A primary feature of a disembedding mechanism is that people have faith in expert systems, despite the fact that they know little about them. But, as we have seen, the money system is anarchic, and without adequate regulation the system is open to abuse and sometimes prone to disaster.

History shows that there is always someone who is willing to take advantage of the money system. When money primarily consisted of gold and silver, dishonest traders would shave the edges off coins and sell the remainders for a tidy profit. In order to combat this thievery, mints placed ridges or embossed print around the perimeter of the coins (this ridge is still apparent on Canadian quarters and dimes, but not nickels or pennies because of the low value of their metals). It would appear that currency speculation is the modern equivalent of coin shaving, and this activity, arguments about its usefulness notwithstanding, is about equally beneficial. Galbraith writes that 'If anything is evident from [the history of money], it is that the task attracts a very low level of talent ...' (1995: 310). Coin shaving and currency speculation serve as good evidence of this.

Stocks and Bonds in Canada

While currency speculation is a concern of international regulation, stocks and bonds remain primarily a national affair. Governments are the biggest issuers of bonds, and they continue to legislate and regulate how bonds and shares are issued. These instruments are not vital to international trade the way currencies are, and therefore national control is much easier to attain. The degree to which these financial markets are globalized is another question. We have already examined FDI, and will now take a closer look at stocks and bonds. Generally,

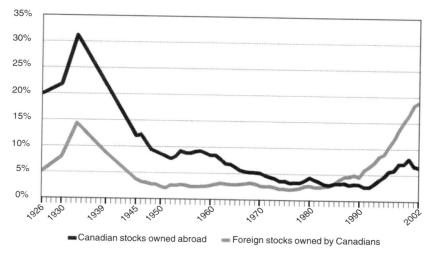

Figure 6.1. Stocks owned abroad and foreign stocks owned by Canadians as a percentage of GDP, 1926–2002

the evidence shows that domestic investment (stocks, bonds, and direct investment) continues to be highly correlated to domestic savings. Within the OECD, 60 per cent of variation in investments can be explained by domestic savings rates. In contrast, within the United States, where the capital market is fully integrated, this relationship is essentially zero (Wade 1996: 74). Furthermore, interest-rate differentials among countries remain significant, and there is little evidence of a decline from a hundred years ago (ibid.: 74–5). In other words, international market integration is far from being achieved.

Stocks

In 2001, Canada's stock market was worth approximately $1.7 trillion. In comparison to the trading of currencies and government bonds, the trading of stocks remains relatively local, as few companies are able to boast a global reputation (Wade 1996: 73). Figure 6.1 shows that, as a percentage of GDP, investment in Canadian stocks is relatively low and has been so since figures have been available. Investment in stocks outside of Canada has increased in the past few years, probably because stock markets have performed better abroad and because some American corporations, such as Microsoft and IBM, do have a global reputation. The same cannot be said for Canadian companies. It is easy to understand, given misadventures such as BreX, Livent Inc., and Nortel, why foreign investors would be reluctant to buy Canadian stocks. Foreign stock ownership in Canada did increase in the 1990s, but it is still less than levels found previous to 1950.

While international ownership of stocks has changed little, there have been some significant changes in the structure of institutional ownership. One of the classic problems of corporate ownership has been the separation of owners (stockholders) and managers. Traditionally, managers have paid little attention to the welfare of stockholders, who were often scattered geographically and incapable of acting as an organized group. This has changed significantly over the past few decades as ownership has become concentrated in collective funds (in the United States, 60 per cent of stocks are owned by pension and insurance funds). In this way, stockholders have been able to band together and direct the actions of managers, resulting in a wave of mergers and takeovers. The motivation behind these actions is that bigger corporations are considered more efficient. Companies whose stocks are undervalued are the most vulnerable to these kinds of takeovers. Fear of takeover has encouraged many corporations to buy their own stocks and retire them. It has been estimated that between 1995 and 2000 more than U.S. $1 trillion was spent by corporations in buying their own stocks. Interestingly, the retirement of stocks has outgrown the issuing of new ones over the past years, meaning that in the United States there were fewer stocks on the market in 1996 than in 1980 (Henwood 1997: 72). Though often wrongly blamed on globalization, downsizing can be traced to this change in stock ownership: 'Public justifications for these downsizings have almost always pointed to technological change and global competition, which takes human interest and agency out of the picture, but in fact the proximate cause has more often been pressure for higher stock prices coming from Wall Street portfolio managers' (ibid.: 290). Or, as Henwood writes elsewhere, rather than a product of globalization, a leveraged buyout (LBO) can be better described as a 'form of class struggle' (ibid.: 274).

Business professor Peter Drucker (1996) claims that this change in ownership of the means of production, from individual to institutional, constitutes a fundamental shift in the capitalist economy, the most meaningful in the postwar economy. He also points to the consequence of mergers and takeovers. Ownership, he writes, has now become 'socialized' without being 'nationalized.' What is of note here is that many of these pension funds are owned by workers (e.g., teachers' unions, Ontario Hydro), making for an odd kind of 'class struggle,' as Henwood would have it.

Statistics Canada does not calculate the distribution of wealth according to population groups (quintiles or deciles), which makes it difficult to know what percentage of the population owns the majority of stocks (*Globe and Mail*, 7 Oct. 1996). However, the United States does keep tabs on the distribution of stock ownership. In 1992, the top 5 per cent of individuals who held stock owned 94.5 per cent of all stock held by individuals. Once the whole of the population is considered, only 1 per cent of the population can be said to own stock in any meaningful way (these figures do not include pension funds) (Henwood 1997: 67, 10). Another way to look at distribution is to consider dividend income from stocks. In Canada, in 1995, 71 per cent of all dividend income went to the top 11.5 per cent of tax-filers and 45 per cent went to the top 1.5 per cent. The Thomson family alone claimed more dividend income in 1995 than the bottom 52 per cent of income earners combined (as before, these figures do not include pension funds) (Stanford 1999).

Bonds

In Canada, the bond market is worth over a trillion dollars – approximately $1,100 billion, including corporate, federal, provincial, and municipal bonds. Figure 6.2 shows that bond ownership presents a somewhat different picture from that of stocks. Canadians own few bonds abroad, but Canadian bonds are popular among foreign investors, precisely the opposite of what we just saw with stocks. The reason for this is quite simple: interest rates have generally been higher in Canada over the past two decades than in the United States, which is good reason for foreigners to invest here. At the same time, lower interest rates in the United States have provided little incentive for Canadians to invest abroad. In 2001, in Canada, about 37 per cent of the total Canadian bond market was foreign owned. This is relatively high but, historically speaking, not unusual. As the graph shows, foreign ownership of bonds was markedly higher before the Second World War. As was noted earlier, the recent rise in foreign ownership of bonds can be explained by the relatively high interest rates in Canada, particularly in the early 1990s. By the late 1990s, however, Cana-

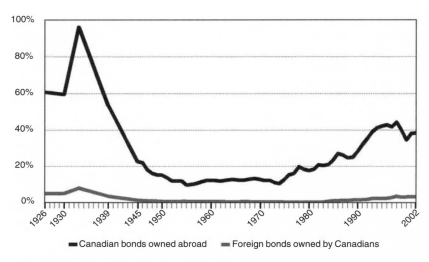

Figure 6.2. Bonds owned abroad and foreign bonds owned by Canadians as a percentage of GDP, 1926–2002

dian rates had dropped below those in the United States, making Canadian bonds less attractive to foreign investors. This resulted in Canada's net debt dropping a 'startling 7.9 percent' in 1999 from the previous year (*Globe and Mail*, 30 Mar. 2000: A1).

Another, and probably the most accurate, way to assess foreign investment in Canada is to add up all foreign-owned assets in Canada, including foreign direct investment, stocks, bonds, loans, bank deposits, and international reserves. In 2001, this amounted to $1.1 trillion, a hefty amount indeed – approximately the same as the GDP that year. As a proportion of all assets, however, which was $11 trillion in that same year, this amounted to only 10 per cent.[2] This means that around nine-tenths of our economy, including liabilities (debts), is owned within this country. At the same time, Canadians owned assets worth $919 billion abroad, for a net deficit of only about $189 billion. Overall, then, the amount of outside ownership in this country is minimal, even trivial. To put this into some kind of perspective, a family worth $1.1 million on paper would spend little time worrying about a $110,000 mortgage, especially if it had $91,900 in a savings account.

In summary, although the Canadian bond and stock markets are far from global, this is not where the real story lies. It must be remembered that for every dollar of liability there exists an equivalent dollar amount in assets. In other words, the flip side of large bond markets is equally large debts. The next section examines how contemporary politics can be better explained by the dynamics behind debts than by globalization, the more usual scapegoat.

Debt and the Class Struggle

Many people, and financial advisers in particular, marvel about the magic of compound interest without reflecting much on its larger social context. In his book entitled *Investing for Income: A Guide to Earning Top Interest on Your Savings* (Anderson 1998), the author calculates that, had the Natives who sold Manhattan to the Dutch invested that money (roughly U.S. $35) at an interest of only 3 per cent per annum, their little nest-egg would have grown to be worth U.S. $8.4 trillion today. Given current exchange rates, this is nearly as much as all the wealth in Canada combined ($11 trillion). It is hard to imagine that millions of Canadians toiling away for centuries would end up producing less wealth than a paltry U.S. $35 kept in the bank.

But this rather sanguine view glosses over such 'anomalies' as the bank failures that have a tendency to happen every once in a while. This is another instance where the market proves inept at communicating potential disaster. Had the $35 in question been invested in one of the 5,500 banks that went bust in the United States during the Depression, the descendants of our Native friends would have been left with literally nothing. Even with the introduction of deposit insurance (currently $60,000 per depositor in Canada), the balance would essentially be wiped out. More importantly, the excitement about compound interest completely ignores the other side of the story: compound debt. The wealth produced by compound interest has to be paid for by someone. Unfortunately, if the burden of interest payments becomes too high, debt renunciation may result. The possibility of such an unpleasant scenario has kept many a banker awake at night, for when a failure occurs, the domino effect can potentially result in the collapse of the banking system, and even put the whole economy in jeopardy. When such a disaster does happen, extensive government – or even IMF – intervention is required.

It is also important to understand that the interest rates are not solely established by supply and demand but are dependent upon the larger political and economic context. In the late 1980s and early 1990s, interest rates rose as a result of an almost neurotic fear of inflation. Although interest rates appeared lower in the 1990s than in the 1970s, they were in fact much higher once inflation was factored into the equation. Real interest rates actually wandered into negative territory at one point in the 1970s, but hovered around the 5 per cent mark for most of the 1980s and 1990s (Stanford 1999).

Money accrued from interest rates is referred to as imaginary wealth by Daly and Cobb. Whereas there are physical boundaries on how much real wealth can grow, this is not the case for imaginary wealth. To use an example provided by the authors (Daly and Cobb 1994: 423), to invest in a pig (or any commodity for that matter) takes a considerable amount of effort in terms of time and work: you have to feed the pig, provide it with a place to live, tend to it when it becomes ill, and so on. None of this effort is necessary in the case of imaginary wealth – that is, financial wealth. There is no need to rent or buy land, erect buildings, or maintain them; there is no chance that fire, strikes, or labour unrest will destroy your investment, as is the case with productive resources. To return to our compound interest example: it is just as easy to imagine $8.4 trillion as it is to imagine $35.

But even imaginary money has implications for the real world. As Marx noted, money and capital bring with them enormous social power. As debt increases so does the power of the rentier. The growth of debt has had dramatic repercussions on the distribution of resources, not only within individual countries but between them as well. Another way to expose the downside of investing is to ask where the money for compound interest comes from. The answer is, from massive debts incurred by governments, corporations, and even individuals (banks sell cumulative credit-card and mortgage debt on the bond market). These debts, in turn, are owned by pension funds, banks, financial institutions, and mutual funds, which, in turn, are owned by individual households. This brings to light that debt and interest are part of a larger distribution scheme that involves significant transfers of wealth. Credit has played an important role for both rich and poor since the 1980s: 'for one to reduce their poverty; the other to increase their prosperity' (quoted in Henwood 1997: 65). Equally important, credit has helped 'to nourish both the appearance and reality of a middle-class standard of living in a time of polarization' (ibid.: 66).

But individuals are not the only ones who have encountered perilous levels of debt. First on this list is Third World debt. While this crisis may have been solved from the perspective of the First World by means of 'debt restructuring,' it continues to be a serious problem for the countries that have incurred those debts. The rapid increase of corporate debt in the United States also reached critical proportions recently, a crisis only averted by the lowering of interest rates by the Federal Reserve (Henwood 1997). The 9/11 attacks in the United States in 2001 prompted a further lowering of interest rates, which fell to below 1 per cent at one point. But low interest rates have only encouraged people and institutions to take on more debt. The U.S. budget deficit in 2004 is projected to come in at close to half a trillion dollars, and the federal debt was approximately $7.3 trillion in the middle of 2004.

Canadian economist Jim Stanford has written that the deficit and debt hysteria of the 1980s and 1990s pushed the left into a position of defending the status quo and 'waxing nostalgic of better days gone by' (Stanford 1995: 48). But the left was incapable of offering an alternative model, and Stanford suggests that the left needs to go on the offensive and use the public debt to criticize the whole economic system.

Borrowing money can, in fact, stave off a recession, but this tactic may be shortsighted, as interest payments eventually crowd out spending on consumer products. In this way, credit puts a drag on the economy and restrains growth, particularly future growth. Once interest rates rise, and there is no reason to believe that they will not, debt payments will rise in lockstep. Even though Canada's public debt is lower than most, spending on interest payments is still nearly as high as spending on health and education and constituted the number one government expenditure for a short period in the early to mid-1990s (see chapter 7).

Winners and Losers

When it comes to the politics of debt, there are obvious winners and losers. Who are the losers? Workers, organizations, and individuals with high debt loads, as well as businesses vulnerable to takeovers. Harvey (1982: 285) quotes Marx by referring to mortgages and consumer credit as 'secondary forms of exploitation' that have obvious distributional consequences. Debts of all kinds – private, public, corporate – are high in Canada, but, as we saw, the majority of debt is still held within Canada. In that respect, foreign investors and globalization are not a threat. High debts do make governments more dependent on the financial community, but in the case of Canada, this financial community is primarily domestic.

Who are the winners? There are primarily two groups. One is the firms and traders who buy and sell stocks, bonds, and currencies, as well the firms that design the computers, software, and telecommunications technology that make the system work (Kurtzman 1993: 204). To an extent, then, Stehr (1994) is right: knowledge workers are becoming more powerful. But this is not enough to elide class distinctions, as Stehr would have it, as there is a second set of winners: those who own the bonds, mortgages, and other forms of debt. It is these investors who were able to multiply their holdings because of high interest rates throughout the 1980s and 1990s (Stewart 1997). But interest rates have been relatively low for the past few years; this has been generally good for the economy but, one would suspect, less so for investors. Low interest rates have also had an impact on the stock market in that many investors buy on margin. As a result, there are fears that, once interest rates rise, stock markets will be affected negatively.

Conclusion

When global talk first found its way into popular parlance it was primarily about the productive economy: about corporations that were shopping around the world for cheap labour, about de-industrialization in the West, and so on. As time went on, the focus shifted to the sovereignty of the state and, finally, to the financial realm. But while the terrain of the debate has shifted, assumptions about the state's inefficacy remain. This is despite some major differences between the globalization of production and the globalization of finance. First, in the financial realm the actors involved are primarily in the First World and constitute a small financial elite situated in New York, London, and Tokyo, as well as lesser centres such as Hong Kong, Frankfurt, and Toronto. While money can easily move around the world, these financial centres are solidly anchored to their locations and are dependent on technology and a well-educated workforce. Moreover, wealth follows wealth, which is already highly concentrated in the West, effectively crushing any global dreams that Third World countries might have. In other words, threats about moving to the Third World because of more compliant governments or low labour costs fail to play a significant role here. Unlike in the globalization of production, where workers in the First World are placed in direct competition with workers from the Third World, financial globalization hurts those who are in debt, which includes nearly everyone: most of the First World and virtually all of the Third World. In this sense, globalization of financial services is a misnomer, in that it offers opportunity to only a small group of individuals concentrated in the First World, while distributional issues, other than Third World debt, remain primarily national.

Despite a considerable backlash against globalization, the regulation of financial markets has failed to find support among the most powerful players. Yet as the Asian crisis has shown, financial liberalization can easily result in disaster (Stiglitz 2002). As the examples of Thailand and Indonesia show, the negative consequences of marginally higher growth associated with deregulation far outweigh any benefits. And such disasters are not confined to the Third World. The Savings and Loan debacle in the United States cost American taxpayers upwards of U.S. $100 billion, to say nothing of the losses incurred by banks and investors (Stiglitz 2003: 63). This money did not simply disappear into thin air; it made some people rich, while the taxpayer was left to pick up the tab. This effectively socializes the risk of investing and further encourages reckless speculation.

All this is to say that financial regulation is an inherently political task, as its consequence determines how profits are shared between capital and labour, between industrial and money capitalists (Harvey 1982), and among countries. Bienefeld (1992) claims that neoclassical theory would actually oppose deregulation because deregulation impedes information flows, favours short-term over long-term investments, and makes sentiment a variable, resulting in market volatility. But opposition to the orthodoxy is difficult to mobilize, as many economists and politicians see regulation as a backlash against globalization, fearing it could slow down economic integration and, therefore, growth (James 2001). Yet some of the most successful emerging economies in recent years continue to have regulated financial sectors. Moreover, the countries that best survived the Asian crisis – China and India – did so largely because of 'their long-standing capital controls' (Stern 2004: 495).

Helleiner (1995) contends, based on Polyani's *The Great Transformation*, that 'laissez faire was planned' and that liberal markets will be reigned in once governments decide they cause too much social unrest. Helleiner adds that Bretton Woods attempted to make finance the 'servant' and not the 'master' of society, a relationship that has since been reversed. As was noted earlier, the United States and Great Britain were instrumental in bringing about market liberalization in the 1970s and 1980s, mostly because it was these two countries who had the most to gain. Once they end up at the losing end of this equation, Helleiner speculates, support for re-regulation will mount.

The above discussion paints a picture of financial markets that are volatile and disorganized, with only a few firms and individuals profiting from the mayhem. How can governments let this go on? No doubt this activity keeps the economy, no matter how fragile, humming, and to interrupt it might risk an economic slowdown. Why does the public put up with this? Probably because most people believe that regulation is ineffective based on the myth that these developments are due to technology and globalization. As was argued above, however, this is likely not the case, and all this turmoil can be better explained by a blind faith in the market.

Chapter 7

The Retreat of the Nation-state

Introduction

One of the most powerful myths associated with globalization is that national borders have become so porous that governments are no longer able to properly manage their own affairs. So, either by choice or by force, states will eventually cease meddling in the economy, a development that has been observed with some glee by the right. Although less enthusiastic about such an outcome, commentators from the left have, by and large, reached similar conclusions. Based on the assumption that capital has become too mobile for nation-states to control, the left has declared that social policy is dead. The title of Teeple's book (2000), *Globalization and the End of Social Reform*, well illustrates this position. In a similar vein, Mulvale (2001: 11) notes that 'The growing reach of global capital ... brought an end to the social-democratic welfare state project.' Tabb (2002: 10) observes that 'At the start of the twenty-first century the inadequacy of the nation-state as the sovereign unit of political organization and economic regulation is increasingly clear.' Ohmae (1995: 4) sees governments as mere middlemen whose rule is now 'largely unnecessary' in the global economy. Or, as Daniel Bell (1987: 116) has famously identified the problem, the nation-state is too small for the big problems in life and too big for the small problems.

The claim that we are witnessing the end of the nation-state is a bold one, and I aim to show through detailed examination of individual government programs that it is also a claim that is untenable. In short, my argument is that the end-of-the-nation-state thesis is no more than an idea, a product of wishful thinking actively promulgated by the right. And like many ideas, this one, too, fails to coincide with an always intransigent reality. Government continues to loom large at the beginning of the twenty-first century and, when we bring to light the politics that undergird state expenditures, we see why its overwhelming presence is likely to endure.

This chapter is divided into two sections. The first section examines the premises and conclusions of the end-of-the-nation-state argument made in the globalization literature. It begins with a quick overview of how the state has been theorized and then focuses on the Marxist perspective. As was discussed in the chapter on definitions, some globalists have held globalization responsible for both the birth and the end of the nation-state, a position that I subject to some scrutiny. With the growth of supranational organizations such as the United Nations come assumptions about the state's autonomy, the theoretical basis of which is questioned. An examination of the role of NAFTA for Canada closes this section. The second section looks directly at state expenditures and how these have changed in recent years. The growth and importance of government spending in the past fifty years is a topic conveniently overlooked by globalists. Once raised, however, this issue poses serious obstacles for the end-of-the-nation-state thesis. The data trace government expenditures going back to 1933, first divided along non-welfare-state and welfare-state lines, and then according to individual programs. Various programs of the welfare state are featured.

Contemporary Discussion of the State

The nation-state did not become a universal phenomenon until after the Second World War (Wallerstein 1991: 92), and already globalists are busy writing its obituary. While estimates of the starting date and the causes of globalization vary, the observation that we are now living in an age (or on the cusp of an age) that marks the end of the nation-state is one detail the myriad theories of globalization share. Whether in academic theories or more popular versions, the conclusion consistently points towards this end. The reasons given for reaching this conclusion may vary slightly from one theory to the next. In some accounts, this conclusion is predicated on the spread of markets; in others the flow of information is highlighted; in yet others, the ascendency of supranational institutions is cited. But the undermining of state power is an observation that is consistent among all theories.

Even Lash and Urry, who otherwise make incisive observations about national differences in *Economies of Signs and Space*, write that 'national governments are increasingly unable to control cross-border flows generated by these transnational practices' (1994: 280). In preceding chapters they compare and contrast trajectories of post-industrial societies, social rights, and ethnic conflicts in liberal democracies, giving ample evidence of how the nation-state still matters. Yet these authors fall into the common trap of believing that 'nation-states can no longer govern their borders and prevent the extraordinary flows of ideas, images, capital, technologies, environmental hazards and people that are the contemporary experience' (Lash and Urry 1994: 312). Finally, they ask the all-important question central to the globalization thesis: 'Is there such a thing as a national economy left?'

This raises a host of issues, some of which have already been discussed in previous chapters. First, it is misleading to lump 'ideas, images, capital,' and so on, into one homogeneous mass, as the consequences for each differ in their impact. Second, an increase in transnational flows is usually matched by a concomitant increase in national flows that often serves as a force that binds. Third, how exactly do these flows undermine the autonomy of the state? Borders have always been open with respect to economic activity and, as we saw in previous chapters, this is not a new development. Yet many accounts of globalization assert a connection between the two. There is a tendency to list an array of flows and from this conclude that the national economy is in jeopardy. And while it may be true that borders are becoming more porous, the conclusion that this necessarily affects the state's ability to govern does not logically follow.[1] The state manages many other aspects of daily life besides the flow of goods and services. Foremost among these responsibilities is the well-being of its citizens, which it maintains by providing education, health, and other social services. It is this aspect of the state that is conveniently ignored in end-of-the-nation-state arguments. (This point is highlighted in the second half of this chapter.) To put this slightly differently: Rather than focusing on the apparent weakening of the state by enumerating what passes through its borders, we need to redirect the spotlight onto developments occurring within those borders, thereby highlighting what makes a state strong.

State Theory

The perceived inefficacy of the state is built on the assumption that the state was at one time capable of managing its internal affairs independently of outside influences (Panitch 1994). Yet events this past century, such as the two world wars and the Depression, reveal that states never had that level of autonomy to begin with. Canada's own history shows that economic interdependence goes back well into the nineteenth century. The *1870 Canada Yearbook*, for example, tells us that trade was down because of a 'world-wide depression of demand for products' (193).

Not only have economies been interdependent for a long time, the state continues to be one of the key players in organizing both international and domestic affairs. A development that globalists are hard pressed to explain is the increased role of the state, particularly in the past half-century. As we see later on in this chapter, the state continues to manage a considerable portion of the national economy in advanced capitalist economies. Moreover, intervention on a grand scale is a relatively recent development, one that began during the Depression and did not come into full force until after the Second World War. Before that time, the state's role was relatively laissez-faire, especially with respect to redistribution (although many states, Canada among them, have long played an important role in establishing markets through programs such as the National Policy, first introduced in 1879; see, for example, Brodie 1990; Saul 1997).

The Great Depression brought to the fore the impact a major economic downturn can have on an industrial economy, in contrast to the past, when mostly rural populations were better able to survive by depending on their own devices. Labour uprisings and social unrest in general, coupled with the threat of socialism, made state intervention during the Depression an attractive alternative (Hobsbawm 1994). In short, the Depression made it evident that the hands-off approach was no longer feasible, a point most famously made by Keynes. From that point on, governments took a more active role in shaping their economies, a role that continues to this day. This capacity is strangely ignored by globalists. Interestingly, the rise of government intervention parallels the decade – the 1960s – that many globalists peg as marking the acceleration of globalization (Waters 2001; Albrow 2004; also see Gough 1979 on the expansion of the welfare state throughout the 1960s).

A related shortcoming of the end-of-the-nation-state thesis is that the state is poorly theorized, apart from its role of keeping capital within its borders. Although this is a very public role of the state, it is also relatively minor. In many accounts of globalization, trade is presented as evidence of the continual weakening of the state. Logically, it follows from this that states should oppose trade. But, if anything, governments have been only too eager to secure trade deals and open their borders. Why would states do this if it truly undermined their power to govern? Furthermore, there is little logic presented to explain the perceived relationship between an increase in trade and a decrease in the power of the state. In fact, there is nothing inconsistent about the behaviour of states. As Wallerstein observes, the division of labour with respect to production, labour, and commodities requires that state borders be permeable (1991: 98). The simple fact is that states have actively pursued trade policy in the hope of reviving their economies. As domestic demand declined in the 1970s, governments sought to keep their economies growing by focusing on exports (Brenner 1998).

So, even in the age of globalization, the state continues to perform many indispensable duties. But exactly where and when the state should intervene in the economy continues to provide the basis for much political acrimony. The political right advocates only a minimal role for the state, usually confined to military and legal affairs, and generally opposes state interference in the economy, in particular when it comes to taxation and income distribution. In contrast, the left champions state-sponsored social programs for health, education, and income support. The left also fears that the relationship between the state and capital is often too comfortable. This observation was certainly appropriate in the past. In the age of mercantilism, which lasted well into the middle of the nineteenth century, the state was primarily a tool of the economic and aristocratic elite, a circumstance that prompted Marx and Engels to observe that 'The executive of the modern state is but a committee for managing the common affairs of the whole bourgeoisie' (1986: 36). Despite profound changes in the political economy since then, the relationship between capital and the state continues to be hotly debated to this day, the globalization controversy being the most recent variant. In general, much Marxist literature is critical of the state and, particularly the work of Miliband, perceives the state to be subservient to capital. Whether or not one accepts the instrumentalist version of the state is not the point here. More important for our discussion is the fact that the argument for a weak and subservient state is not new but has deep historical roots. This literature anticipates by many years the theory of globalization, with its emphasis on the domineering power of capital. Globalization accounts of the state are akin to instrumentalist versions in that both have a tendency to ascribe excessive power to capital. In the instrumentalist literature, the state is subservient to national capital; in the globalization literature, and particularly in the corporate globalization variant, the state is subservient to multinational capital. Starr, for example, writes that 'corporations have slipped their moorings and are no longer responsible to nations' (2000: 23). Contemporary writers on globalization would be well advised to read criticisms of the instrumentalist accounts; such criticisms stress how state officials deliberately try to distance themselves from capital, making them relatively 'autonomous' from the capital class; how the state serves many diverse interests and not just capital; and how the state often acts against the immediate short-term interest of capital in order to serve its own long-term interests.

Of course, the state is constantly changing and evolving. As writers such as Offe and O'Connor have pointed out, the state has taken on a variety of responsibilities, some that are supported by the capital class (such as the provision of infrastructure) and some that are not (such as social programs, in particular social assistance). And while the state often appears to respond to the demands of the capital class, this class itself is often divided and frequently makes contradictory demands on the state (Porter 1965). As the literature on the welfare state illustrates (e.g., Pierson 1994), the state has to answer not only to capital but also to voters, the elderly, the sick, civil servants, and a litany of other interests, which often end up overriding the interests of the capital class. Furthermore, it is increasingly recognized that the state is a self-determining actor in its own right, and that it has the power to act independently of the wishes of other institutional actors (Skocpol 1986). Finally, states throughout the world differ vastly one from another, and it is unlikely that capitalism can 'render all this variation irrelevant' (Mann 1997). As we analyse the upcoming data on state expenditures, we see that any kind of explanation that views the state as an instrument of the capitalist class, whether domestic or international, is far too simplistic. We revisit some of these issues throughout the data section as well as in the discussion that follows it.

Contemporary accounts of the state contrast the present period to the immediate postwar era, when the state appeared to be more willing to fund social programs. This is true to some degree, for the threat of another depression provided much of the impetus for these programs. However, as the political economy literature on the welfare state demonstrates, the state did not provide these programs voluntarily, but only after workers, often through political organization, had fought for them (see, e.g., Myles 1989). In other words, social programs are the result of class-based politics and rarely, if ever, of the largesse of the state.

Finally, one should avoid confusing the pessimism directed towards state action in North America and Great Britain as a universal development. In Western Europe (Germany and Sweden) and Asia (Japan and Taiwan), industrial policy continues to play an important role in the structuring of the economy. In Germany, for example, the state continues to take an active part in labour market policy, ensuring a steady supply of skilled workers for industry. Things are similarly coordinated in Japan, where business and government work hand in hand to reduce their huge trade surplus with the United States, with state subsidies available to help companies relocate overseas (Weiss 1997: 15). Speculations about the state's demise may therefore be unduly influenced by Anglo-American thinking, where the state does indeed play a relatively minor role.

The Creation and Demise of the Nation-state

Many commentators recognize the immense power of the state and appreciate that claims about its demise are likely to be exaggerated. These authors have therefore adopted a softer and more tentative language. Instead of predicting outright the end of the nation-state, they prefer words such as 'weakening,' 'powerless,' and 'impotent' – a vague approach that, according to Becker (1986), is typical of much academic writing. However, while this language is less emphatic, its message is essentially the same: a reversal of fortunes for the nation-state.

This hesitation has led to some confusion, even contradictions. Waters writes that 'it is not absolutely necessary to demonstrate that the nation-state is in decline in order to support a case for political globalization' (2001: 127). Yet he also writes that 'If states survive globalization then it cannot be counted the force that it currently appears to be' (ibid.: 157). While these two positions may not be a complete contradiction, the second position appears much less self-assured and leaves room for doubt about the globalization thesis. In any case, Waters's observation about the state's possible survival is incompatible with his definition of globalization as the receding of 'constraints of geography on economic, political, social and cultural arrangements ...' (ibid.: 164). This is not to single out and attack Waters, but to illustrate the inconsistencies that a comprehensive and historical theory of globalization must overcome.

The difficulty in the end-of-the-nation-state argument lies not in providing details about how the world has changed but in making a coherent argument about how and why present state structures cannot survive these changes. Nowhere are these inconsistencies more apparent than in accounts that implicate globalization as responsible not only for the demise of the nation-state but also for its creation. The most obvious example of this is Robertson, who sees no need to address this contradiction (see chapter 1 above). Waters, however, attempts to do just that. Waters acknowledges that the nation-state is itself a product of globalization, but then goes on to add that it is also responsible for its expiry. In the hope of reconciling this contradiction he suggests that globalization found its seed in the nation-state but eventually outgrew its borders. This is predicated on the logic that increased interaction among states necessitates the growth of international organizations that will, in turn, ultimately render the nation-state ineffectual.

> Nation-states are bounded social systems; they will compete for resources and markets and they will not necessarily be materially self-sufficient; they will therefore engage in economic, military, political (diplomatic) and cultural exchanges across the boundaries that are both co-operative and conflictual; differential outcomes and therefore cross-national mimesis will ensue; states will seek to systematize international relations in order to secure the conditions of their own existence. (Waters 2001: 126)

The allusion to the 'systematization of international relations' refers to institutions such as the United Nations, the World Bank, and the IMF, which Waters discusses in some detail in the pages preceding the above passage.

But this approach both misunderstands and exaggerates the role and the power of supranational institutions. First, as in pluralist theories of the state, the assumption here is that these organizations are neutral and act in the interests of the globe rather than of individual states, thereby overriding national self-interest. In this sense, these institutions are far from supranational, as they entrench the already exploitive relationship between the First World and the Third. Neither is power shared equally among countries in the First World. Many of these institutions are headquartered in the United States, a country that plays a significantly more important role than most, if not all, in the running of international organizations. The IMF (originally established to help countries work out their balance-of-payments problems) now aims to impose a free market on Third World countries, its interventions in Indonesia, Argentina, and Russia being only a few recent examples. The Third World plays only a negligible role in the running of these institutions, while the United States has veto power in both the World Bank and the IMF (George and

Sabelli 1994). Certainly, the IMF is indicative of how power flows from the First World to the Third, and not vice versa. When was the last time that a Third World country, or any other country for that matter, was able to force its will onto the United States through one of these institutions? The IMF and the World Bank are not the only institutions that reinforce First World dominance. The UN Security Council was unable to stop the United States from invading Iraq, despite opposition from most of the world. Interestingly, the one so-called special organization under the aegis of the United Nations that has proven to be progressive, the International Labor Organization (ILO), has had its funding withdrawn by the United States.

Another misunderstanding is theoretical in nature and assumes that, as states hand over authority to supranational organizations, they undermine their own. But this is simply not the case, as power is not a zero-sum game. As Giddens observes, international organizations such as the United Nations should be seen not as threatening the sovereignty of states but rather as confirming the securitization and institutionalization of sovereignty (Giddens 1985: 255–7). The analogy of the relationship between the state and the individual citizen serves to illustrate the point. When individuals surrender some of their rights to the state they do not give up their autonomy; they enhance it. This conceptualization of rights is the organizing principle behind Hobbes's *Leviathan*, in which he argued that a powerful state was a prerequisite for a peaceful society. While an individual may lose some freedoms by conferring certain rights to the state, she or he simultaneously bolsters other freedoms. The fact that I cannot enslave another person means that neither can others enslave me. In the end, the state works to everyone's benefit by enforcing certain rights. Individuals are better able to conduct their day-to-day activity without the constant worry of being cheated or having their safety jeopardized. In much the same way, at least in theory, international treaties ensure that countries do not arbitrarily invade others, pollute each other's air, or engage in unfair trade practices. From a theoretical standpoint, then, there is no logical reason to think that supranational institutions will work to undermine state power.

Deregulation

We must now ask to what degree increased trade and attacks on social programs can be traced to globalization and to what degree they are a necessary consequence of the adherence to a free market model. In the next chapter, I argue in some detail that the globalization explanation is just another variant of free-market proselytization. In this scenario, the state willingly relinquishes control over economic activities and invests its faith in the market. In theory, a free market applies to the free movement of goods and services based on supply and demand, but in the real world it means that powerful actors such as corporations are better able to exert their will, especially vis-à-vis labour. (A case in point is that NAFTA governs the free movement of goods and services but for the most part excludes labour.)

Exactly how effective the free-market approach has been is another question. As we recently saw in Asia, countries with a regulated investment climate (Japan, China, and Taiwan) were in a much better position to weather the currency crisis than countries that had adopted a more liberal approach (Thailand and Indonesia). Ironically, the failed economies have now been bailed out to the tune of U.S. $95 billion by the IMF (Stiglitz 2002), an organization that preached the liberal model to begin with. Also witness the bailing out of the Savings and Loan institutions (again, billions of dollars) by the U.S. government, and a similar intervention by the Canadian government when both the Canadian Commercial Bank and the Northland Bank failed in 1985. Thus, we are forced to conclude that the 'free' in 'free market' remains a relative term in that intervention is condoned the minute the stability of the system itself is jeopardized. (Then again, it is difficult to blame governments or international organizations for attempting to avert the panic associated with a run on a bank or a currency.)

Examples such as Japan or Germany illustrate that the laissez-faire model favoured by the Anglo-American nations is neither universal nor all that successful (Weiss 1997: 15, 26). The point to keep in mind is that events such as the currency crisis that affected Asia, Russia, and Brazil are problems long associated with capitalist economies. There is nothing new about such predicaments, and blaming them on globalization sheds no new light on finding a solution or achieving a better understanding of the problem.

Globalization and Free-trade Zones

Related to the argument that recognizes globalization as responsible for both the creation and the demise of the nation-state is the belief that the establishment of free-trade zones or the birth of new states are reactions to or manifestations of globalization. This demonstrates that a theory of globalization wants it all. The fall of the Soviet Union is adduced as an example of globalization's power to bring borders down, while a development such as NAFTA, which effectively establishes borders, is explained as a natural reaction of countries seeking to shield themselves from globalization. In other words, whether borders go up or down, globalization is implicated. At worst, this is intellectually dishonest; at best, it makes the theory unfalsifiable.

Giddens (2002; 1990) acknowledges the contradictory ways of globalization and explains the revival of local nationalisms as a reaction to it. But what exactly distinguishes these new nationalisms from older versions? The Scots, for example, have long aspired to be independent, for reasons that have probably been consistent for centuries: culture, economics, and autonomy. Nationalism has a long history, and globalization theory adds little to our understanding of it. As usual, we find that the process of globalization is left vague, and we are called upon to fill in the blanks. What is needed is something more specific, a theory that explains in detail how a process that dismantles borders can also be implicated in their creation.[2]

As was noted earlier, NAFTA is often put forward as evidence of globalization, yet the two scenarios offer vastly different challenges for a country like Canada. First, in an 'ideal type' of globalization, Canada is in competition with many other, some of them low-wage, countries. With NAFTA, however, Canada has become a relatively low-wage site itself, much of this because of the low dollar that prevailed throughout the 1990s and into the early 2000s. Many industries benefited from the advantages associated with a lower dollar and, as soon as it rose again, as it did throughout 2003, an immediate outcry emanated from industries that all of a sudden found themselves to be less competitive. Second, with NAFTA Canada stands in the shadow of an economic giant, whereas in a globalized economy Canada's economic prowess would be more strategically dispersed vis-à-vis the rest of the world. Canada is the world's seventh-largest economy, and its economic and technological superiority are an obvious asset in a pool of approximately 190 countries; whereas in NAFTA, Canada is in competition with only two other countries, one of them the most powerful economy in the world. This, in effect, greatly weakens Canada's economic strength. Third, in a truly global economy there exists a diversity of economic cultures including those of workplace organization, capital-labour relations, and workers' rights. With NAFTA, Canada is deluged by an American version of economic liberalism. And fourth, as we saw in chapter 4, NAFTA speaks more to the power of the Canadian elite's strategy for further continentalization than to the power of multinational capital to create a globalized economy (see Clement 1975; G. Williams 1986).

Data

The question underlying this chapter is whether there exists any empirical evidence that points towards the retreat of the state. One way to answer the question is to examine state expenditures. If the state is indeed being squeezed out of most economic activities, this should be reflected in a decline in expenditures. Furthermore, a detailed examination of government programs should provide us with a sense of the state's changing priorities – if the state is distancing itself from funding social programs and is focusing its attention on further abetting capital accumulation, this should be apparent. To determine if this is the case, both welfare-state and non-welfare-state expenditures will be scrutinized. The focus, however, will be on social programs, as these are most often the intended targets whenever anti-state rhetoric is invoked. To measure state strength by correlating it with state expenditures may be criticized as an overly positivistic approach (see Esping-Andersen 1990), as one could argue that no matter how much governments spend, their efforts continue to be futile. In other words, government expenditures can be seen as a desperate measure to stem the inexorable tide of globalization. This criticism is difficult to counter in the abstract but becomes considerably less damaging once individual programs are examined. For now, let us say that without government services there would not be much of an economy left to invest in. Certainly, government intervention may prove futile in some instances, but just as often it is indispensable. This section focuses on some of these indispensable areas.

Throughout this chapter, I make the argument that the state continues to answer to many diverse interests (e.g., labour, voters, the elderly, bureaucrats, NGOs) in addition to practical considerations such as fiscal constraint and the possibility of social unrest – all variables that have been discussed in the welfare-state literature, from Piven and Cloward to Pierson. In this context, capital is only one of multiple interests the state has to consider, many of which are contradictory. Globalization, as it were, has not dramatically altered this mix.

In order to properly assess various programs, we need to keep in mind a series of questions throughout the analysis. These questions will be highlighted again at the end of the chapter:

- Will state abdication in this area be supported by the voting public? Often support for a program makes it politically foolhardy to cut it, as it translates into lost votes.
- Will state abdication be supported by business (i.e., all sectors of capital)? Business, after all, needs an educated and healthy work-force and up-to-date infrastructure; moreover, it often benefits from government contracts.
- Is this program a likely candidate for privatization? Even where a case can be made that the private sector can do things more effi-ciently, funding still comes from general tax revenues.
- Will elimination of public funding for a particular program make the economy more competitive? To put it slightly differently, how well will the economy perform without publicly funded education or health?

State Expenditures

After twenty years of what seems like interminable cuts, one could eas-ily get the impression that public spending is way down. But this is not the case. Even in Great Britain, a country that pursued the neoconserva-tive agenda much earlier and with considerably more vigour than Can-ada, government spending remained virtually unchanged throughout the Thatcher era. In 1980, shortly after Thatcherism arrived on the polit-ical scene in the United Kingdom, government expenditures amounted to 43 per cent of GDP. After more than a decade and a half of slashing, this figure decreased to 42 per cent, a mere one percentage point drop (*The Economist*, 20 Sept. 1997: 7).

A similar scenario has unfolded in Canada. In 1960, the date given by Waters for the beginning of globalization, government expendi-tures amounted to approximately 27 per cent of GDP. Two and a half decades later, around the time when the Mulroney Conservatives first started to chip away at government spending, it had increased to 48 per cent of GDP (figure 7.1; and see appendix). After nine years of Pro-gressive Conservative downsizing, this figure had *increased* to slightly over 51 per cent. It was only in the 1990s that government expendi-tures were reigned in to any significant degree (and that was, as we shall see, primarily the result of lower interest rates). Throughout the same period (1960–2003), as we saw in chapter 4, trade doubled from approximately 15 per cent to 30 per cent of GDP. Obviously, the increase in trade has had little impact on government spending. Nei-

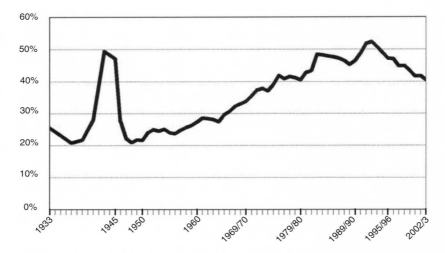

Figure 7.1. Total government expenditures as a percentage of GDP, Canada, 1933–2002/3

ther have what seem like interminable cuts made much of a difference. At around 40 per cent of Canada's GDP, the state continues to hold considerable sway over national affairs. Roughly half of these government expenditures go towards the three pillars of the welfare state: education, health, and social services. The other half is spent on more mundane programs such as infrastructure and resource management. It is this second, less newsworthy, half of government expenditures that we examine first.

The following figures represent consolidated government spending and include federal, provincial/territorial, and municipal spending. To break these figures down further by level of government is difficult because of overlap. For example, funds are transferred by the federal government, through the Canadian Health and Social Transfer (CHST), to the provinces, which in turn pass them to municipal governments, where they are spent on social assistance. In effect, this one expenditure is counted three times, an overlap that consolidated expenditures successfully averts.

As was the case with trade, the data in this section are presented as a percentage of GDP. As already mentioned, the advantage of this method is that it takes into account the growth of the economy, including inflation and population growth. A disadvantage is that it tends to downplay where the government is setting its spending priorities, decisions that are, no doubt, very political. For example, as a percentage of GDP, spending on infrastructure declined from 3.3 per cent to 2 per cent between 1965/66 and 1994/95. But as a percentage of total government expenditures it decreased from 12.5 per cent to 4.4 per cent, a cut of a much different magnitude. Another common way to present the data is on a per-capita basis, although the overall trends would be very similar. Overall, no matter what method is chosen, these data essentially paint the same picture: government expenditures have increased unabated since 1960 until the downturn that started in the early 1990s.

A systematic breakdown for other than the largest government programs is not available until 1965/66. For the years spanning 1933 to 1964, only the total, welfare-state services (health, education, and social services), and debt maintenance expenditures are available. Beginning in 1965/66, Statistics Canada began to list seventeen distinct services, four of which are welfare-state services and thirteen of which are non-welfare-state services. These services, and the percentage of the GDP they consume, are listed in table 7.1. Beginning in 1995/96, Statistics Canada introduced new categories for government expenditures. It eliminated the 'other expenditures' and 'transfers to own enterprises' categories and included them in more relevant categories. For example, in the old accounting procedure, pension outlays made by foreign affairs would have been included in 'other expenditures' but were moved to 'foreign affairs' beginning in 1995/96. Expenditures on education and health made by departments such as the military are now included in the 'education' or 'health' categories rather than in 'protection of persons and property' as they were in the past. Because of these changes, table 7.1 and table 7.3 show only figures up to and including 1994/95 so as to keep the categories consistent. The figures in the graphs include categories that remained unchanged, so they present less of a concern. Still, the reader should be aware that Statistics Canada warns that the two different accounting systems are not directly comparable. However, the years for which both categorizations are available show that the numbers are quite similar. And finally, Statistics Canada does not include CPP/QPP figures in its expenditures records (though for some reason it does include EI, which is also funded by contributions). Since pensions constitute some of the important programs provided by the welfare state, I have added these figures to the social services category.

Table 7.1
Categorization of expenditures as used by S tatistics Canada from 1965/66 to 1994/95; and consolidated federal, provincial, territori al, and local government expenditure, fiscal year 1994/95 (March to March) as a percentage of GDP

Function	Where spent	Percentage of GDP 1994/95
General services	Executive and legislature, general administrative	2.39
Protection of persons and property	National defence, courts of law, corrections, policing	3.21
Transportation and communications	Air transport, road transport, rail, water transport, telecommunications	2.06
Resource conservation and industrial development	Agriculture, fish and game, oil and gas, forestry, mining, water power, tourism promotion, trade and industry	1.85
Environment	Water purification and supply, pollution control	1.05
Recreation and culture	Libraries, art galleries and museums, broadcasting	0.95
Labour, employment, and immigration		0.43
Foreign affairs and international assistance		0.65
Regional planning and development		0.21
Research establishments		0.27
Transfers to own enterprises		0.67
Other expenditures		0.10
Health	Hospital care, medical care, preventive care	6.18
Education	Elementary, secondary, postsecondary, retraining	5.76
Social services (inc. CPP and QPP)	Social assistance, income maintenance, social security, family allowance, workers' compensation, employee pension plans, veterans' benefits	13.85
Housing		0.50
Debt charges		9.36
Grand Total		**49.51**

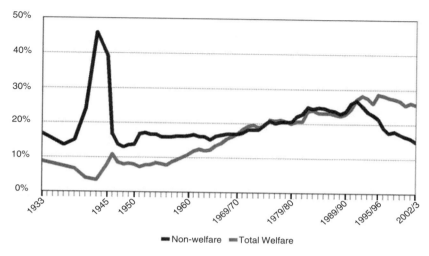

Figure 7.2. Total welfare and non-welfare expenditures as a percentage of GDP, Canada, 1933–2002/3

An Overview

Figure 7.2 shows that in the first few years following the war, government expenditures on non-welfare-state services were considerably higher than on welfare-state services. As more comprehensive and generous welfare-state programs were introduced throughout the 1950s and 1960s, these figures gradually converged, with both growing in lockstep throughout the 1970s and 1980s. However, things changed dramatically in the 1990s. The downturn in government spending that we saw in the previous graph can primarily be traced to non-welfare-state spending, while welfare-state spending levelled off. We will now look at both of these two major spending categories in turn.

Non-welfare-state Spending

Figure 7.3 shows that currently, including debt payments, slightly less than one-fifth of GDP is directed towards non-welfare-state spending. As we saw in the preceding graph, this is the result of slow but steady growth in spending across all sectors, with a sharp decline in the 1990s. However, once interest payments are deducted from non-welfare ex-

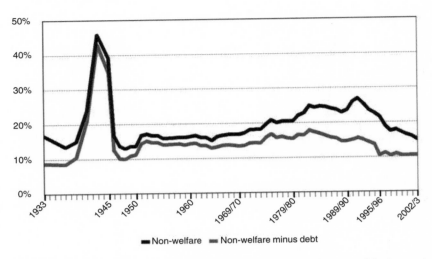

Figure 7.3. Total non-welfare-state expenditures (plus and minus debt interest payments) as a percentage of GDP, Canada, 1933–2002/3

penses the picture changes somewhat. Now, rather than experiencing an abrupt decline, expenditures peaked in 1980 and then underwent a much more gradual decline up until the mid-1990s when expenditures levelled off at around 10 per cent. Non-welfare expenses are now lower than they were at any time in the 1950s or 1960s, and only marginally higher than before the Second World War. Also worth noting is how the distance between the two lines increased throughout most of the 1980s and early 1990s, coinciding with the era of high interest rates, but converged with the lowering of interest rates in the mid-1990s. In other words, high interest rates have a tendency to crowd out spending on other programs. Whereas politicians have made minor cuts to this and that program, they cannot arbitrarily renege on interest payments. In an era when high interest rates prevail, the government cannot simply ignore debt maintenance payments, for refusal to pay only means bigger payments further down the road.

Government services that make up non-welfare spending are, on the whole, much less politicized than social programs. This is not to say that these programs are impervious to a backlash when under attack, as cuts to the public service suggest, but these are the exception rather than the rule. Rarely have we heard anti-government rhetoric that targeted spending on police services, management of resources, or foreign affairs. In many ways, such mundane activities make for uninteresting news. 'Resource conservation and industrial development' is not a topic that arouses strong public opinions. Other areas, such as policing and the military, are avoided because they are incongruent with a right-wing platform, although these programs have not been spared. These programs are also glossed over because expenditures for each amount to relatively little – even if these expenditures were completely elimi-nated, the change in total expenditures would be insignificant. Yet despite this silence, or maybe because of it, this is where some of the big-gest cuts have occurred over the past few decades.

Areas such as culture, research, foreign affairs, labour, the environ-ment, 'own enterprises,' and 'other expenditures' consume less than 1 per cent of GDP each (see table 7.1), figures that have not undergone sig-nificant changes in the past thirty years. While expenditures on the environment did increase considerably over the past decades, at mar-ginally more than 1 per cent, they continue to make up only a relatively small portion of GDP. Non-welfare-state programs that demand larger portions of the pie are the debt, 'resource conservation and industrial development,' 'transportation and communications,' 'protection of per-sons and property,' and 'general services.'

Not surprisingly, as a consequence of monetarist policies pursued by the Bank of Canada starting in the mid-1970s, the biggest increase in expenditures has been in debt servicing, which tripled from around 3 per cent of GDP in 1965–6 to more than 9 per cent of GDP in 1994–5 (although it has dropped significantly since interest rates have been lowered). 'Labour, employment, and immigration' and 'foreign affairs' are a further two areas where spending has grown significantly. All other areas experienced cuts. Cuts to 'resource conservation and indus-trial development' were most dramatic in the early 1980s, reflecting the hands-off approach practised by the then reigning Progressive Conser-vatives. 'Resource conservation and industrial development' is an important area because it reflects the government's commitment to shaping industrial policy. As one would expect from the Conservatives, who have long advocated the market-based exploration of resources, cuts in this area were deep during their tenure. The various levels of government invested 3.3 per cent of GDP in 1984/85, a figure that was almost halved by 1994/95 to 1.8 per cent of GDP.

Another sector hit hard has been infrastructure ('transportation and communications'), which has experienced a steady decline in expenditure since 1965/66, from 3.1 per cent of GDP to just over 2 per cent in 1994/95. One would expect expenses to have risen somewhat in this area based on the promise of infrastructure investments made by the Liberals in the 1993 election, but this is not the case. Ongoing cuts in this area are somewhat surprising given that infrastructure is also important to business. Much publicized cuts to the civil service are not reflected by equally deep cuts in expenditures. In 1965/66, expenditures in this sector stood at 1.5 per cent of GDP and more than doubled, to 2.4 per cent, by 1994/95, down only marginally from a high of 2.7 per cent in 1990/91.

In summary, we can see that cuts to non-welfare services have been relatively effective. Even programs that are traditionally supported by the right, programs that fall under the aegis of the 'nightwatchman state,' such as policing and the military, have endured their share of cuts. In addition, programs that benefit capital, such as infrastructure, have not been able to evade cuts, suggesting that the government's zeal for cutting spending knows few friends. However, the biggest decline in spending has occurred in interest payments.

Welfare-state Services

One of the biggest oversights in the globalization literature is the welfare state. Accounts by Robertson (1992) and Waters (2001) fail to allude to it, while the political economy literature for the most part ignores it too. The exception is Teeple (2000), but even he provides no empirical evidence – his work is primarily a lament for the end of the welfare state. Albrow views the attack on the welfare state as evidence of the declining faith in the nation-state, but again, provides no evidence. Given that the development of the welfare state is one of the most significant developments in politics in the past half-century, this oversight is more than a bit surprising.

In order to make up for this shortcoming, this section examines welfare-state spending with an emphasis on the postwar period. The figures are further subdivided into what may be termed the three pillars of the welfare state: education, health, and social services. (The last item includes contributory and non-contributory pensions, family allowances, social assistance, and veterans' benefits.)

Figure 7.4 illustrates the continuous and gradual rise of expenditures on social programs from 1955 onwards. Whereas figures were below the 10 per cent mark before the mid-1950s (with only one exception), they have not approached anywhere near single digits since.

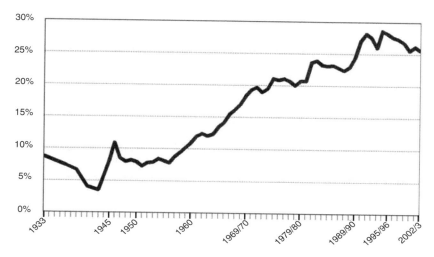

Figure 7.4. Total welfare-state expenditures as a percentage of GDP, Canada, 1933–2002/3

This is in stark contrast to the figures for non-welfare-state spending, which, as we saw above, are now lower than in the 1950s. Welfare-state expenditures grew rapidly from the late 1950s onwards until well into the mid-1970s, but even after that date, despite well-publicized cuts and many laments about the demise of the welfare state, expenditures continued to increase. The first cuts came in 1977/78, but expenditures rose again with the recession in the early 1980s, after which they declined once again, but then only negligibly. In the early 1990s, there appeared to be a sudden upsurge in spending, with figures rising to 28 per cent of GDP, but there was a subsequent decline back to one-quarter of GDP, at which level they remain in 2002/3. In general, then, the right's attack on the welfare state cannot be considered all that successful given that expenditures rose from 20 to 25 per cent of GDP between the time the offensive first began in earnest in the mid-1970s up until the present. Nor has globalization made much of a difference.

Viewed from a slightly different angle, welfare-state programs accounted for less than 40 per cent of all government spending before 1960 and increased to about one-half by 1970. Surprisingly, this share fell somewhat throughout the late 1970s and early 1980s, only to regain its former 50 per cent share in the early 1990s. Both figure 7.1 and figure 7.4 suggest that social reform is a long way from being committed to the dustbin of history. In order to further assess why this may be so, we now take a closer look at each of the three pillars of the welfare state.

i) Education

The first area of spending we examine in detail is education, primarily because it introduces some obvious contradictions to the globalization thesis. For a variety of reasons, education has been publicly funded for more than a century in industrialized economies and continues to be so to this day. In the year 2000, Canada spend 6.2 per cent (including both public and private expenditures) on education as a proportion of GDP. Even a country like the United States, a welfare-state laggard in so many other respects, spent 6.9 per cent of its GDP on education that same year. The country with the lowest spending in the OECD world is Japan, which still spends 4.7 per cent of its GDP educating its citizens. The average for the OECD world is 5.9 per cent, indicating that there is little variation among industrial countries. In Canada, as in most industrialized countries, a relatively high proportion of education is funded by the government: 89 per cent compared to the OECD average of 80.1 per cent in 1998, and 75 per cent for the United States. Please keep in mind that all the following data are for public expenditures only. In 2000, these figures amounted to 5.5 per cent of GDP for Canada and 5.0 per cent for the United States, with the OECD average being 5.2 per cent (OECD 2003a; OECD 2001).

Figure 7.5 shows that public funding for education has long been a major item of the welfare state. In 1945, funding was down slightly from the levels found before the war but then began a steady rise. Expenditures peaked in 1960 and then levelled off somewhat, only to rise again towards the middle of that decade. Near the end of the 1960s, they reached almost 7 per cent and then settled in at around 6 per cent. As a matter of fact, there has been little change in education expenditures in Canada over the past twenty-five years; they have hovered consistently around the 6 per cent mark. This amounted to around $65 billion in 2002/3. The consistency of these figures may appear somewhat surprising, particularly to those who either work at or attend a university, where cutbacks have been felt to be relatively deep. Students across the country have been faced with higher tuition fees, and the workloads for faculties have increased. Everyone – including students, teaching assistants, and professors – has had to contend with larger classes. One reason cutbacks are perceived to be worse than they actually are is that the number of students enrolled in universities has increased while expen-

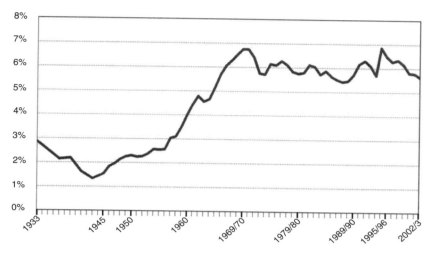

Figure 7.5. Public education expenditures as a percentage of GDP, Canada, 1933–2002/3

ditures have failed to keep up. Apart from that, universities present a somewhat skewed picture of education in general. Approximately one-third of education expenditures (32.8 per cent) are directed towards tertiary education, with the other two-thirds going to primary and secondary education. Cuts at the tertiary level have been easier to implement because they present the path of least resistance. Universities are able, at least to some degree, to compensate for these cuts by offloading costs to students by way of tuition fees, an option not readily available to primary and secondary institutions. University funding has also been the victim of free-market rhetoric, which claims that university education is a commodity that primarily benefits the individual. Consequently, public opinion has countenanced a shifting of expenditures from the state to the individual consumer.

An equivalent shifting of expenses to primary and secondary students has not been the case (the other two-thirds of public expenditures), and this is unlikely to be the case in the future. For a politician to even suggest that students or parents should pay tuition fees for twelve years of primary and secondary education would be political suicide. As we are constantly reminded by the ongoing teachers' disputes across Canada, education is a highly sensitive and emotional issue. Cuts to education, compared to funding cuts overall, have been relatively trivial and have translated into less preparation time for teachers and larger classes (as was the case in Ontario in the mid-1990s and in British Columbia in 2001). Yet even at these relatively small levels, cuts have provoked vigorous opposition from teachers, parents, and even students.

Furthermore, education is unlikely to undergo major cuts or elimination because public, private, and business support for education is high. Seldom do we hear about the need to take the responsibility of education away from government. Even among the charter school movement, which aims to bring control of schools to a local level, the assumption remains that these schools will continue to be funded by the various levels of government. What we do find is that control of education is becoming simultaneously more centralized and more decentralized. In other words, power is being squeezed from the middle (Davies and Guppy 1997: 459). That is, government continues to play a central role in the funding of education.

These developments are a direct refutation of the globalization thesis that predicts the end of the state. Education is conveniently neglected not only by advocates of globalization but also by its opponents. Why is this so? One can only speculate. One possible reason is that public funding for primary and secondary education has been in place for so long that it is taken for granted, and its opposite – the complete absence of publicly funded education – is unimaginable to most people. In the minds of the majority of Canadians, public education is so integral a part of modern industrial society that few even consider how it is funded, and even fewer are able to imagine a world without it.

Education raises other important issues besides funding for the globalization thesis. Globalists trace many of the changes they observe to advances in technology, in particular, computers and telecommunications. Two criticisms can be made with respect to this thesis. First, the 'constant revolutionizing of the forces of production,' as Marx and Engels observed, is an integral part of capitalism and can hardly be considered a new development. Furthermore, changing technologies cannot be properly exploited without a well-educated workforce, and education is, as we saw, primarily publicly funded. Judging by regular complaints about a lack of skilled workers in Canada (complaints that are, no doubt, highly exaggerated), business is fully aware that a high-quality education system is essential to the smooth functioning of the economy, and hence business is unlikely to support major cuts in this area.

In terms of both funding and technology, education presents a major obstacle to the globalization thesis. Education guarantees that the state will continue to play a central role in the management of the economy for some time. Technology may have made borders more porous, but at the same time the state needs to intervene and ensure that these technologies can be successfully harvested. In short, all levels of education – primary, secondary, and tertiary – are unlikely to be abandoned by the state precisely because education remains a lynchpin ensuring the competitiveness of our technologically driven economy. The onus should be on globalists to clarify who will fund education once the government has packed up and left the country.

ii) Health

Governments began to take an active interest in the funding of health care only after the Second World War. The United States is often presented as a notable exception to this, yet almost 45 per cent of its trillion-dollars-plus expenditures on health is publicly funded. Still, the majority of the U.S. system is privately funded. Our proximity to this country sometimes blinds us to just how exceptional a largely privately funded health-care system is. While the system in the United States has provided the best health for some, in many ways it has proven to be a failure. The United States spends more on health care, by a considerable margin, than any other country in the OECD (14.6 per cent of GDP in 2002, 44.9 per cent of which is publicly funded), yet this lavishness does not mean that all Americans have access to health care.

Canada's health-care system, on the other hand, is more comprehensive than the U.S. system, at least in the sense that it does cover everyone.[3] When both public and private spending are taken into account, Canada spent 9.6 per cent of its GDP in 2002 on health. This is slightly higher than the OECD average. In 2000, Canada's health expenditures came in at 8.9 per cent, which was slightly higher than the OECD mean of 7.9 per cent that same year. In Canada, in 2000, public expenditure amounted to approximately 69.8 per cent of all health expenditure, which is within a percentage point of the OECD average (70.6 per cent) that same year. Canada suffers somewhat by comparison with countries such as Sweden or Norway where public coverage amounts to around 85 per cent. In Canada, areas that are primarily privately financed include dental care, some prescription drugs, some eye care, and some visits to chiropractors, physiotherapists, and the like. The public-private mix in Canada has changed in past decades, but not dramatically so. In 1970, the proportion of total health expenditures in Canada that was privately funded amounted to approximately 30 per cent, but this decreased to 20 per cent in 1980 and 1990, only to return to a 30 per cent share by 2003. Again, please note that only public expenditures are shown in the graph; these amounted to 6.5 per cent of GDP in the year 2000/1, nearly the same as the OECD figure of 6.3 per cent for 2001 (OECD 2004).

As a single program, health consumes the largest share of all government expenditures. Health-care spending has long been a responsibility of the various levels of government in what could best be described as a stop-and-go approach (see Myles 1988). The private sector's role in health care is already more evolved than in education and has the potential to become even more so. Approximately 30 per cent of health care is paid for by private sources, compared to only 10 per cent for education, but this does not indicate a trend towards the privatization of medical services. As politicians have found, Canadians value their health-care system above all else, and those in favour of privatization or major cuts meet firm public opposition at every turn. Not surprisingly, health care was the major issue in the 2004 election. Privatization has considerable support from the right, usually in the form of a two-tier health system, but this support is insignificant when compared to that for a publicly funded system. The dearth of support for a private system may in part be linked to the inefficient and inequitable example found south of the border.

As figure 7.6 shows, health expenditures rose slowly but steadily in the 1940s (the average for the decade was 1 per cent) and 1950s (average 1.3 per cent). Expenditure growth did not start to accelerate until the late 1960s, about the time the Canada Health Act (1966) was introduced by the federal government (the average for the 1960s was 3 per cent). In the 1970s, expenditures rose another two percentage points to 5 per cent and nearly another point in the 1980s (average 5.8 per cent). At the beginning of the 1990s numbers continued to rise, averaging around 6.5 per cent for the decade.

As with education, we find that health expenditures have not taken a dramatic downturn. If anything, the rise in health-care expenditures has been more steady than in education. Even so, however, we find that funding has not kept pace with rising demand. One reason is an aging population. Another, according to the Canada Health Institutes, is the increased cost of pharmaceuticals as a result of Bill C-22. On the

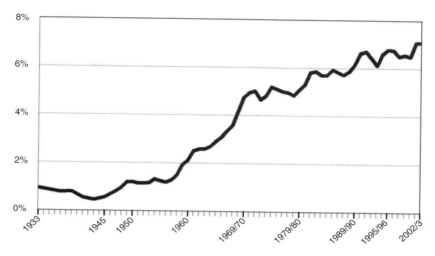

Figure 7.6. Public health expenditures as a percentage of GDP, Canada, 1933–2002/3

other hand, funding to hospitals has stagnated. Hospital closures throughout the country have been well publicized, making it appear as though cuts have been deep throughout the whole system, but figures reveal that funds have merely been diverted elsewhere. And if the claims of nurses across the country are true, they have been taking the brunt of the cuts. In other words, it is not so much that health has experienced deep cuts across the board, but that funds within health care have been reallocated, from hospitals to pharmaceuticals and from nurses to doctors.

For most of the past half-century, health-care costs have lagged behind education costs. This was true right through to the mid-1980s, at which point the two converged (5.5 per cent for education and 5.8 per cent for health). One reason for the continued growth in health care is the public support already mentioned. Another reason, often overlooked, is that public funding for health care makes business more competitive. Certainly, there are institutional actors who would gain if the system were privatized (e.g., insurance companies), and there is little doubt that support for privatization there is highest. But support for the privatization of health care is not uniform across the business community. Opposition comes from firms that would have to pay health insurance for workers if the government abdicated its role. To these firms, publicly funded health care constitutes a considerable subsidy, and the existence of this program partially explains the large numbers of car manufacturing plants that continue to thrive in southern Ontario (see the chapter on trade above). A recent study by an American investment firm shows that it costs an additional U.S. $930 to produce a car in the United States because of costs associated with private health insurance (*Globe and Mail*, 12 Feb. 2002: B10).

Once again the evidence does not support the weakening state theory. Governments show few signs of getting out of health care, partly because of popular support, partly because it is good for business, and partly because it is more efficient in terms of costs. In the First Ministers' Meeting in September 2004, Paul Martin promised another $18 billion in health-care funding over the next six years, suggesting that a decline in funding is not likely to occur in the near future. As with education, we find that a publicly administered health system makes a country *more*, not less competitive. It also ensures that the investment made in education stays around for some time. In short, the abstract claim that the state is becoming obsolete is refuted once a concrete responsibility such as health care is examined.

iii) Social Services

Social services comprise the kind of programs most commonly associated with the welfare state. Mention welfare and most people think of social assistance, although many other programs, such as pensions, are included in this group. Strongly held ideological beliefs about individual initiative make social services the most vulnerable to cuts. Of course, social assistance makes up only a small portion of social services expenditure, which also includes social security (i.e, pensions), veterans' benefits, employment insurance (EI), and family allowances. All programs that fall under the rubric of social services, with the exception of family allowances, entail transfers to individuals (or families) who do not work, whether they are too young, too old, infirm, sick, or simply unable to find employment. In short, these programs decommodify the worker from the labour market (Esping-Andersen 1990). It is worthwhile noting how attitudes differ towards the various programs that make up social services. The distinction between deserving and undeserving poor, or in the past between the potent and the impotent, can serve as a useful example. While all social services programs decommodify the worker to some degree, some recipients are considered more deserving (e.g., the elderly) than others (e.g., able-bodied males between eighteen and sixty-five). This distinction plays a crucial role in what programs can be exploited for political gain – or, alternatively, which are best left alone.

EI and social assistance continue to be most vulnerable to cuts, not because of excessive costs but because they are intimately linked to the labour market. Most often these programs fall victim to ideological opposition that disparages them as 'labour market disincentives.' Expenditures for these programs are minimal, as they are relatively affordable, in the case of social assistance, or are self-funded, in the case of EI. In other words, recurrent attacks on these programs stem more from ideology and opportunism than from fiscal probity or globalization. The constellation of support for these programs is also weaker than for education, health, and even other social service programs such as pensions. Social assistance and EI have several weaknesses that tend to undermine their popularity: they are not universal, their recipients are geographically dispersed and poorly organized, and they have little support from either the general public or business, a state of affairs that can be traced back to the very beginnings of the market economy. In point of fact, business enthusiastically endorses cuts to these programs on the grounds that it disciplines the workforce and lowers wages.

Figure 7.7 shows that social services expenditures grew slowly between the 1950s and the mid-1960s, a period of rapid economic expansion. Disbursements started to grow more rapidly in the mid-1960s with the introduction of the Canada and Quebec pension plans (CPP/QPP) and the Guaranteed Income Supplement (GIS).[4] Expenditures accelerated when unemployment insurance benefits (now EI) were expanded generously in 1971, and even more so when unemployment rose later that decade. As the economy contracted in the early 1980s, social services expenditures rose correspondingly. Between 1969/70 and the present, we can identify a pattern that is the mirror image of the economy: expenditures increase during recessions and abate during booms. After each recession, however, expenditures stabilized above their pre-recession level – the result of factors such as an aging population and ever-increasing rates of unemployment – making for an almost staircase-like pattern. It is also important to note that expenditures in this sector failed to plateau as they did in education and health, and have continued their seemingly inexorable climb (see figure 7.8). To get a better understanding of why this may be so, we examine two major cate-

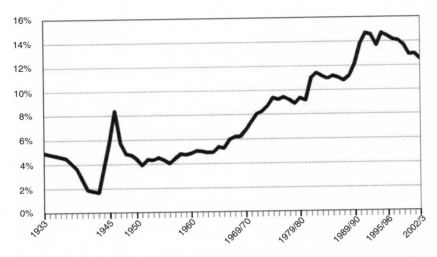

Figure 7.7. Social services expenditures as a percentage of GDP, Canada, 1933–2002/3

gories of social services spending in turn: (1) pensions and (2) labour market programs (social assistance and EI).

a) Pensions
Despite the gloom and doom surrounding most discussions on pensions, the reality is that these programs continue to be well funded and their growth has been less hindered by cuts than that of any other government program. In the fiscal year 2002/3, pension expenditures, including CPP, QPP, OAS, GIS, and SPA,[5] amounted to $54 billion. Currently, pensions account for 37 per cent of all social services expenditure, or 4.7 per cent of GDP. Most of this growth has occurred in the CPP/QPP, which went from less than a billion dollars ($792 million) in 1975 to $28 billion in 2002/3. Part of this impressive rise in expenditures is, of course, due to the aging of the population, but some can also be explained by the large number of workers who have been forced into early retirement because of limited opportunities in the labour market. Pensions are also indexed to inflation, and to change this has proved difficult. The grey public keeps a sharp eye on the government to ensure it does not even consider such a move. Pensions are also directly funded by the federal government and dispensed to indi-

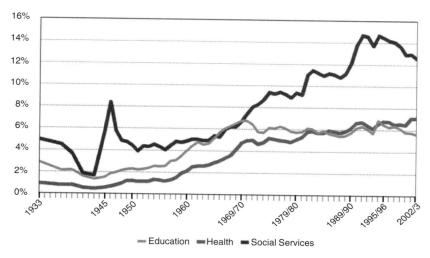

Figure 7.8. Public health, education, and social services expenditures as a percentage of GDP, Canada, 1933–2002/3

viduals, rather than paid through the more usual block funding (e.g., CAP or CHST), making it politically much more difficult for the federal government to cut funding or offload expenses to the provinces as it has done with education, health, and social assistance. When de-indexation or cuts to pensions are attempted the political backlash is usually forceful and immediate, as then Prime Minister Mulroney found out in 1985 when he tried to de-index the OAS. This is not to say that pensions have been immune to cuts, as Mulroney did successfully implement clawbacks to the OAS in 1989. In general, however, as the rise in expenditure clearly indicates, politicians are hesitant to meddle with pension programs and appear content to hunt for weaker prey.

Of all the different pension programs, the government would have the least to gain by cutting the CPP/QPP. These programs are funded directly through contributions (as opposed to the other pensions, which are funded out of general revenues). When pensions were first introduced in Germany by Bismarck in 1889, some commentators cynically referred to the system as a forced savings plan, which the CPP/QPP essentially continues to be to this day. If the government were to distance itself from contributory pensions it would have to make up for this shortfall in other areas anyway (which it already does to some degree with the GIS and social assistance), and this would then show up in an increase in expenditures elsewhere. The way the CPP/QPP is presently structured works well for the government. It is well funded as well as popular. No politician with even a modicum of intelligence would attempt to tinker with this program in a major way for there is very little to gain and a whole lot to lose. Interestingly, the CPP/QPP and EI are alike in that they are both self-funded through contributions, and both decommodify the worker. The crucial difference between the two is in the amount of public support they receive.

This does not mean that the business community is happy with the status quo: privatization threats are more real with respect to pensions than for most other social services programs – at least in theory. Overall, Canada's public pensions are less generous when compared to those of other industrialized countries, particularly in Western Europe (Myles 1989). The relative inadequacy of public funding has meant that the Canadian pension system is already partially privatized. Private pensions are either directly tied to employment or are purchased on an individual basis (RRSPs). Even then, there are ongoing pressures to privatize the system, with the end-goal of shifting the burden completely away from government. But in the long run, complete privatization would prove unfeasible. While there is always a portion of the population fortunate enough to be able to invest for its own retirement, others are not so lucky. This means that, in the end, the more penurious elements of society would end up collecting some form of social assistance anyway. In other words, if public pensions were eliminated, government responsibility would merely be shifted to another sector. Furthermore, the government would lose valuable tax revenue if RRSP limits were increased, resulting in little overall change to their budget. And last, the majority of private pensions are invested in the stock market, and as the bear market starting in 2000 well illustrates, millions of people in North America find themselves in the position of having to delay their retirement dates. If the whole system were privatized, millions might be left without adequate pensions, meaning that once again the government would be forced to provide assistance. As Henwood (1997) says, why not simply have government take care of pensions in the first place?

b) Social Welfare and Unemployment Insurance
Social welfare has historically proved to be the most disdained of welfare-state programs, a prejudice that persists to this day. Recently, the

attack on the poor has been most viciously rehearsed by Premiers Harris in Ontario, Klein in Alberta, and Campbell in British Columbia. Cutbacks to social assistance were also implemented by the NDP government in British Columbia (in the form of a three-month residency requirement),[6] and the current B.C. Liberals have attempted to introduce a two-year limit on the collection of benefits, a policy they later withdrew because of public pressure and the scheme's impracticality. While the motives for these cuts are primarily ideological, social assistance remains vulnerable because of the stigma attached to being 'dependent'. By comparison with the elderly, doctors, or even students, poor people are not well organized, and this makes them easy targets. Paradoxically, attacks on the poor mount as the economy worsens – that is, when social assistance is most needed. These assaults continue despite the relatively low cost of social welfare, especially in comparison to big-ticket items such as health, education, and pensions. Even if all social assistance programs were eliminated, it would barely put a dent in government spending. Throughout the various levels of government, welfare consistently consumes around 2 per cent of GDP. In 1993, it accounted for just under 2 per cent of GDP (National Council of Welfare 1995). In 1995 it cost $19.5 billion, or 1.7 per cent (Clark 1998: 26), and in 1999, 1.98 per cent, according to the HRDC website.

Unlike pensions, social assistance payments vary among provinces, as individual provinces and territories (and sometimes municipalities) set their own standards. This has meant that the attack on social assistance has largely depended on the ideological position of the provincial government in power. How successful these cuts have been is not easy to measure. Much was made of the cuts made by the Conservatives in Ontario. In 1995, the Harris government successfully pared social assistance payments by 21.6 per cent (Sossin 1998). However, this merely served to wipe out the 23.6 per cent gain made between 1986 and 1991 (Courchene 1994: table 23). Even with the Harris cuts, the remaining benefits were still more generous than in most other provinces (see Clark 1998: table 1).

And while those cuts may have somewhat eased the financial burden of the Ontario government, they could not compensate for the increase in expenditures due to the higher caseload that was generated by the recession in the early 1990s. The number of social assistance recipients in Ontario doubled between 1988 and 1993 (Courchene 1994), a trend that could be found across Canada. In the early 1980s, 6 per cent of Canadians were on social assistance, a figure that rose to 10 percent by the early 1990s and hovered there until 1994. Since 1995, this number has steadily declined, with only 5.6 per cent of Canada's population receiving social assistance in 2003 (National Council of Welfare 2004).

A number of provincial governments have successfully tightened eligibility requirements, but if anything, this has increased the role of the state in terms of surveillance and increased administration costs. While causing distress to individuals and families, the cuts have done little to improve the overall fiscal health of the various levels of government. They have also failed to lower unemployment, as unemployment is primarily the result of a slowing economy and structural changes that occur within the labour market. Social assistance expenditures have also increased as fewer unemployed workers are eligible for EI (see below).

Another way to measure the effects of social assistance cuts is to inspect poverty rates and income distribution. Ken Battle's (1994) research shows that poverty rates declined substantially between 1961 and 1991; while rates have stabilized for most groups, they have decreased dramatically for some, such as the elderly. Statistics also reveal a remarkable stability in the distribution of income among the quintiles over the past forty years (Urmetzer and Guppy 2004). Once again, the health of the economy plays an important role. Figures released by the National Council of Welfare (2004) show that increases and decreases in the number of people on social assistance reflects the larger ebbs and flows of a market economy.

We must now ask how likely it is that social assistance will be reduced drastically in the future, or even eliminated, and how susceptible it is to privatization. If the past is any indication, these programs will be around for some time. Social welfare provisions have a long and tenacious history in the capitalist world, starting before the Elizabethan Poor Laws of 1572. While these programs have always suffered from some degree of ideological opposition, they have nevertheless endured. According to Piven and Cloward (1993), their persistence can be explained by the fact that they contain social unrest. Additional reasons, such as the high cost of incarcerating people who turn to crime, cannot be overlooked. California, for example, now spends more on the prison system than on higher education (Hacker 1997: 235). In short, the danger of social turmoil and the political and financial expense that accompanies it make it unlikely that these programs will ever disappear.

Since few profits are to be made by giving away money, there is little chance that social services will be replaced by the private sector. Private charity (e.g., food banks) does take up some of this slack, but historically this type of service has been wanting. Moreover, our predominantly urban and secular society is much different from the society of past centuries, and the church, the institution historically responsible for doling out alms, has few social welfare responsibilities in today's world. Even then a considerable amount, if not all, of funding to the parishes came from taxes (paid for by occupiers of land referred to as ratepayers). If the state did abandon its responsibility in this area, conditions would indeed be grave for the poor, resulting in a situation similar to that in many Third World countries.

Meanwhile, cuts to EI have been more successful. Part of the rise in expenditures in social assistance can be directly linked to cuts in EI, serving to illustrate the interconnection between government services. EI is similar to social assistance in that both are explicitly linked to the labour market. Interestingly, while pensions are as much of a labour market disincentive as EI, people have generally come to accept that the elderly should enjoy their retirement free of toil. In the 1990s, EI experienced deep cuts, in terms of both eligibility and expenditures. Expenditures decreased by 43 per cent between 1992 and 1997 (from 2.8 to 1.6 per cent of GDP). As a percentage of GDP, however, figures for EI are less meaningful than for other social services as the number of clients can fluctuate dramatically with the health of the economy. For example, both in 1990 and 1996, EI expenditures amounted to $13 billion, or a moderate decrease from 1.9 to 1.7 per cent of GDP. However, in 1990, 87 per cent of the unemployed were covered by EI, a number that was almost halved by 1996 (to 46 per cent of unemployed) (Pulkingham 1998: 20) and that declined further to just 36 per cent by 1997 according to a study done by the CLC (*Globe and Mail*, 27 Jan. 1999: A1).

There are many other programs in the social services sector, including the family allowance, veterans' benefits, and workers' compensation, and most have successfully avoided major cuts. The bulk of these programs, especially the family allowance and veterans' benefits, are generally immune because they are politically sensitive. The Mulroney administration de-universalized the family allowance and attempted to channel funds towards those who needed them most, a process that in the end provided no savings for government and few benefits to clients, with expenditures remaining relatively unchanged (Battle 1993).

The overarching conclusion to be drawn from these data is that most social services are difficult to cut and impossible to eliminate. Despite the ideological posturing normally associated with the politics of the welfare state, cuts to these programs are strikingly more difficult to implement than would appear on first sight. 'Ideology' is etymologically and semantically related to 'idea,' and in the political arena, ideas are poor competition to practical considerations such as social unrest, voter backlash, and even public opinion. Five centuries' worth of opposition to social services, often passionate and acrimonious, testifies to the fact that ideology alone is not able to secure their elimination.

There is always the (slight) possibility that governments will get out of social services altogether, resulting in what has been aptly referred to as the Brazilianization of the economy (Therborn 1986). More pessimistic accounts of globalization overtly take this position, but such a scenario is improbable. It is, of course, difficult to predict the future, but one can make some reasonable observations about the future by looking backwards, and if the last half of the past millennium is any indication – essentially the whole of capitalist history – the probability is high that even the most disdained of social programs will stay around for some time.

Is the Welfare State History?

Much of the literature on the formation of the welfare state has emphasized the role of politics, as well as the general balance of class power, a theory commonly referred to as the power resources model. In the late 1980s, advocates of this theory concluded that the welfare state was at an impasse, based on the observation that neoconservatives were unable to dismantle it, while its defenders, usually labour or the left, were equally unable to enlarge it. Pierson (1994) accepts the assessment that the welfare state is neither growing nor shrinking and agrees that the success of conservatives in dismantling the welfare state has been greatly exaggerated. He writes that, while 'the welfare state has been battered, its main components remain intact.' But Pierson also strongly disagrees with the usual reasons given for this impasse, particularly with the notion that the left has actively defended the welfare state. He accurately points out that even in countries where labour is weak, such as in the United States and Great Britain, attempts at retrenchment have markedly failed. Rates of unionization in both these countries have declined, and labour has been weakened politically as well. So while the power resources model may explain the expansion of the welfare state, it falls short of explaining why its opponents have found it so difficult to dismantle. Canada fits Pierson's argument well. While levels of unionization in Canada have held steady at around 30 per cent of the workforce over the past few decades, Canada's party on the left, the NDP, lost considerable support throughout the 1990s (although it gained some of it back in the 2004 election). Still, as we saw, during the neoconservative reign from 1984 to 1993 and beyond, the welfare state has endured.

Pierson relates the failure to substantially dismantle the welfare state to a number of reasons that can best be summarized as the persistence of the status quo. He argues that the process of disassembling the welfare state is fundamentally different from that of its creation. First and foremost, politicians are reluctant to engage in major cuts because of the potential political fallout (1994: 29). Taking someone's education or health services away is tantamount to political suicide. Programs bring with them their own support, and politicians are loath to tamper with that support for fear of losing votes. In contrast to the boost in voter popularity that comes with the introduction of social programs, political costs have to be endured when cutting them. Politicians are acutely aware of such negative repercussions and consequently are compelled to rely on a variety of tactics that make cuts less visible. When cuts do happen, they are only marginal. More often than not, politicians are forced to resort to stealth, tinkering with eligibility requirements or implementing clawbacks. This task is most effectively performed by spreading cuts over time, an example being the de-indexation of benefits (that is, benefits no longer keep pace with inflation). Another way of minimizing public backlash is to shift blame elsewhere. The need for fiscal restraint in order to balance the budget is probably the most favoured rationale when it comes to making cuts, even when, as was the case in British Columbia in 2001, that wound was self-inflicted.[7]

Last, Pierson stresses that any contemporary political action is straitjacketed by past decisions. Promises made cannot be easily dismissed or broken, thereby leaving the choices available to politicians 'path dependent'. Myles and Pierson (2001: 306) find in their study of old-age pensions that 'choices made in the past systematically constrain the choices in the future.' This literature draws heavily on the work of economists Paul David and Brian Arthur, who demonstrate through examples such as the arrangement of the keys on a typewriter or the use of a technology such as VHS (as compared to BETA), that a superior product does not naturally win out over an inferior one. History often determines how and where a product is made, and subsequently 'locks in' and constrains people's choices in the future (Krugman 1994: 222). To summarize, past practices matter, whether in the production of private goods or public services.

Equally important when it comes to implementing change is the existent political structure. Is there an opposition party, and if so how effective is it? Are politicians accountable to their constituents or their leader? In Canada, the prime minister has considerably more power than his or her presidential counterpart in the United States. In the United States, the president faces several roadblocks when introducing policy, and his wishes can be thwarted by either the Senate, the House of Representatives, or both. In contrast, in the Canadian parliamentary system, the prime minister can force policies through as long as his party has a majority. The division of power is also important, and determines whether a country has a weak or a strong state (Olson, 2002: 143). Canada and the United States both have adopted a form of federalism, in which powers are divided between federal and provincial or state governments. The British system, on the other hand, is more centralized in that it does not share power with any regional entities. In a country with only a central government, at least in theory, it should be easier to achieve one's objectives than in a system where power is shared with other jurisdictions. Yet even in a country like the United Kingdom, which is considered to have a strong state, Thatcher's Conservatives were unable to cut social programs to any significant degree.

Furthermore, as I have repeatedly noted throughout this chapter, it makes a great deal of difference if the groups that are the potential targets of cuts are well organized. As Pierson documents, the grey lobby in the United States, the American Association of Retired People, with currently more than 35 million members, showed itself to be a formidable foe when attempts were made to cut pensions throughout the Reagan era. As well, the bureaucracies associated with the public and para-public services are a political force in their own right. Those who work in the delivery of government programs – civil servants, teachers, professors, doctors, nurses, judges, police officers – are often able to mobilize enough resources, through strikes and use of the media, to put up an effective fight. In Canada, more than a million people work for the various levels of government in some capacity. Whether civil servants are on board or not can play a crucial role when it comes to implementing social policy. Their specialized knowledge, or ideological perspective, can potentially spell success or failure (Olson 2002).

Not only are workers able to facilitate or frustrate the introduction of new legislation, workers are also voters. In Canada, for example, there are more than 300,000 full-time primary and secondary school teachers. In addition, teachers potentially have the support of the parents of the close to 5 million primary and secondary students in this country (Guppy and Davies 1998). In face of such multifaceted opposition, tinkering with social programs can be risky and implementing cuts considerably more difficult than it first appears.

From this perspective it is interesting to note how unresponsive the welfare state has been to changing trends in economic inequality. In the immediate aftermath of the Second World War, a large proportion of the elderly lived in poverty. Consequently, new social programs were introduced and existing ones enhanced in order to combat this problem. Roughly five decades later, in 1999, wealth statistics indicate that the elderly are fast becoming the wealthiest segment of society, having made some of the biggest gains since the last survey was taken fifteen years ago. In contrast, the twenty to twenty-four age group has experienced the biggest decline in wealth. As a matter of fact, most people in that age group have negative wealth – that is, debt – which would logically call for some redistribution of income. But that is unlikely to happen. The elderly are well organized and continue to collect their pensions. Moreover, they vote. In the 2004 election, 80 per cent of seniors voted, compared to only 25 per cent of those under the age of twenty-five (*Globe and Mail*, 19 July 2004: A15). Younger adults are currently faced with higher costs in the form of tuition fees and less support in terms of grants and loans. If anything, this inequality between age groups is likely to worsen as the baby boomers age, showing the importance of past decisions.

Weber

The preceding data document that the welfare state has survived many attacks – be they from neoconservatives or globalization – remarkably well. Why is this? As the above discussion shows, and as many sociologists have noted, change is difficult to implement. Max Weber traced this difficulty to bureaucratic structures, which he stated were a by-product of all modern societies, whether capitalist or socialist. He remarked that the primary objective of bureaucracies is the efficient execution of tasks, the process he referred to as rationalization. Weber also noted that bureaucracies, once established, were next to impossible to destroy. Not only are bureaucracies 'practically unshat-terable,' but they have a tendency to grow (quoted in Ritzer 2000: 233). Also important for our purposes is the fact that – as politicians can attest – bureaucracies (such as those associated with the welfare state) are easier to introduce than to eliminate; this explains the relatively rapid growth of social programs, and their obdurate presence once established. Over the past fifty years, in the context of the tremendous growth in state services, thousands of state bureaucracies have become established and have turned into what Weber called legal-rational institutions, each with its own clientele and sets of rules and regula-tions to enforce and oversee. Based on this incapacity to change, sociol-ogists have come to compare society to physical phenomena – for example, the inexorable progress of a glacier or an oil tanker – in order to illustrate the persistence of existing institutions. While social scien-tists have generally lamented the process of rationalization and the rise of bureaucracy, the upside is that any kind of change is difficult to implement, be it good or bad. With all the bureaucracy, red tape, over-lap of jurisdictions, and democratic checks and balances that are part of modern political systems, politicians find that their hands are tied and the status quo endures, including, in this case, the welfare state.

Summary and Discussion

As we saw, the possibility of eliminating or even making sizeable cuts to social programs is remote. We can now summarize the information above in matrix form. Table 7.2 shows the three major components of the welfare state in the rows and the different measures of support in the columns. Each cell is scored from −1 to +1 depending on the pro-gram's public support, likelihood of remaining publicly funded (that is, not being privatized), and importance to economic competitiveness. The discussion above tells us that support is strongest for education and weakest for social services. But even for social services, a score of 0 in the 'total' column suggests the status quo rather than elimination, for while social assistance may not be popular, pensions are.

Elimination of any one of the three pillars of the welfare state would certainly translate into a loss in competitiveness for the Canadian econ-omy; the elimination of all three would be disastrous. Globalization theory notwithstanding, most people would quickly realize what a threat this would pose to their own well-being, and to the economy, once these services were no longer available.

Table 7.2
Support for various welfare-state programs

	Public support	Business support	Likelihood to remain publicly funded	Importance to c ompetitive workforce	Total (range from −4 to +4)
Education	high 1	high 1	high 1	high 1	+4
Health	high 1	medium 0	medium 0	high 1	+2
Social services	medium 0	low −1	high 1	medium 0	0

As we saw at the beginning of this chapter, globalization is often viewed as a force that has turned the state into a veritable eunuch. The main actors responsible for this scenario are purported to be multinational corporations, although technology, currency traders, and consumers are also frequently implicated. For now let us focus on corporations, which are often deemed the most powerful actors in the global economy, supposedly having garnered their power at the expense of labour and the state. The intentions of business are difficult to deny, as it has orchestrated an ongoing and concerted attack on the welfare state. In Canada – whether under the guise of deficit cutting, globalization, productivity enhancement, or just plain market ideology – welfare programs are the consistent targets of the C.D. Howe Institute, the Canadian Council of Chief Executives (formerly the BCNI), the Fraser Institute, the Canadian Taxpayer's Foundation, and other similar organizations. The success of these attacks, however, is another matter.

Rather than declining, spending is up, and most noticeably spending on welfare-state services. When the three pillars of the welfare state – education, health, and social services – are plotted side by side, we see, somewhat surprisingly, that while spending for education and health has levelled off, spending for social services is up. As figure 7.8 shows, expenditures in all three pillars grew gradually from the close of the Second World War until the beginning of the 1970s. From the 1970s onwards, expenditure growth slowed in some areas, such as health care, or failed to increase altogether, as in education. Social services, however, continued to grow unabated. More importantly, none of the three pillars experienced a major downturn at any point. Once we consider all government programs, the sector that experienced the biggest growth over the past few decades was social services. Given how relentless the attack on the welfare state has been, particularly on social services, this finding is certainly counter-intuitive.

Another way of illustrating the resilience of social programs is to separate welfare-state from non-welfare-state spending. Going back to figure 7.2, we can see that spending on welfare services matched non-welfare expenditures from the late 1960s onwards. Once debt charges are deducted, we see that welfare expenditures have risen considerably while non-welfare-state expenditures have shrunk (see figure 7.3 and figure 7.4). This is precisely the opposite of what one would expect given what we hear about the increased power of capital in an age of globalization. Both neo-Marxist theories of the state and contemporary accounts of globalization, such as Teeple's, attribute undue influence to capital, a power that has not translated into the realization of projected goals. We can reasonably assume that business supports funding for education and health since, in the long run, capital does benefit from these programs, but this same argument does not hold true for social services. It is precisely these programs, stigmatized as labour market disincentives, that supply-side economists implicate as a major drag on the economy (Brenner 1998). Yet these are the programs that have experienced the most vigorous growth in the past decades. Obviously, business interests, at least in this instance, are not powerful enough to overcome the momentum of public support, bureaucrats, and the diverse interests of the state.

Another way to approach the data is to consider each of the seventeen government programs individually and determine how much change each has undergone since the welfare state entered its period of 'crisis.' (This is a good opportunity to remind the reader that Statistics Canada changed the way it categorizes expenditure data in 1995/96; for that reason the numbers in the table are only included up to the preceding year. For more information please see p. 137.) Expenditures grew almost without interruption from the Second World War onwards, and it was not until 1977/78 that the first set of cutbacks occurred, making this an appropriate year for comparison. Percentage changes, whether positive or negative, are shown for each spending category in table 7.3. The table is further subdivided according to welfare-state and non-welfare-state programs. Immediately apparent is the increase in welfare-state services and the decrease in non-welfare services. Nine out of the twelve non-welfare-state services have experienced cuts while only one of the welfare services has (education). Once aggregated, non-welfare services suffered a 15 per cent cut, while wel-

Table 7.3
Consolidated federal, provincial, territorial, and local government expenditure, fiscal year 1994/95 (March to March), in millions of dol lars, as a percentage of GDP, and percentage change since 1977/78

Function	Expenditure 1994/95 (millions of dollars)	Expense as percentage of GDP	Percentage change from 1977/78
General services	18,236.70	2.39	−20.0
Protection of persons and property	24,476.50	3.21	−7.5
Transportation and communications	15,689.30	2.06	−31.8
Resource conservation and industrial development	51,619.00	1.85	−26.0
Environment	14,119.30	1.05	−8.0
Recreation and culture	7,214.90	0.95	−9.5
Labour, employment, and immigration	3,310.80	0.43	+65.4
Foreign affairs and international assistance	4,933.60	0.65	+27.4
Regional planning and development	1,614.80	0.21	−25.0
Research establishments	2,072.80	0.27	−23.0
Transfers to own enterprises	5,112.70	0.67	−15.0
Other expenditures	791.20	0.10	+1000.0
Total Non-welfare-state Expenditures	105,612.70	13.86	−15.2
Health	47,100.00	6.18	+21.7
Education	43,919.60	5.76	−9.4
Social services (inc. CPP and QPP)	105,544.10	13.85	+44.7
Housing	3,827.60	0.50	+38.9
Total welfare-state Expenditures	200,391.80	26.29	+23.1
Debt charges	71,325.00	9.36	+112.0
Grand total minus debt charges	306,004.50	37.55	+1.3
Grand total (non-welfare, welfare, and debt charges)	377,329.50	49.51	+17.5

fare services grew by 23 per cent. Once debt charges are deducted, we find that total expenditures have barely changed – an increase of only 1.3 percentage points. During this period the biggest change, in constant 1992 dollars, occurred in the social services sector, a gain that is double ($57 billion) the combined losses incurred by all non-welfare-state services ($25 billion).

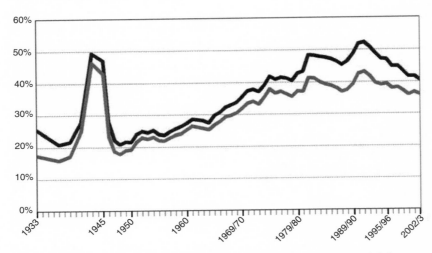

Figure 7.9. Total government expenditures (including and minus debt) as a percentage of GDP, Canada, 1933–2002/3

The biggest percentage increase occurred in debt maintenance (excluding the 'other expenditures' category, which consumes only one-tenth of a per cent of GDP even after growing tenfold). Debt payments more than doubled in terms of GDP between 1977/78 and 1994/95. Figure 7. 9 shows that total spending, including and excluding debt, first started to diverge significantly in the mid-1970s, a trend that became more pronounced throughout the 1980s. Once debt payments are subtracted, we see state expenditures stabilizing in the mid-1970s, with only slight fluctuations since; these are probably explained by economic recessions.

Spending as a percentage of GDP was lower in 1994/95 than in 1977/78 primarily in the areas of non-welfare services and education. Even 'protection of persons and property,' an area one would suspect is favoured by the right, has experienced cuts. According to O'Connor (1973), infrastructure is another area where one would expect to see a rise in expenditures, given the benefits that accrue to capital. Yet even there we can see substantial cuts. It is somewhat ironic that, with all the anti-state bashing the right has engaged in, it has been more successful in cutting programs it endorses than those it denounces (welfare-state programs in general and social services in particular). Clearly, this is precisely the opposite of what one would expect from a theory of globalization that emphasizes the burgeoning power of corporations and capital.

I do not mean to diminish the attack on the welfare state. At the same time, however, the evidence indicates that the power of capital is often overstated. Even from the mid-1980s onwards, when deficit bashing first began in earnest, welfare-state expenditures grew while non-welfare expenditures shrank. This is certainly not what the right was striving for when it first mobilized its attack on the welfare state, but it is what they got. So even if business, at times, has appeared to be relatively powerful (it did get government to fight inflation and lower taxes), it was only partially successful in achieving other objectives (the cuts to the welfare state have been sporadic and less than significant).

Canada is certainly not an isolated case, as the state remains firmly entrenched in national economies throughout the industrial world. What does this say about the right, about business, or about politics in general? Why has business failed to rid the world of the welfare state? In Canada, one conclusion that can be drawn is that the right does not adhere to a well-coordinated plan of attack. Business has been most successful in its fight against inflation, but this success has been far from unqualified and has come with some unpleasant and unintended side-effects. High interest rates, the primary tool used to wrestle down inflation, pushed unemployment to its highest level since the Depression throughout the 1980s and into the early 1990s, and with it came an increase in demand for social services. As well, interest payments on the debt spiralled. These two programs were also the fastest-growing areas of government expenditure (although that changed with the gradual lowering of interest rates in the mid-1990s).[8] By no standard does this qualify as a success. Let us not forget that the neoconservative revolution began in Great Britain, with Thatcher promising to get rid of the 'nanny state.'

The failure of the right's agenda should not come as all that much of a surprise to sociologists. Except under totalitarianism, and even then, it is very difficult to create a society according to one's wishes. Yet some of the more pessimistic analyses of globalization have done exactly that, painting a picture that features an all-powerful multinational capitalist class. But, as we saw, there is opposition to such an agenda at every turn. Second, there are structural limitations to what capital can do, and third, once implemented, social actions are likely to bring about unintended consequences (Giddens 1984). The failing of the right's biggest success, the fight against inflation, was that it was won in a theoretical vacuum. Taking what philosophers might call a deontological approach, the right fought this battle as being right on its own merits, no matter what the outcome. But the suppression of inflation came with some unpleasant, albeit unintended, consequences, foremost among them an increase in expenditures on social programs as well as debt payments (see Mimoto and Cross 1991; also McQuaig 1995). The fact that low inflation (via high interest rates) and low social expenditures are difficult to attain simultaneously is seldom acknowledged by policy makers. Paul Hellyer, a high-profile MP in both the Pearson and the Trudeau governments, writes that 'If central bankers had any understanding of how the real world works, they would know that there is no practical way for governments to cut expenditures precipitously every time central banks bring economic growth to a grinding halt' (Globe and Mail, 6 Apr. 1995: A19). The lack of coordination between various government departments, in this case finance and human resources, also seems to be a major shortcoming here. There is little doubt that these policies were driven by an ideology of economic liberalism: inflation is inimical for investment, and social programs undermine the efficacy of the labour market. Both these points may be true in isolation but, as Giddens suggests, within a larger social and political context policies are likely to clash in unintended ways. And so they did.

Prospects have somewhat improved since the mid-1990s; interest rates have been lowered, and there has not been a major recession since the Liberals were elected in 1993. But to a large extent, the damage inflicted by the high-interest-rate policies cannot be reversed. Between 1979 and 1998, the amount of interest payments generated by the debt on a yearly basis exceeded that of any social program, even education and health. During the recession in the early 1990s, the high cost of debt maintenance effectively crowded out program spending in other areas; at the same time, demand rose because of increased unemployment caused by high interest rates. Most interesting is that the return to balanced budgets across the country had less to do with program cuts than with lower interest rates. Interest payments reached a high of 9.2 per cent of GDP in 1990/91, and were less than half, 4.5 per cent, in 2002/3. It seems that what is good for the average consumer in terms of more affordable mortgages and loans is also advantageous to governments. It is unlikely that the Liberals would have been able to balance the budget had it not been for the sharp drop in interest payments.

Nevertheless, cuts did happen. And it was the non-welfare spending that was affected the most: policing, transportation and communications, research, resource conservation, and industrial development.

But even within various welfare-state programs, such as education or health, a considerable amount of redistribution went on. In short, each category of government spending comes with its own story, and each comes with its own set of winners and losers.

Conclusion

Imagine the counterfactual to what exists today: a world without a state. Then try to envision what measures would have to be taken in order to arrive at that destination. At every turn there would be insurmountable obstacles. Take education, for example. Support would be split among ideologues, politicians, media, and business interests. But opposition to cuts would be both firm and uniform from teachers, professors, parents, and students. And this is true for each and every service the government provides: a different constellation of support and opposition would lead to raucous disputes and make elimination unrealizable. The turmoil resulting from the eradication of any major program would also make the re-election unlikely of any political party responsible for such havoc.[9] (Of course, logically, complete elimination of the state would obviate the need for re-election.)

The data serve as strong evidence that the role of the state in the economy has not experienced a significant decline no matter where one puts the date for the beginning of globalization: the 1960s, the 1970s, even the 1980s or 1990s. Government involvement is so firmly entrenched in so many facets of political and social life that it is often taken for granted, and this may explain why globalists have succeeded in ignoring it. Nevertheless, whether one chooses to acknowledge it or not, government intervention continues to play an indispensable role in education, law, public transportation, roads, the regulation of food, trade, construction, transportation, communication, and so on.

Services that make a country more competitive are precisely the same services that require state participation, for the private sector is not likely to provide them on its own. Infrastructure such as roads, bridges, and airports, to say nothing of services such as health, education, and welfare, are often too costly or unprofitable for the private sector to provide, at least initially. In this respect, the existence of the state is guaranteed for some time to come. Moreover, the Canadian economy remains national in the sense that most government services are provided by Canadians for Canadians, with little foreign involvement. The vast majority of people consume the bulk of their education, health services, culture, police protection, housing, and many other services within Canada. Globalization, if there is such a thing, has not significantly altered this fact.

And it is not only the individual citizen who benefits from state services; business also benefits. As O'Connor (1973) suggests, in a mixed economy like ours, costs are socialized while profits remain privatized. Free-market ideology notwithstanding, business has little interest in drastically altering this relationship, for it knows it would suffer. Furthermore, many businesses rely on lucrative government contracts for their economic survival. Telephone companies, computer firms, the media (governments are profligate advertisers), construction companies, airlines, law firms, hotels, restaurants, pharmaceutical companies, manufacturers of medical equipment, polling firms, and on and on – almost any business of significant size has had a lucrative contract with the government. If Ohmae is right and the consumer is king, then government still has some ruling left to do.

Globalists rarely look at these state services in detail and focus solely on the state's responsibility to attract capital. They treat the state in rather abstract terms and ignore the interests of bureaucrats, the public, labour, the unemployed, and the unemployable – people and groups that form the very foundation that makes politics what it is. On an abstract level, contradictory claims made by capital or voters can easily be ignored. But these contradictions clash forcefully in the real world. The state has many responsibilities and answers to a variety of interests that constrain it to act in sometimes contradictory ways. No matter how powerful capital appears to be among these other interests, the objectives of capital are rarely accomplished easily, and often not at all. This holds true even for multinational capital in an age of corporate globalization.

Globalization theory is obviously not up to the task of explaining the changes the nation-state or, for that matter, the welfare state has undergone since the Second World War. Its observations and predictions do not correspond well with contemporary political and economic events. A theory of globalization must explain how a process that at one time provided the conditions for the nation-state to flourish has now suddenly turned against it. It must then provide some convincing evidence of exactly how the state has been weakened and why this trend is not likely to be reversed. And, probably most important, it must explain the increased presence of the state in the economy over the past forty years, the beginning of a period that is often given as the date for the inauguration or acceleration of globalization.

The data just presented are completely incongruent with a theory that predicts the weakening of the state. The fact that social programs, as well as political and civil rights, continue to thrive in Canada testifies to the continuing strength of the state and the relative weakness of multinational corporations. There is little evidence that capital has made significant inroads in reversing the trend of state intervention that began after the Second World War. This is particularly true with respect to the welfare state. The more logical conclusion to be drawn from the data is that, rather than witnessing the end of social reform, we are seeing the continuing impasse of the welfare state. Reform-minded political parties have found it impossible to institute cuts in face of opposition from various quarters and have had to confront several obstacles: an established political system, opposition parties, the judiciary, voters, bureaucrats, unions, binding contracts, business lobbies and other interest groups, alternative media, and sometimes even the mainstream media.

There are, in fact, few reasons to believe that globalization has had a negative impact on the welfare state. As a matter of fact, the precise opposite could be argued. As we just saw, there has been an increase in both social spending and trade in the postwar years, prompting at least one commentator to argue for a causal relationship between the growth in trade and social spending (Iversen 2001: 46). But such a relationship is almost certainly spurious, as the two are the results of quite different policy trajectories. Iversen (2001) suggests that, rather than globalization, it is the process of de-industrialization and its disorienting impact on the labour market that was crucial when it came to the provision of welfare-state services. This transition, first from agricultural to industrial jobs and now to post-industrial ones, was more evident in Sweden than in the United States, prompting the adoption of a different set of policies for each country. Pierson (2001) makes a similar argument against the relationship between globalization and the pressures on the welfare state. In addition to de-industrialization, he focuses on the aging of the population and the changing demographics of the household. In summary, the welfare state has endured, and alarmist accounts of its demise generally exaggerate the power of either economic liberals, multinational corporations, or globalization. In the end, it is more mundane variables, such as demography and technology, that have significant explanatory power. That does not make for a very exciting story, but that's how it appears to be.

Chapter 8

The Postwar Economy

Everything in economic history suggests that inflation is as great a threat
to the social and economic health of a country as war.
Rowland Frazee, Chairman and CEO of the Royal Bank, 1979–1986

What on Earth Is Happening? Alternative Explanations

When testing hypotheses in the social sciences, researchers are advised
to keep in mind the possibility that an alternative, more plausible explanation may exist. An alternative explanation could well render the
present hypothesis invalid. The task of this chapter is to search for such
an alternative, one that better explains current political and economic
developments than globalization. There is little doubt that things are
different now than they were in the 1950s or 1960s. Canada's economy,
like most economies around the world, has suffered from slowed
growth, higher unemployment, and declining business profits for more
than three decades. This has resulted in a change of attitude that can
best be summarized as a shift from confidence to uncertainty. Many
claim that this uncertainty can be attributed to globalization. As previous chapters have shown, however, that is not the position taken here;
instead, it is argued that, while there has been a long-term contraction,
there has been no fundamental change in the economy. First, we take a
closer look at this contraction, examine its structural features, and then
outline how it has played out in the political arena. Against this back-
drop, alternative explanations to that of globalization are developed.

I argue that the current contraction can be better understood as a
structural downturn that, at the same time, has also significantly altered

the dynamic between capital and labour. One of the major objectives of this chapter is to reintroduce agency back into the debate. The globalization argument has been successful in stealing away agency from contemporary politics: many people, including, as we saw in the introduction, former prime minister Chrétien, may disapprove of globalization yet believe there is little anyone can do about it. This fatalistic attitude allows the government to distance itself from making decisions, conveniently avoiding those it did not want to make in the first place.

A look at the actions of various social actors such as business, government, and labour enables us to offer a better explanation for the current uncertainty that is commonly linked to globalization. First, we examine some of the contradictions of capitalism and how their emergence has altered capital-labour relations. Then we explore how the right has interpreted the current downturn and how economic liberals have attempted to revitalize the economy by curtailing market intervention and, in a somewhat contradictory fashion, have used the state to fight inflation. The chapter concludes with an assessment of the success of these policies.

Assessing the Problem: Structure and Agency

Immediately following the Second World War and up until the early 1970s, the world economy experienced its most robust growth ever, commonly referred to as the 'Golden Age.' According to Maddison's (2001) analysis, the period between 1945 and 1972 stands as the most prosperous in the history of capitalism. This growth came to a gradual halt in the 1970s, as Western economies entered a contraction sometimes called, in contrast, the 'Leaden Age.' How has the problem of slowed growth manifested itself? First, unemployment has increased substantially. According to the International Labor Organization, there are currently 189 million unemployed workers around the world, or 6.2 per cent of the global workforce (ILO 2004). Canada provides a fitting example, as it experienced double-digit unemployment, with few exceptions, throughout the 1980s and early 1990s. Second, real wages (that is, adjusted for inflation) have failed to grow significantly since the mid-1970s. In Canada, family income has stagnated, despite an increase in the number of women joining the workforce (Urmetzer and Guppy 2004). Throughout the 1990s, wage growth was generally negative for men but positive for women (*Vancouver Sun*, 21 Feb. 2000), and in the decade spanning 1993 to 2002, the real average hourly wage (before taxes) in Canada fell by 2.4 per cent (BC Checkup 2003). In the United States, between 1973 and 1990, the real hourly wage in private business fell by 12 per cent, back to mid-1960s levels, and productivity growth fell to its lowest level in American history (Brenner 1998). Third, profits have slumped, particularly in the manufacturing sector, decreasing by an average of 40 per cent for the years 1970 to 1989 in comparison with the two preceding decades (1950–69) (Brenner 1998), a development commonly referred to as the profit squeeze. Profits rose throughout the 1990s, but at nowhere near the rate achieved in the 1950s and 1960s (Brenner 2002: 20 figure 1.2). Cumulatively these problems – high unemployment, stagnating wages, and falling profits – have created an atmosphere of uncertainty that is often blamed on the globalization of the economy.

The political economy school in general, and Marxist writers such as O'Connor and Harvey in particular, have attempted to illuminate contemporary developments in light of the structural features of capitalism, features they believe to be self-defeating. These contradictions are said to result in crisis if not properly managed. Harvey (1990: 180) enumerates the following three contradictions: (1) capitalism is growth-oriented, and lack of growth equals crisis; (2) capitalism is technologically dynamic, and progress is seen as both inevitable and good; and (3) growth is predicated on profit and, based as it is on the exploitation of labour, contributes towards tensions between capital and labour. Thus we can understand contemporary events as the emergence of a series of contradictions. We will discuss each in turn.

i) The Limits of Growth

The history of capitalist economies is littered with depressions and recessions. Extensive research on the cyclical nature of capitalist growth – from Kondratieff and Kuznets to Wallerstein – shows that contemporary events could well be explained as just another contraction in a perpetual cycle of boom and bust. Marxist economists perceive this problem as endemic to capitalism and rooted in overproduction. Economies cannot grow forever, and as growth slows – the 'essential cornerstone of capitalism,' according to Harvey – fiscal pressures mount. The fact is that people are only able to purchase a finite amount of consumer products and eventually must stop buying: a household can own only so many cars, fridges, and VCRs. But even when few people are buying, factories continue to churn out products. Economists refer to this as the lack of aggregate demand. Marx and Engels characterized this as the 'absurdity ... of over-production' (1986: 39).

Overproduction also lay at the root of the Depression in the 1930s. While similar ideas were circulating at the time, it is Keynes who is best known for his interventionist prescription for managing the crisis. He argued that the market was ill equipped to deal with the problem of overproduction, a point relevant with respect to both goods and employment. Keynes demonstrated that, as wages were driven down, workers had less money to spend on products, pulling profits down with them, resulting in more layoffs and even lower wages, and so on. In other words, without some kind of government intervention, it would be some time before the market was able to work through the crisis of unemployment on its own. Instead, Keynes argued, funds needed to be redirected towards workers so they could once again purchase goods, thereby increasing demand. To various degrees, the Keynesian orthodoxy was adopted by most industrial countries following the Second World War, and economies grew briskly (although the fact that economies had entered an upswing also played a major role).

Today the situation is not so different from when Keynes wrote his treatise in the 1930s: we are experiencing a contraction. Not all busts and booms are alike, however. What distinguishes this economic contraction from preceding ones is its lack of severity. This may be attributed to two factors: increased wealth and its more equitable distribution. Canada's experience throughout this period is typical and serves as an illuminating example. Wealth surveys by Statistics Canada show that wealth in this country has exploded since the Second World War. This gradual accumulation of wealth makes Canada a vastly different place from what it was during the contraction experienced in the Depression. While it is true that the wealthy are accumulating disproportionately more wealth than others, in terms of income, distribution continues to be quite stable, primarily because of an array of programs associated with the welfare state (Urmetzer and Guppy 2004). The scourge of absolute poverty is now, with a few exceptions, virtually non-existent in Canada. Social assistance, unemployment insurance, and much-improved pensions are universally available in Canada and ensure that people have at least a modicum of income to survive on. In the 1930s, this was not the case. For example, food shortages in the Depression were pervasive, to the point that scurvy broke out in the Prairies. Also, unemployment during the Depression was more than double the rate found now – it is estimated to have reached a high of 25 per cent in the Depression compared to 11.8 per cent in the present contraction (Norri and Owram 1996).

The growth of the welfare state can be seen as a direct attempt to avoid a recurrence of the problems that plagued the Depression. Furthermore, labour uprisings in the 1930s and the threat of communism following the Second World War provided an atmosphere receptive to social and economic tinkering (Hobsbawm 1994). The result was the introduction of an unprecedented number of social programs in the 1950s and 1960s. Once in place, the welfare state also had the effect of cushioning business cycles and rendering them less severe. It is somewhat ironic, then, that economic liberals are so bent on dismantling social programs, the very ingredient that contributed to the rapid post-war growth in the first place.

ii) Technology

At one level the problems of technology are obvious. The 'constant revolutionizing of the means of production' invariably leads to changes in the labour market and to unemployment. The Luddites realized this more than two centuries ago when they smashed machinery in the hope of saving their jobs; so did governments that chose to tax more efficient looms in the seventeenth century (Heilbroner 1980). The contemporary approach towards technology is precisely the opposite. Technology is now heralded as a saviour, and economies around the world are in stiff competition with one another to attract whatever high-tech industry may be out there.

Technology is generally regarded, as Harvey points out, in a positive light, and its negative consequences are wilfully ignored. This view is shared by commentators from both left and right, some of whom have hoped to solve the current crisis by stressing the role of technology. Both Mishra (1984) and James Laxer (1984) have urged social democrats to become more active in the productive side of the economy rather than focusing only on distribution. Mishra suggests that unions start cooperating with firms when new technology is introduced rather than opposing it, as is traditionally the case. On first sight, opposition to technology does indeed appear counterproductive. Unions in Germany, for example, have successfully forced car manufacturers to pay the wages of workers displaced by machines, but in the end everybody – the firm, workers, the whole economy – loses (Turner 1991). Jessop (1993) draws much the same conclusion as Mishra and contends that, as economies become more technologically sophisticated, labour needs to embrace technology, not fight it. But this attitude feeds directly into Harvey's second contradiction, the reverence for progress. At the core of this contradiction is the notion that the more efficient an economy becomes, the sooner the threshold of surplus of production is reached. This technological fetishism can also be criticized on the grounds that resources are automatically directed towards activities where productivity increases can be realized, thereby diverting them away from activities that are technologically neutral such as health care, education, and child care. Last, the conflicting attitudes of capital and labour towards technology underscore just how different the interests of these two groups are. To suggest that workers cooperate with business on this issue is tantamount to counselling unions to be more cooperative with respect to wage cuts. In capitalism, technology serves as a major weapon used by capital against labour. From this perspective, technology is integrally related to distribution. To give in to technology means that all the spoils go to those who own it. This brings us to the last of Harvey's three contradictions, the tension between capital and labour.

iii) Agency: Capital and Labour

Globalization pays little heed to the power of agency, and Harvey's third contradiction, that capital-labour relations become intensified when profits shrink, presents us with the opportunity to document how the dynamic between the two social actors has changed. A growing economy is inherently different from one that is contracting and, while the struggle over resources is ongoing, it is heightened when resources shrink. In this way, the conditions were markedly different throughout the Golden Age than in the era that followed it. Furthermore, while the structural characteristics of capitalism bring with them certain limitations (for example, an economy cannot grow forever), actors offer different interpretations of how these problems can best be solved. The central question is whether we need more or less capitalism in order to ease the current contraction; or to phrase it slightly differently, Is capitalism a cause or a cure? When profits shrink, the state is forced to make difficult decisions about distribution. In this struggle, based on its interpretation that the market is over-regulated, capital has made a powerful case for making capital accumulation a priority.

This has resulted in a concerted attack – sometimes effective, often not – on the working class and the welfare state.

While robust economic growth and industrialization were both necessary ingredients in the generation of wealth in the immediate postwar era, it is important to recognize that this wealth was not shared voluntarily by capital or the state. Central to understanding these distributional issues is the strength and political organization of working-class movements (see, for example, Myles 1989; Esping-Andersen 1990). Institutional arrangements such as tripartism in Sweden and corporatism in Germany, where business and labour made a long-term commitment to labour peace, were also important. But whatever arrangements were in place, these started to corrode atop the industrial economies they were built on. Even in Sweden, the exemplar of social democracy and the welfare state, the cooperative relationship between capital and labour deteriorated, and business mounted a relentless effort to break labour.

In Canada, as in other industrial countries, capital was better organized than the working class when it came to mobilizing its resources, and it effectively broke the postwar social contract (Mullaly 1994). A number of campaigns were waged to cut social programs, ingeniously dressed up in the guise of the national interest. First, Canadians were told that social programs had to be cut in order to reduce the deficit and save the country from financial ruin. This effort was mounted principally by business lobbies such as the Business Council of National Issues (recently renamed the Canadian Council of Chief Executives) and the C.D. Howe Institute (Langille 1987; Ernst 1992). Globalization has also been used as a justification in this ongoing battle, based on the assertion that Canada's economy must become more internationally competitive. For a short while, it looked as though 'productivity' would serve as the next 'crisis' but, for whatever reason, it failed to catch on. While the left in Canada has been reasonably astute in piercing the veil of the deficit argument, it has been less incisive with respect to globalization. The overarching point is that politics continues to be a decisive variable in the ongoing battle over resources. No matter what the 'national crisis' – inflation, the deficit, globalization, productivity – the solution consistently and without fail entails the channelling of more money towards capital, be it through high interest rates, tax cuts, social program cuts, deregulation, or privatization. So the solution always remains the same; it is the problem that varies.

Harvey's three contradictions of capitalism are illuminating in that they offer a different interpretation of the contemporary political economy. However, to recognize these contradictions is one thing – to find a solution is quite another. The most obvious way to rid the economy of the contradictions of capitalism is to abolish capitalism itself, hardly a feasible prescription. Given experiences in socialist countries and the fate of the Soviet Union, it would be an understatement to claim that support for such an undertaking would be weak. Moreover, there is no guarantee that any system that would replace capitalism would not be rife with its own contradictions (Mishra 1984). Yet Harvey's observations should not go unheeded. The next section will argue that the way these contradictions have been dealt with, based primarily on prescriptions from the right, has only served to exacerbate their severity.

Solutions by the Right

The interpretation presented above does not, of course, stand alone. Not everyone agrees that capitalism is rife with contradictions or that an economy cannot grow forever. Market advocates offer a much different explanation for the current downturn. Given their long-held opposition to government intervention, the right welcomed the economic downturn as an opportunity to exact their revenge on the Keynesian orthodoxy. Rather than finding fault within capitalism itself, as neo-Marxists or social democrats would have done, the right pointed to an excess of state interference as the root of the problem, and the focus became the market. Economic liberals have long preferred that the market be left to its own devices and have eschewed government intervention when it comes to resource allocation.

> Equipped with ... inferior intellectual baggage and a toolbox containing nothing more than four large hammers (deregulation, privatisation, tax reductions and free trade), the international economic organisation set about transforming the world according to the American model. In this endeavour, no account needed to be taken of the history and geography of that world, with its various tensions and conflicts. The cult of the 'new' allowed ignorance of all precedents. The rule of the market and openness to the market would guarantee prosperity and democracy everywhere.
> (*Le Monde Diplomatique*, Oct. 1998: 1, 10)

For as long as liberals have been championing the free market, opponents have been criticizing it as too abstract an idea, one that completely ignores differences in social power (Macpherson 1977). As with

the globalization thesis, the free market argument assumes that everyone is equal. Moreover, the solution for every economic problem, even
macro-economic problems such as recessions, is said to lie within the
irreproachable workings of the market.

Despite obvious intellectual and practical shortcomings, the liberal
market philosophy continues to provide a powerful ideological back-
drop for contemporary politics. Overpowered by Keynesianism in the
1950s and 1960s, economic liberalism made a resurgence beginning in
the 1970s and arrived with full force in the 1980s. This time around, the
perennial ideas about the free market appeared in the guise of neoconservatism. The belief that the market naturally coordinates supply and
demand was carried over into the labour market. Motivated by a long-
standing faith in the market, neoconservatives intensified their attacks
on social assistance and unemployment insurance – widely disparaged
as labour market disincentives – and even identified them as a cause of
unemployment (McBride and Shields 1993). A consequence of these
attacks, intended or not, was to put downward pressure on wages. A
further, and this time unintended, consequence was that workers had
less money to spend on consumer goods. Ironically, the proposed cure
(cutting programs) only served to exacerbate the problem of a stagnating economy by taking even more money out of circulation, further
undermining demand.

What is often understood to be the result of globalization is, in fact,
the result of cyclical changes and the adherence to free-market doctrines. From this perspective, neoconservatism can be seen as the most
recent expression of an economic liberal ideology, an intellectual lin-
eage that goes back centuries. The only thing new about neoconservatism is its emphasis on the strong state, and then only when it comes to
promoting private enterprise (McBride and Shields 1993: 37). But the
'conservative' element of neoconservatism is classic laissez-faire economics: belief in the supremacy of the market, hostility towards organized labour, and glorification of the individual (Marchak 1988). On
this point, liberalism, neoliberalism, and neoconservatism have more
similarities than differences. It might have been through neoconservatism that the free-market ideology came to the fore in the late 1970s,
but the ideas that define it are as old as capitalism itself. From Locke
and Smith to Hayek, Rand, and Nozick, this ideology is an integral
constituent of capitalist culture. And so are reactions against it.

The ideology of free markets has served as a guiding light throughout
the history of capitalism. With the failure of the market in the Depression, this ideology was temporarily overpowered, at least to some

degree, by the force of Keynesianism, but with two important qualifications. First, there were always deep rumblings of dissatisfaction associated with the welfare state. Hayek, for example, wrote his famous *Road to Serfdom* in 1944, well before the introduction of most welfare-state programs. Furthermore, opposition to welfare-state services did not originate only among fringe elements but also surfaced among mainstream political parties. In Canada, for example, conservative MPs in the Liberal party opposed the introduction of the Family Allowance (Guest 1985: 123). Also, much of the social-policy legislation introduced during the heyday of the welfare state was written with an eye on the market. Social programs were meant to 'assist rather than suppress market forces' (Howlett et al 1999: 36). In other words, liberal markets, especially in the United States and Canada, were always recognized as an important feature of the economic culture, and its relative abatement throughout the years of welfare-state growth was only a matter of degree.

In Canada, the attack on the welfare state began under Trudeau's Liberals, long before the Progressive Conservatives came to power (Myles 1988: 140). This offensive was well organized, not only in Canada but around the world. From the very beginning, these ideas were 'skilfully managed by the government with help from the corporate sector and the corporate-controlled media' (Cohen 1997: 35). And international capitalists made sure the ideas of the right were 'assiduously propagated and well funded' (Marchak 1991: 11).

The perceived weakening of the state and the attack on the welfare state did not come from outside but originated within the nation-state. Under the guise of neoconservatism, business mobilized a four-pronged attack in an attempt to revive the ailing economy: cut taxes, cut social programs, privatize government programs, and fight inflation. The first three of these are consonant with a free-market ideology, while the last, the fight against inflation, is not. The next section is going to examine each of these solutions in turn.

i) The Free Market: Tax Cuts, Social Program Cuts, and Privatization

Tax cuts, the assault on the welfare state, and privatization combine to squeeze government out of the economy. Of these policies, the most popular has been, and continues to be, tax cuts. The reasons for this are manifold: tax cuts are purported to free up money for private investment and consumer spending, or as in the case of Canada, to make the economy more competitive with other jurisdictions.[1] As government policy, tax cuts were most vigorously pursued by Thatcher in the United Kingdom and Reagan in the United States. In Canada, the combination of wide public support for social programs and growing deficits made tax cuts less feasible, although governments did succeed in lowering corporate taxes and shifting the burden onto individual taxpayers.[2] Tax reform has also been popular in the provinces, particularly under Klein, Harris, and Campbell. Not surprisingly, however, once implemented, tax cuts did little to resuscitate long-term economic growth, given that this strategy tends to favour high-income earners and starve the revenue side of the equation.

The attack on the welfare state constituted another attempt to recapture economic growth. In what has disparagingly been labelled the 'nanny state' by Margaret Thatcher, social programs were identified as a fetter on the economy. This is believed for a variety of reasons. First, government is perceived as rigidly bureaucratic, in contrast to the more efficient alternative of private enterprise. Thatcher's success at the polls can, in part, be linked to her exploitation of this platform (Mishra 1984). Second, welfare-state services, in particular unemployment insurance and welfare programs, are considered to be labour market disincentives. Poor relief has always been about regulating the labour market, and for this reason, the singling out of these programs should not come as a surprise (Piven and Cloward 1993). While the success of these attacks has varied, they have been widespread, especially throughout the Anglo-Saxon world. It is no coincidence that, in every province that initiated major tax cuts throughout the past decade and a half, programs for the poor also came under attack.

Yet another alternative invoked in the ongoing quest to revive economic growth has been the call to privatize government services, a tactic that works hand in hand with the call for tax and program cuts. In the United States a combination of tax cuts and military spending and in Canada high interest rates and unemployment ran up deficits, leaving government budgets vulnerable to private-sector censure. And, not surprisingly, business stepped in and offered a solution: privatization. Traditionally, expenses in capitalist economies are socialized and profits are privatized, but when profits started shrinking near the dusk of the Golden Age, business increasingly felt encroached upon by government (O'Connor 1973). By the end of the 1970s, it was not unusual for economies to route upwards of one-third of their GDP through government coffers. As a consequence, business eyed the public sector as an area of lost opportunity and profit. This resulted in a wave of privatization that has swept the world, and one that shows few signs of abating. In the West this occurred through government edict, and in the Third World under the aegis of the IMF and the World Bank.

The first step towards privatization of the economy entails the selling of government corporations, including public utilities, public airlines, and oil companies. Other paths towards privatization are less obvious. Business pressures government to cut spending, and spending cuts eventually result in a shortage of services, a gap that business is only too eager to fill. Cutting health care opens space for private services; threats of pension reform force individuals to rely on private pensions and RRSPs; cuts to tertiary education result in increased debt loads for students, held by private banks. In all these instances, private corporations are destined to make a profit. Program cuts also provide business with numerous opportunities to fund public institutions and increase their corporate presence. The Pepsi/Coca-Cola war on campuses throughout Canada is one example. Corporate donations to libraries and museums are others, the UBC library and the Vancouver Public Library being some local examples. On first look, such activities appear innocent enough. However, as business increasingly decides who gets funding, this form of privatization slowly gnaws away at the democratic decision-making process. Business has narrower interests and answers to fewer constituents than government does, leaving unpopular programs, so designated by business, more susceptible to neglect. Thus we find well-funded computer science departments and underfunded English departments. Because of the positive exposure, a public library is more likely to receive funding than a women's shelter, a sports complex more so than low-income housing.[3] Private funding has the added benefit of portraying business in a charitable light, *and* it is good advertising.

In summary, tax cuts, the attack on the welfare state, and privatization are a well-coordinated set of policies that follow a consistent free-market logic. In combination, they work to squeeze government out of the economy by choking off its funding (tax cuts), attacking its output (social programs), and providing alternative funding (privatization). There is one very important policy, however, that is inconsistent with a free-market logic, and that is the ongoing fight against inflation.

ii) Inflation

Harvey (1982) writes that the central bank sits atop a hierarchy that oversees the sometimes unstable world of finance. But this control is not always used wisely and is vulnerable to abuse. This is apparent in the ongoing fight against inflation, which reveals that the faith economic liberals profess to have in the market is rather selective. When Margaret Thatcher urged that unemployment should be left to find its natural rate (the non-accelerating inflation rate of unemployment or NAIRU), she was obscuring how much effort she was willing to invest in the battle against inflation. The willingness to manipulate interest rates in order to regulate the money supply is indicative of how quickly free-market doctrines can be abandoned once the interests of investors are threatened. It is surprising how this obvious contravention of free-market principles remained unchallenged throughout the Thatcher era in Great Britain as well as here in North America under Mulroney and Reagan.

The fight against inflation in the postwar period was primarily motivated by investors who were faced with negative real interest rates in the 1970s. This laid the groundwork for what Smithin (2004: 172) has called the 'revenge of the rentier.' This ongoing battle against inflation has obvious class consequences. As was discussed in the chapter on finance, the use of high interest rates to fight inflation primarily works to the advantage of the investment class and to the detriment of both workers and productive capital. The fight against inflation has particularly troubling implications for workers. Unemployment, investors wrongly believe, is the simplest way to keep inflation in check (Glyn 1995). One should also not forget that the same faction of the capitalist class that keeps pushing for higher interest rates also benefits from higher returns. By putting pressure on governments to cut taxes and keep interest rates high, business wins every time (Stewart 1997).

Efforts to control inflation border at times on the obsessive, with little concern for the consequences. In Canada, this policy was enforced with particular zeal throughout the tenure of John Crow, who headed the Bank of Canada between 1987 and 1993. The bank abandoned its original mandate of regulating employment levels and inflation and focused its energies exclusively on the latter. This policy shift, primarily instituted by the governor of the Bank of Canada, was undemocratic in the sense that the Canadian public had little say in the matter (Babad and Mulroney 1998). A similar scenario played out in the United States, and 'there is little doubt that many of the postwar recessions have been caused by the Fed ... in its fixation that ... inflation will break out' (Stiglitz 2003: 67).

In summary, the high-interest-rate/low-inflation policy has a fourfold impact on the economy. First, high interest rates put an immediate brake on the economy, as people and businesses are discouraged from investing by the high cost of money. Second, reduced investment often leads to higher unemployment, the effects of which were particularly hard on the Canadian economy in the early 1990s (see McQuaig 1998; Keil and Pantuosco 1998). Third, as we saw in chapter 7, high interest rates divert money from investment in production and towards paper investments (Stanford 1999). And fourth, as was explained in the section on the state, high interest rates precipitate the ballooning of the deficit and debt (Smithin 2004: 173; Mimoto and Cross 1991).

a) Inflation: Its Causes

This is not the place to enter into a detailed discussion of the causes of inflation. Suffice it to say that, as with most debates in economics, there is little consensus. Heilbroner (1980) claims that if unemployment was the formidable economic problem of the first half of the twentieth century, inflation filled those shoes in the second. He adds that it will take an economist of Keynes's stature to successfully solve this problem, which remains far from solved now. Historically, economies have experienced inflation during war and deflation during peacetime, and this has hitherto happened without exception. Deflation, however, failed to materialize in the peace following the Second World War, and inflation persisted even when demand fell in the 1970s, a phenomenon frequently referred to as stagflation. The onset of inflation has often been blamed on the oil shocks that occurred in the 1970s, but as Galbraith (1995) points out, inflation was already well under way by the time the first shock hit in 1972. Galbraith puts forward the widely accepted explanation that when growth first slowed in the late 1960s, neither corporations nor unions were willing to take a cut in their share of the economic pie, a stalemate that resulted in inflationary pressures. In other words, the fault for inflation cannot be pinned solely on labour, for capital did its part by raising prices.

The political right fears inflation (or claims to do so) because it undermines investment confidence, and blames it on something as simple as an overabundance of money in the economy. Front and centre in the attack on inflation was a style of economics variously referred to as supply-side economics, neoclassical economics, or simply monetarism. Chicago school economist Milton Friedman has come to be known as the most fervent defender of monetarism, and his writings were instrumental in convincing governments around the world that all that was necessary to revive economic growth was to focus on the money supply. Central banks became key players in the fight against inflation and were handed the responsibility of revitalizing both investor confidence and economic growth. The foremost tactic used in the fight against inflation was the manipulation of interest rates. It should be kept in mind that the monetarists offered only one explanation for inflation, and neither their interpretation nor their prescribed solution is widely accepted or uncontroversial.[4] But it is the version that ruled the day.

b) The Consequences of a Zero-inflation Policy

There is equally little consensus about the exact point at which inflation becomes detrimental to an economy. While few people would countenance runaway inflation the likes of what was found in Germany during the interwar years, there is less agreement on the level of moderate inflation that is tolerable. The crux of the matter is whether lower is always better, with zero being the ultimate goal, or whether there may be some advantages to a more moderate inflation policy with targets ranging somewhere between 3 and 8 per cent.

Glyn (1995) highlights some of the implications of a zero per cent inflation policy for Sweden, points that may be generalized to other economies. First, very low inflation targets undermine the viability of the class compromise. As he puts it, moderate inflation serves as a 'lubricant' to the economy. For example, it is reasonable to assume that during times of 4 per cent inflation, a labour union will settle for a 2 per cent pay raise, but in an environment of only 1 per cent inflation a union is considerably less likely to take a 1 per cent cut in pay. Of course, the two amount to the exact same thing – a 2 per cent cut in real wages.[5] From this perspective, moderate inflation can actually be quite beneficial to the economy. Economic historian Robert Brenner (1998: 249) is equally critical of a low inflation policy and points to its class consequences:

> In should be noted first that even contemporary economic orthodoxy has failed to establish that inflation rates up to 8 per cent have *any* negative impact on the economy's vitality. As even the International Monetary Fund has been obliged to admit, there is no evidence that reducing inflation below 8 percent yields any gains whatsoever in terms of growth or living standards. For this reason, there are strong grounds for believing that the grand crusade to control inflation, while very costly to most people, has little positive effect, except, of course, for the owners of capital.

As an aside, it is interesting to note that most Western economies, at least until a few years ago, have looked at Asia's rapidly growing economies with envy. It was rarely noticed that this growth was, and continues to be in isolated cases, accompanied by what is generally considered medium to high rates of inflation. In 1995, when Canada had an inflation rate of 2.2 per cent, Hong Kong's rate was 9.2 per cent, Indonesia's 9.4 per cent, and the fastest-growing economy of all, China, had an inflation rate of 17 per cent (although those rates have all settled considerably by now).

Zero tolerance towards inflation has also undermined the ability of the welfare state to work effectively. As originally conceived, the welfare state consisted of two mutually supporting principles, the social-program component (or Beveridgian side) and the full-employment component (or Keynesian side) (Mishra 1984). The abandonment of the full-employment commitment has increased the stress on the social safety net. As expenditures for unemployment and social assistance soared, attacks on social programs increased in concert. Rather than implicating high interest rates, economic liberals put the blame on workers and social programs.

High interest rates, as argued above, also serve as an incentive for paper investments, which, in turn, funnel money away from productive endeavours. Between 1960 and the late 1970s, both paper and real investments constituted between 350 and 400 per cent of GDP. From the late 1970s onwards, paper investments almost doubled to over 600 per cent of GDP while real investments remained stable at 350 per cent (Stanford 1999).

Furthermore, high interest rates on massive public and private debts have contributed to mushrooming interest payments (which Brenner describes as 'manna from heaven' for leading capitalist interests [1998: 251]). This has contributed to increased deficits, which are then unfairly blamed on profligate social programs, further fuelling anti-welfare-state sentiment. In effect, social programs were attacked on two fronts. They were held responsible not only for the budget deficits but also for breeding indolence. The irony is that high interest rates and the fight against inflation had little to do with the 'invisible hand' of the market, but were the direct consequence of government intervention. Moreover, planned unemployment and social program cuts took money out of the hands of the very segment of the population most likely to spend it, further dwindling demand. Thus a downward spiral was created: higher interest rates led to higher unemployment, which in turn led to higher social expenditures, which led to social program cuts, which led to shrinking demand, and so on.

Galbraith writes in a book on the history of money, banks, and monetary policy that the clearest lesson of the recent past is the 'unusefulness of monetary policy' and that its consequences this century have been 'patently disastrous' (1995: 313). As evidence, he contrasts periods of strict monetary policy (the interwar years, including the Depression) to periods of more lenient use (during the Second World War until the late 1960s, a time of robust economic growth). With the power of governments, business, and unions, the effect of prices is no longer solely controlled by money, thus making monetary policy futile. But, he concludes, monetary policy bears 'strongly on the question of who controls economic rewards' (1995: 311). Brenner (1998: 251) draws similar conclusions, arguing that continued profits have only been possible because of the 'repression of wages' brought about by the 'fight on inflation.' The above serves as strong evidence that the struggle over the allocation of resources was a salient feature of late-twentieth-century politics, and that class politics continues to play a central role. The poor health of the economy in the past quarter-century testifies to the failure of monetary policies. Not only has monetary policy failed to manage the contradictions of capitalism, it has often aggravated them, in particular capitalism's tendency to concentrate wealth. From this perspective, far from mitigating social inequality, suffocating inflation has resulted in higher unemployment and placed unnecessary strain on the welfare state.

For now it seems that inflation has been temporarily wrung out of the system, and interest rates are at historic lows in both the United States and Canada, a trend accelerated by the terrorist attacks of 2001. But concerns about inflation are starting to reappear. *The Economist* (19 June 2004: 11) cautions that monetary policy around the world is 'dangerously lax' and warns of a return to the kind of inflation experienced in the 1970s. The message of the editorial is obvious: central banks must raise interest rates or run the risk of fuelling 'bubbles in house prices or equities.' It is laudable that *The Economist* seeks to avert such situations, but why do similar concerns not apply to the consequences of currency speculation or the distribution of resources, both globally and domestically. Why is it that only inflation is given this kind of attention?

But then again, central banks can do no right. Alan Greenspan, the chair of the Federal Reserve, has been blamed for fuelling the financial boom in the stock market during the late 1990s because of his low-interest-rate policy (Brenner 2002: 173). At the same time, he now has little room to manoeuvre, as raising interest rates would likely grind the economy to a halt, given the record high debt loads of governments, corporations, and individuals, in particular stock market speculators who buy on margin. However, as *The Economist* fears, with rising oil and gas prices in 2004, the spectre of inflation and higher interest rates looms large. There are also widespread concerns about the current-account deficit that the United States has with the rest of the world, with some economists speculating that the value of the American dollar could drop another 25 to 50 per cent (*Globe and Mail*, 26 June 2004: B1). The need to defend the currency would put central bank policies to the test, and the Fed would have little choice but to raise interest rates.

In Canada, the fight waged against inflation in the late 1980s and early 1990s had particularly serious consequences for labour in terms of high unemployment and slowed growth. But this was not the first time interest rates had been used as a policy instrument. Myles cautions that there is nothing new about the Canadian state's use of high interest rates to raise unemployment as a tactic to discipline labour (1988: 140). In this disciplining process, he writes, the 'most important and successful strategy was the tight money policy adopted by the Bank of Canada in 1975' (139). Neither is there anything new about the bank's obsession with a tight money policy. Ever since its inception, the bank has believed that its sole purpose was to enforce price stability, although some governments have resisted that urge (Stewart 1982). In 1961, James Coyne was forced to resign as the governor of the Bank of Canada based on a strong difference of opinion with Diefenbaker about monetary policy (Stewart 1997: 92–4).

But a difference of opinion between the Department of Finance and the bank is a rarity and has proved to be the exception rather than the rule. This can be directly traced to the fact that the federal government appoints the governor of the Bank of Canada, thereby ensuring that the candidate shares its own views on monetary policy. Consequently, a convergence of policy objectives tends to be the norm. Michael Wilson, for example, has admitted that the Conservatives worked side by side with the Bank of Canada to fight inflation during his reign as finance minister (*Globe and Mail*, 22 Mar. 1999: B4).

In Canada, interest rates were higher than those south of the border under the Conservatives from 1984 to 1993, but were lower on average from when the Liberals came to power until September 2001. This shows that though interest rates are affected by international factors, central banks continue to have considerable autonomy, but only if they have their own currency (Smithin 2004: 173). Lower interest rates alone greatly contributed towards balancing the budgets of provincial and federal governments. As we saw in chapter 7 on the state, the largest reduction in expenditures during the 1990s was in interest payments.

But the Bank of Canada is also greatly influenced by a banking culture that vigorously eschews inflation. Furthermore, the bank has strong ties to the business community and corporate think tanks. Rowland Frazee, CEO of the Royal Bank and author of the delusional quotation at the beginning of this chapter, was at one time chair of the Business Council of National Issues, and John Crow was appointed to a research post with the C.D. Howe Institute following his appointment at the bank. All this reveals a web of social and ideological networks that connect the interests of the Bank of Canada with those of the private banks and the financial community in general.

To Regulate or Not to Regulate

The economic uncertainty of the past thirty years is often traced to globalization. According to this theory, firms are moving away from the industrial nations to the Third World, taking jobs with them. Fear of being left behind by footloose corporations has prompted governments to lower taxes and provide lavish incentives, but to no avail. Consequently, globalization is said to have resulted in an increase in unemployment, social program cuts, and privatization. Yet, ironically, corporations are doing the exact opposite of fleeing. Tax cuts and privatization have led to an ever-increasing number of corporations in our midst. A dwindling tax base in combination with spending cuts has provided business with the opportunity to encroach on terrain traditionally occupied by governments, and business is infiltrating our lives as never before. Public places are now adorned with the names of corporate sponsors, from exhibits in museums to bookshelves in libraries. These developments, however, have little to do with globalization and everything to do with the fact that corporations are entrenching their power base right within Canada's borders.

Deregulation has been important to the burgeoning corporate presence, but this is far from a new trend. Polyani (1944) was concerned about the impact of deregulation during the interwar years. A completely free market, he wrote, is unattainable, merely a utopian fantasy. Without regulation, a society is doomed to fail; once trust fails, business and social relations soon follow. Eventually, people lose faith in the system and social unrest ensues, bringing about pressures to regulate once again (Piven and Cloward 1993). A breakdown of regulation ushered in the Depression, and it took a considerable amount of state intervention to restore confidence in the system. On the other hand, overregulation, as was the case in the erstwhile Soviet Union, can put a choke-hold on the economy. These and other developments led Polyani to observe that there is constant tension between regulation and deregulation.

Blind devotion to a low-inflation policy clearly illustrates that the right is against not regulation per se but regulation that constrains capital or cuts into profits. Deregulation can more accurately be described as re-regulation.[6] In the world of politics we also find that the conflict is less about regulation versus no regulation than about *regulation for whom*. As the example of monetary policy clearly illustrates, financial capital is quick to reject a hands-off approach when the absence of regulation fails to work in its favour. Business is unabashedly hypocritical about this. It openly encourages international regulation of intellectual property law and investors' rights, yet expects everyone to rely on the virtues of the free market when workers' rights or environmental protection are at stake. The attitude of business towards regulation also underscores that, at times, everyone finds some kind of regulation necessary. A completely free market is a fiction that would not be supported by even the most radical free-market capitalist, as the free market itself and attendant private property rules need to be enforced by somebody.[7]

Another way to understand current events, then, is that we are witnessing a swing of the pendulum towards more regulation and away from market-based solutions. Even if the pendulum may not quite be swinging in the other direction, it seems to be exhausting its swing to the right. According to Doug Henwood, 'neoliberalism has taken some blows' (*Left Business Observer*, 24 Jan. 2004: 1). As evidence of these blows he enumerates Argentina's defaulting on its debt, Hugo Chavez's continuing grip on power in Venezuela, and the refusal of President Lula da Silva of Brazil to abide by IMF policies. There are also strong stirrings around the world for a return to some kind of currency regulation. These include support from various central banks, including those of Canada, Japan, and the European Central Bank (*Globe and Mail*, 22 Jan. 1999: B9). The only country that has yet to come out in favour of such an initiative is the United States. Furthermore, the Asian crisis and the collapse of the Argentinian economy, as well as the fiascos associated with deregulation in the United States, have prompted politicians and voters around the world to question the soundness of the free-market model.

In Canada, the free-market ideology reached its apex during the Progressive Conservative rule that began in 1984 and ended abruptly in 1993. Mulroney, like R.B. Bennett in the Depression election of 1935, experienced the voter backlash that is often the result of being too closely associated with 'big business' (Guest 1985:87). However, many commentators believe that things have changed little with the Liberals. Clarkson (2002: 286) is of the opinion that when the Liberal party was elected in 1993, 'Rather than moving to the left ... it nimbly moved to the right to borrow its [the PC party's] ideas and defuse the threat of an ascending neoconservatism.' Similarly, Dobbin (2003) has pegged Paul Martin as being to the right of Mulroney.

But such accusations overlook a considerable policy shift that took place in 1993. After the Liberals came into power, John Crow's appointment as governor of the Bank of Canada was not renewed, and interest rates have been substantially lower since. This suggests that the government has adopted a more sane monetary policy and has moved away from the obsession with inflation. The Liberals have also shown themselves to be less business-friendly than the Mulroney Conservatives. While still finance minister, Paul Martin publicly criticized the proposition that lower taxes would lead to improved productivity as a 'form of escapism' (Globe and Mail, 1 April 1999: B11). Martin successfully opposed bank mergers and refused to let the banks expand into car leasing and insurance. Martin is also a strong proponent of the Tobin Tax on currency speculation and, as prime minister, continues to support Third World debt relief. On the other hand, the Liberals have stayed committed to free trade. Not only did they fail to abrogate NAFTA, as promised, but they have pursued its expansion, which is planned to include most of Latin America. The Liberals are also strong supporters of the WTO.

The above discussion illustrates that political events over the past two decades are better understood in the light of the struggle over resources within Canada than within the larger context of globalization. The right has tried to convince the general public that an excess of state intervention, through social programs in particular, is responsible for the economic downturn. But as the Conservative Party found in the runup to the 2004 election, selling this view is an uphill battle. Canadian voters have grown fond of their social programs and are willing to defend them at the ballot box.

The need to compete, based on the threat of globalization, is often used as a justification to cut social programs and wages. The above argument presents a somewhat different picture of the events of the past thirty years by examining class interests and identifying who is likely to benefit and who is likely to lose from various policies. How effective the free-market approach has been at revitalizing a stagnating economy is another question entirely. The fact is that the economy has failed to return to its pre-recession splendour. Of course, there is little the right, or anyone for that matter, can do to rescue the economy from a downswing in a business cycle. That is the nature of capitalism. The best one can hope to do is cushion the fall.

Conclusion

Now that we have examined an array of data, let us tie it all together to see how this evidence fits with the theory of globalization. In order to do so, let us revisit a typical observation made about the topic: 'Commentators ... link the decline of the nation-state to the process of globalization, often deploring the loss of national control ...' (Albrow 2004: 475). In the broader context of globalization and all its complexities, exactly what does this proposition mean? How does the process of globalization lead to the 'loss of national control?' First we must ask, the globalization of what? The globalization of everything is just too vague and incorporates many, often contradictory, developments. The impact of globalization differs from one activity to the next, and we need details about what particular strand is being discussed in order to assess whether it actually hinders the state's role to govern. Coca-Cola, email, and CNN are global developments, but they hardly limit a state's ability to rule. The unfettered movement of people across borders could feasibly undermine the power of the state, but immigration is more tightly controlled now than at any other time in history, and the prospect of the unrestrained movement of people is highly improbable.

Neither is there a reason to believe that trade has a negative impact on national sovereignty. Canada has long had voluminous trade and has not only survived but thrived. Canada's trade with the rest of the world has increased considerably since the Second World War, but this rise looks much less impressive when the time span is lengthened to include the past 133 years. Neither is Canada's trade at an all-time high, having been higher during the First World War. Current trade levels are high, but only in comparison to the relatively low levels found in the 1950s and 1960s. Once disaggregated, we find that almost all of the increase in trade in the past-half century has involved trade with Canada's nearest neighbour, the United States. 'Global trade,' as such, has stayed mundanely stable since 1870.

In comparison to the volume of trade with the United States, imports from the Third World are negligible, and there is little reason to believe they are detrimental to the Canadian economy. Moreover, imports are offset by a concomitant increase in exports to those same areas. Trade with the First World continues to dominate, and here the fears about low-wage competition expressed by the globalists just do not apply. Furthermore, governments have actively engaged in the implementation of various trade agreements, gambling that neoclassical prescriptions about comparative advantage will prove to be right and save the day. Free-trade agreements notwithstanding, voluntary trade barriers indicate that powerful states such as the United States are still able to impose their will on other countries, and trade is anything but 'free.' Moreover, as the Canadian economy becomes increasingly service-oriented, the importance of trade is likely to diminish in tandem.

Globalization talk has meant that international trade has become increasingly politicized. On the one hand, the left has identified trade as a threat to Canadian workers and national sovereignty. After fifteen years of free trade, this has not turned out to be the case. On the other hand, the right presents free trade as a panacea for all economic problems. This uncritical optimism is, in my opinion, also unwarranted. The increase in trade over the past decade and a half has done little to improve Canada's economic performance. While trade increased substantially throughout the 1990s, corresponding economic growth has remained unimpressive. In contrast, when economic growth was most robust – in the 1950s and 1960s – Canada participated in relatively little trade. These figures suggest not only that the relationship between free trade and economic growth is a weak one, but that it might actually be a negative one (Urmetzer 2003).

Also noteworthy is the increased role of the state in the economy. The lockstep rise of trade and government expenditures in the second half of the twentieth century makes the proposition that the flow of goods undermines the power of the state somewhat implausible. Here the facts just do not fit the theory. Not only has the government presence remained dominant, there exists no logical argument for why nation-states ought to be threatened by the flow of goods, ideas, or services. This becomes especially evident once individual state programs are examined and the competing interests of capital and the country as a whole are taken into consideration. We must then ask, precisely what aspects of national control are undermined? States may have less control over what goods cross their borders, but they continue to govern many other essential activities, many of which are vital to a competitive economy. Education, health, and infrastructure are just a few examples.

Another reason commonly given for the loss of national control is the rise of supranational institutions such as the IMF and the World Bank. There is ample evidence that these institutions can compromise national sovereignty, and have done so by enforcing their authoritarian will in the name of the free market, as manifested in the use of the notorious austerity programs. But this type of enforcement is only practised on poor countries, which compels one to ask whether such activity is the result of globalization or is merely a residual form of colonialism.

Commentators often link the loss of autonomy to the imperatives of foreign investors, but once numbers are taken into consideration, it turns out to be primarily domestic investors' interests that are at stake. Blaming foreign investors is no more than a sleight-of-hand used by domestic capital to camouflage its own self-interest. Foreign investors do play a role, but it is unlikely that this dispersed group is capable of banding together to make demands about social programs or tax cuts. Their power resides primarily in the fact that people believe that they have it. The threat of fleeing capital also needs to be looked upon with suspicion. It treats all investors as a homogeneous group with consistent interests, but this, as we have seen, is far from being the case in the real world of economics, where interests vary widely. Foreign corporations that invest in production are interested in a well-maintained infrastructure, an educated workforce, welfare-state services, and low interest rates. Moneylenders, on the other hand, and not surprisingly, prefer a higher rate of return on their investments – that is to say, higher interest rates. Stockholders seldom venture past their own borders, and if they do, they are more interested in the performance of an individual firm than that of a country.

Still another way that national control is said to be subverted is by currency speculation. It should first be noted that the governance of the world's financial system has long been a thorny issue, and in this sense the occasional spurt of anarchy is not new. And while there is little that any single government – with the notable exception of the United States – can do about this problem on its own, countries can band together and reimpose order. The only ingredient missing is the political will. In order for this political will to gain momentum, it must be understood that speculators are more interested in volatility – that is, in having currencies or interest rates go up or down – than in fundamentals. The fact is that decisions about when to buy or sell are often made by machines that have no interest in any kind of economic fundamentals. For this reason, the importance of currency speculators should not be overstated, because, as New Zealand found out, they never can and never will be pleased.

Another major weakness of the globalization argument is the ambiguity about whether globalization is a new process or the continuation of an old one. Not knowing exactly what globalization stands in contrast to leaves the term on shaky ground, as it is difficult to know on what basis to judge whatever claims are made. This is true with respect to time (i.e., When exactly did globalization begin?), and in contrast to other social theories such as modernism. Loosely defined, as it so often is, the term 'globalization' packs a political punch but lacks the rigour required to explain contemporary political and economic events.

Much of what globalists identify as new has been going on for centuries; that is to say, globalization is not a new process but one that has been known as either modernity, capitalism, industrialization, or simply progress. The following passage is of note because it is written by Lawrence Summers, president of Harvard University and a former chief economist of the World Bank, an organization well known for its faith in globalization. (The outline Summers refers to is a proposal about globalization originating from within the World Bank.)

What's new? Throughout the outline I struggle with the evidence showing *what* exactly the proclaimed revolution [in production] has revolutionized. FDI has always existed and many of the world's largest firms have been transnational from birth. The 'globalization' of production has happened sure, but has the telecommunications revolution really had a major impact? I would guess the invention of relatively simple things, like steamship transport, did more for world trade than digitalized data transmission through fibre optic cables. How exactly has the nature of manufacturing been 'fundamentally altered?' Aren't people just incrementally better at doing things they've always done, like locate production in the lowest cost location for delivery to markets (now 'globalization of production'), like manage inventories in a least cost way (now 'just-in-time inventory management'), like choose the appropriate level of vertical integration depending on the production process (now 'critical buyer-seller links'), like match production to demand (now 'short product cycles'). Is a 'revolution' really the appropriate metaphor for these changes? I think the detailed evidence from the US about the very small impact of productivity from the large investment in information technology should convince us to hold off on the breathless tone about technology. (quoted in *Left Business Observer*, Apr. 1996: 4)

As has been shown throughout this book, there exists both evidence that points towards globalization and evidence that contests it. But the rhythm of the seesaw between nationalism and internationalism, as Wallerstein puts it, has not, in any discernible way, been transcended. There is no definitive way in which one trend can be said to overwhelmingly dominate the other. However, what is overwhelming is how the rhetoric of globalization, only about two decades old, has taken hold of and pervaded almost every aspect of society and has infected virtually all political and academic discourse. Whether the discussion is about the stock market, the rise of China, the WTO, the welfare state, religion, poverty, or communications, the topic is somehow informed by 'globalization.' Views about globalization have become common currency to the point that even to question the idea is to open oneself to ridicule (see R. Williams 1983).

In the end, the focus should be not about what globalization means but about its intended use. The British philosopher of language H.P. Grice more or less equates meaning with intention, highlighting the difference between connotation and denotation. To complain of a headache, for example, means something different in a doctor's office than in a bedroom. In this way, the battle over the meaning of 'globalization' has become too preoccupied with its literal interpretation, whereas the better question to ask is about intention. More often than not, globalization is used by social actors to deflate opposition or shirk responsibility. 'We cannot do this because of globalization ...' From this angle, ambiguity actually works to heighten the threat of globalization.

Political Fatalism

Globalization is often presented as something mysterious, vague, yet all-powerful. These qualities add not only to its mystery, but also to its potency; it is difficult to oppose something so indeterminate. This is deliberate, I would argue. Ambiguity makes globalization appear to be something beyond our control, to be revered and obeyed. According to this scenario, the choices we are given are painfully constrained: we either fall in line with the demands of globalization and become more competitive (lower wages and fewer benefits) or we perish (no work and no benefits). The danger with this type of account is that it buys into the common misconception that, while globalization may have unpleasant consequences, there is little that can be done about it. It is this 'spreading political fatalism' (Gordon 1988: 64) that proves to be the most distressing aspect of globalization. More accurately, this attitude has been characterized as 'the social construction of helplessness' by Linda Weiss (1997: 15), a phrase that succinctly captures how the idea of globalization and its associated fatalism have been deliberately manufactured and disseminated. Gordon Laxer (2003: 29) cautions that 'much of the political Left and Centre endorsed the neoliberal line that globalization is an objective phenomenon, a qualitative break with the past, that necessarily diminishes or ends nations, nationalisms and sovereignties.' From this perspective, it is critical that political processes are properly understood.

Furthermore, by ignoring agency, we often depict globalization as immutable. Yet despite our pessimism, government, business, and labour continue to function and, for the most part, to conduct politics as usual. In the ongoing tug of war over the economic pie, globalization has been used as just another diversionary tactic to distract the opposition in the hope of gaining some economic ground. At times this has worked but, just as often, people recognize the diversion for what it is and go on about their business as always.

Defining Globalization

Over its short twenty-year lifespan, the concept of globalization has been interrogated to the point of torture. When the term first entered popular and academic parlance in the mid-1980s, it was primarily about the burgeoning power of corporations and was explicitly intended to describe a recent phenomenon. But as evidence mounted, the temporal borders of globalization were necessarily stretched back – first to include the whole of the modern era and eventually to cover all of human history. This has left the semantic boundaries of globalization stretched beyond recognition. As academics from various disciplines jumped into the fray, the concept proved to be exceedingly flexible, as it generously accommodated a myriad of topics, including politics, telecommunications, and culture, to name but a few. This flexibility, however, also proved to be globalization's greatest weakness in that its multitude of meanings eventually led to vagueness and ambiguity. Consequently, globalization gradually lost its force, a victim of its own popularity. As the concept has slowly fragmented into a plethora of disparate meanings, it has gradually been overtaken by more focused discussions on topics such as imperialism, colonialism, and American hegemony. In other words, things are not all that different from the way they were before globalization came onto the scene two decades ago.

In sociology, after years of expanding and tightening definitions, globalization has come to mean 'a growing awareness of deepening connections between the local and the distant' (Steger 2003: 13), a variant of Robertson's global consciousness. After more than two decades of debate, this amounts to pretty thin gruel. In economics, globalization has essentially become synonymous with free trade. Stiglitz defines globalization as the 'removal of barriers to free trade and the closer integration of national economies' (2002: ix). Similarly, the *Globe and Mail* (7 Feb. 2004: A12) suggests that 'Stripped to its essentials, globalization rests on liberalized trade ...' Of course, free trade itself is an ideology, one that is centuries old. Globalization as free trade attempts to neutralize the power differences that exist between countries, and as such pits advanced industrial economies against agrarian ones, as though it were plausible that a farmer from Ghana compete with agribusiness in North America.

The realization that those who demonstrate against globalization are taking part in a long-standing tradition of expressing dissatisfaction with capitalism is slowly gaining currency. The term 'neoliberal globalization,' or just plain 'neoliberalism,' has become popular in academic circles and attempts to describe the prevailing temper of our times. However, it is not altogether clear how either of these terms differs from the traditional 'economic liberalism' espoused by Smith and Ricardo. The advantage of using an unadorned version of the term – that is, simply 'liberalism' – is that it recognizes the extensive history that comes with this ideology, whereas 'globalization' mistakenly conveys the message that something new is happening. The point is that there is nothing novel about free trade, open markets, private property rights, or fiscal prudence.

Corporations and the State

In the ongoing narrative of globalization, two institutional actors are most often identified: the corporation and the state. More precisely, hypermobile corporations are said to have increased their power at the expense of the state. But this approach is profoundly asociological in that it understands both corporations and the state as somehow standing outside of society, rather than being integral parts of it. In order to effectively combat the 'political fatalism' associated with globalization explanations, it is critical to recognize that both these institutions are firmly woven into the fabric of modern society. Contrary to what is often believed to be the case with corporations, they cannot simply move on and leave the country; nor can they disappear from the political landscape altogether, as is frequently believed with respect to the state.

Although corporations are not the omnipotent entities they are often made out to be, they benefit from the common perception that they can dodge borders and ignore regulations. But corporations cannot act with impunity, even though they may find it convenient to pretend to be able do so. Corporations are cumbersome, bureaucratic beasts, as dependent on modern technology and infrastructure as citizens are. Furthermore, corporations rely on citizens not only as workers but also as consumers.

The state is just as important to the functioning of modern industrial society as corporations are – and as unlikely to vanish. The state regulates much of everyday life, performing this task so effectively that most of the time its presence goes unnoticed. Most events transpire without incident only because they are backed by the invisible hand of the state. Every time we sign a contract, get on a plane, or eat a meal, we can be confident that this activity will unfold smoothly because of the forceful presence of the state. At times, we may even forget its existence, only to be reminded of it when things go awry. Without fail, when blood becomes tainted, cows go mad, or water becomes contaminated, we immediately turn to the state to seek justice and rectify the situation. It is somewhat ironic that the state becomes least visible when it performs its tasks best. It is also then, it seems, that it becomes most vulnerable to attacks by free marketeers and globalists.

This is not to say that government intervention is inherently good, or that corporations are inherently bad. What is important to recognize is that both the state and corporations are bureaucracies that, while not always acting in everyone's best interest, perform many useful and essential tasks for society. If our society continues in its present form – being capitalist and democratic and all that that entails – it is highly unlikely that either the state or the corporation will wither away or change in any fundamental way. The primary shortcoming of globalization theory is that it predicts, or purports to describe, a fundamental change in modern industrial society that just does not square with the facts. Society is changing constantly in many different ways, but as we saw, this is precisely what defines modernity. And, for better or worse, we continue to travel along that path.

Capital and Labour and the Distribution of Resources

As the industrial economy is corroding and economic growth has slowed, the fight over resources has become that much more intense. Rhetoric about globalization has successfully diverted attention away from this domestic struggle and has attempted to blame lower living standards and high unemployment on factors outside this country. While it is not untrue that Canada's economy is well integrated into the world economy, the globalization theory glosses over the fact that Canada has been that way from the day Europeans first set foot on North American soil, modern Canada itself being a product of globalization (Watkins 1992).

The economy's lacklustre performance over the past few decades lies at the heart of the increased struggle over resources, manifested in the fight over the welfare state, privatization, and deregulation. Prescriptions by the right are based on the belief that the elimination of social programs, labour laws, and government intervention provides the shortest path to economic prosperity. The targets of this rhetoric, often workers and the welfare state, reveal such attacks to be little more than the usual free-market bromides. It is remarkable how deeply ingrained this ideology remains in the collective consciousness of capitalist society and how firmly it has persisted over the centuries. Despite the many changes that societies have undergone, the unreceptive attitude towards welfare programs is no different today than it was more than 400 years ago when the Elizabethan Poor Laws were first introduced in Great Britain. At least the views of the right have remained consistent in this regard, making it all the easier to expose their ideas for the rhetoric they are.

The right has always deemed that social assistance and unemployment insurance are labour market disincentives. These disincentives must be removed, they urge, to make us more competitive in the global economy. But the behaviour of capital itself is rarely examined. As Myles (1988) has noted, the economic success of Sweden can partially be explained by the high wages paid there. In such an environment, employers are constantly pressured to use labour in the most efficient way possible or to develop technology to replace it. In other words, low wages and a large reserve army of unemployed workers makes capitalists uncompetitive and keeps them from innovating. High interest rates make them even less competitive, as they take away the incentive to invest in productive ventures. To turn the right's rhetoric against them, we need higher wages in order to increase productivity and discipline apathetic capitalists. Nevertheless, despite a professed faith in the market, free marketeers continue to act in a highly interventionist manner. The ubiquitous and prominent role of central banks and the WTO, IMF, and World Bank reveal a faith that is far from inviolable.

The focus on globalization has taken attention away from how indebtedness – and its mirror image, the stock of financial wealth – have increased in tandem. Far from being caused by foreign investors, this redistribution of wealth is the result of high interest rates inspired by an almost neurotic fear of inflation. This policy succeeded in keeping unemployment high and debt servicing unduly expensive throughout most of the 1980s and 1990s. This, in turn, took money out of the hands of workers and effectively broke the production-consumption circle that worked so well in the Golden Age. The only solution offered by the right for the current economic malaise is more deregulation. But given the already skewed distribution of wealth in North America, the further deregulation of markets will likely only move us farther from the balance needed to repair the virtuous circle of production and consumption. As Stiglitz (2003) points out, all of the markets that were deregulated in the United States – electricity, banking, telecommunications – ended in disaster. The same is true in Canada, where the deregulation of electricity markets in Ontario and Alberta failed to lead to lower rates, and required extensive government intervention and financing to avoid a crisis. The often used analogy of globalization as a runaway freight train could well be a metaphor for this type of unchecked capitalism. This said, mounting debts have not resulted in an economic catastrophe, at least for the West, as interest rates have plummeted. But when interest rates do rise again – as inevitably they will – they could dramatically slow economic growth around the world.

Free marketeers may have won some battles, but they are a long way from winning the war. The rhetoric of globalization has been used as a tactic to fight this ongoing war, sometimes with great success. But as we have seen, globalization has little to do with the increase in unemployment in this country, with poverty in Vancouver's Downtown

Eastside, or with the big profits made by the banks. They are all the result of deliberate decisions that are part of the political process, a process that still primarily takes place within the borders of this country. Canada is a wealthy country. The wages of workers in Indonesia or the amount we trade with Taiwan have little to do with how that wealth is divided. Globalization rhetoric has been successful in making Canadians believe that it does. The sooner Canadians are able to debunk this myth, the sooner they will be able to focus on the real issues within Canada's borders and make progress towards solving them.

Appendix

Note on Statistical Sources

The data for the figures presented throughout the preceding pages were collected from a variety of sources, both printed and computer sources, all originating from Statistics Canada. This appendix provides a short overview of where these sources can be located. Please keep in mind that electronic versions are becoming more dominant, while hard copies are increasingly difficult to find.

The figures for Canadian trade for the years spanning 1870 to 1923 come from *Sessional Papers: Third Session of the Fourteenth Parliament* (Canada 1924). For the years 1926–51, data are primarily from a monograph entitled *Trade of Canada* (Statistics Canada 1952) and are supplemented by *Canada Yearbooks*. From 1953 to 1993 the numbers are taken from *Canada Yearbooks* and Statistics Canada (1997b). Trade figures that are broken down by region come from Canada (1924), Canada (1997b) and various *Canada Yearbooks* (Canada 1870–1987). The latter occasionally present summaries that span several years. Trade figures for 1990 onwards, both total and broken down by region, are now conveniently available on the Trade Data Online website housed at Industry Canada (2004). The data for trade in services come from *Canada's Balance of International Payments* (Statistics Canada 1997a) and are supplemented by electronic sources.

For foreign investment flows, data come from *Canada's Balance of International Payments* (Statistics Canada 1997a) The data for foreign direct investment stocks from 1900 to 1925 come from Leacy (1983: G188–202) and Urquhart and Buckley (1965). FDI data for the years 1926–92 are compiled in *Canada's International Investment Position, Historical Statistics* (Statistics Canada 1993). Again, figures for the most recent ten-year period come from electronic sources. The figures for portfolio investment are from Statistics Canada (1997b) and electronic sources. Numbers for Canada's assets and liabilities (stock of wealth) can be found in the *National Balance Sheets* (Statistics Canada 2004).

Government expenditures figures for the years spanning 1933 to 1964 are from Leacy (1983). The figures for government expenditures from 1965/66 to 1991/92 are from Statistics Canada (1993); the data from 1992/93 to 1994/95 are from the *Public Sector Statistics* Series (Statistics Canada 1995). Data for the years spanning 1995/96 to 2002/3 are from electronic sources.

Notes

Introduction

1 There are a number of prominent sociologists, Beck (1992) and Giddens (1994) among them, who have put forward the opinion that many of today's problems are 'beyond left and right.' In some sense this is similar to the 'end of ideology' thesis popular in the 1970s, and it is equally difficult to uphold. While some issues are undoubtably 'beyond' class factions – for example, the environment – this is not the case for matters economic. Rather, what seems to have happened is that the political centre has veered to the right, from a Keynesian to a liberal-market consensus. The Canadian case serves as a good example. When first established, the C.D. Howe Institute espoused Keynesian economics but was forced to take a 'shift to the right' when the Fraser Institute appeared on the scene and started to compete for business funding (Ernst 1992). This has resulted in an atmosphere where everyone, including the left, has been compelled to adopt policies usually associated with the right. But this does not mean that everyone is of the same mind. In fact, nowhere is a split between left and right more evident than when it comes to free trade and globalization, the subject of this book.

1 The Life and Times of Globalization: An Unauthorized Biography

1 Social rights are usually tied to citizenship and entails people's contributions to, and entitlements from, a national system. Unrestrained mobility of people would likely make such practices unfeasible.
2 Ironically, theories of globalization that emphasize time-space compression have been criticized for being a 'western, colonizer's view' (Massey 1994: 147). Massey goes on to write that the importation of cultures from afar has long been experienced by inhabitants of countries that were colonized.

3 Albrow (2004: 471) has interpreted Giddens's comment that 'modernity is inherently globalizing' to mean that modernity causes globalization; this illustrates the confused thinking surrounding this topic.

4 There are many examples of words that have been contaminated by politics. 'Dictator,' for example, is derived from the Latin *dicare*, 'to say,' and up until the rise of fascism merely meant spokesperson or leader (for example, the Pope was referred to as the dictator of the church). This antiquated meaning explains Marx's use of 'dictatorship' with respect to the rise of the proletariat. 'Fascism,' which originally meant any political group, is another instance of a word that has acquired a strong political hue that now separates it from its original meaning (Merriam-Webster 1991: 171–3).

5 The data for popular print sources come from the database Lexis-Nexis. There are isolated uses of the term 'globalization' going back to the 1960s (Waters 2001), but its use did not become systematic until at least the early 1980s. *The American Banker* is of note because it did use the word in a consistent manner.

2 Marx, Globalization, and Modernity: What Is Old Becomes New Again

1 These themes are prevalent in other writings of Marx. I use the *Manifesto* because it is representative of Marxist thought on these issues. This chapter also draws on ideas specifically related to the *Manifesto* as delineated by Berman (1982) and Therborn (1995).

2 I downloaded a copy of the *Manifesto* from the Net, and this greatly facilitated such a count. 'Thirty pages' refers to double-spaced pages.

3 Evidence suggests that it is more difficult to cross borders now than at any other point in history. For example, passports were not used extensively until after the First World War (Zweig nd). Torpey (1998) writes that the state has a monopoly over the 'means of movement' in much the same way that it has a monopoly over the legitimate use of violence. This power may not be absolute, but it is dominant, particularly when it comes to keeping poor people out of rich countries.

4 Trade

1 While it is true that the first United Nations declaration was signed in 1942, the organization's role was vastly different during the war than after. Its forerunner, the League of Nations, was formed in 1920, but the United States, despite President Wilson's best efforts, never did join the organization. Some organizations have been around longer, such as the International

Labor Organization (ILO), which was first established in 1919 but later absorbed by the United Nations. The point, however, remains, and that is that pre-war statistics for trade are not readily available.

2 Export figures used refer to domestic exports only (i.e., they do not include foreign exports or re-exports) and imports include imports for consumption only. Foreign exports are products that go through Canada but originate somewhere else. For example, lumber from Washington state may be shipped through Vancouver, B.C., on its way to Japan.

3 These are Wade's figures, and he provides no reason why Argentina is omitted.

6 The Financial Economy

1 This is not to say that these instruments are new. Futures go back more than a century, options three centuries, and foreign-exchange speculation more than seven centuries (*Left Business Observer*, 6 Jan. 1996: 4)

2 It should be made clear that net worth, once debt is taken into consideration, was significantly less, about $3.5 trillion. However, most of that debt is owed domestically.

7 The Retreat of the Nation-state

1 One aspect of the globalization debate worth noting is the nuclear threat (e.g., Albrow 1996). The fact that these threats are globalized has really little impact on the affairs of the state until they actually happen. But even then, their consequences are likely exaggerated. Chernobyl is often adduced as an example of a global environmental threat (Beck 1992). But if anything, Chernobyl has shown that a nuclear disaster can be survived. As well as in the Soviet Union itself, the disaster caused a great deal of concern in Beck's home country of Germany, but it failed to arouse much attention even in Great Britain, let alone North America. In other words, its implications were far from global.

2 Most globalization accounts are also biased in that they focus only on how technology has made it possible to bypass borders and not the other way around. Technology is a two-edged sword that has meant not only freedom but also constraint. The enduring and ubiquitous presence of the state in the capacity of government spending, surveillance, and as the sole source of legitimate violence (Giddens based on Weber) is often ignored by most globalists.

3 Although residents pay fees in British Columbia, Alberta, and Ontario,

under the Canada Health Act they cannot be refused health care when it is required.

4 The following abbreviations will be used throughout this section: Canada Pension Plan (CPP); Quebec Pension Plan (QPP); Old Age Security (OAS); Guaranteed Income Supplement (GIS); Spouse's Allowance (SPA). All but the CPP and the QPP are financed by general revenues.

5 There are also various means-tested provincial and territorial programs to supplement income for the elderly amounting to a total of $285 million in 1997 (Clark 1998: 77).

6 The three-month residency requirement by British Columbia, however, was more a tactic to persuade the federal government to reinstate funding than an attack on the poor. The Canada Assistance Program (CAP) guaranteed matching funds to the provinces for social assistance if the provinces abided by a few simple rules, the mobility rule being one of them. When the federal government unilaterally capped CAP in 1990, the B.C. government took the federal government to court (Sossin 1998: 153). Imposing a residency requirement was merely a measure designed to reinstate funding.

7 Soon after the B.C. Liberals were elected, they instituted a 25 per cent tax cut, creating a huge deficit. In order to absolve themselves of any guilt, they blamed the budget deficit on their predecessors, the NDP, despite the fact that they inherited a balanced budget.

8 This is in terms of actual expenditures – that is, constant dollars. 'Labour, employment, and immigration' and 'other expenditures' have increased more on a percentage of GDP basis, but both still only amount to less than half a per cent of GDP.

9 Ex-premier Mike Harris found this out the hard way. He encouraged thousands of teachers and nurses to leave their jobs in order to save money, but was forced to lure them back at added expense later. In the late 1990s, the Ontario government spent $375 million to hire 12,000 nurses, a dollar amount only slightly less than was spent to fire them a few years earlier (*Globe and Mail*, 24 Apr. 1999: A10).

8 Postwar Economy

1 In British Columbia, provincial taxes were lowered by 25 per cent with the hope of revitalizing the economy, resulting in the largest deficit in the province's history. As an aside, when these tax cuts did not end up paying for themselves as promised, economist David Bond had this to say: 'I could be tempted to say "I told you so," but I shouldn't. After all, [finance minister] Collins, who was saying there wouldn't be any deficit, is a certified flight

instructor and ... all I've got is a PhD in economics' (*Vancouver Sun*, 15 Dec. 2001: A26).

2 In 1996, corporate taxes accounted for only 12.3 per cent of total income tax revenues, down from 22.8 per cent in 1980 and 46.4 per cent in 1950 (Canadian Global Almanac 1999: 241).

3 Developments on Canadian campuses are a perfect example of this. Philanthropists are happy to donate money to buildings that bear their name (e.g., the Chan Centre and Green College at UBC), while already existing buildings and infrastructures are left in disrepair.

4 This is, admittedly, a simplified version of what happened. Supply-side economists saw labour encroaching on profits and blamed the economic downturn on the inflexible demands of unions. Business believed that the root of the problem was wage demands that outpaced productivity gains and thereby fuelled inflation (Brenner 1998).

5 This is referred to as the money illusion by economists.

6 It is interesting to note that those on the right are all for labour market deregulation but are also the first to object when people participate in the unregulated labour market: drug pushers, sex workers, panhandlers, squeegee workers.

7 This statement applies even to libertarians and anarchists. Whether one believes in the rights of free property or not – as do libertarians and anarchists, respectively – one requires some sort of regulation to enforce these beliefs. The role of the 'night-watchman state' that is supported by most libertarians is a good example.

Bibliography

Albrow, Martin. 1994. 'Globalization' (248–9) in *The Blackwell Dictionary of Twentieth-century Social Thought* (ed. W. Outhwaite and T. Bottomore). Oxford: Blackwell.

Albrow, Martin. 1996. *The Global Age*. Cambridge: Polity Press.

Albrow, Martin. 2004. 'Globalization' (465–91) in *New Society: Sociology for the 21st Century* (4th ed.) (ed. R. Brym). Toronto: Nelson Thomson.

Allen, Woody. 1981. *Side Effects*. New York: Ballantine Books.

Anderson, Hugh. 1998. *Investing for Income*. Toronto: ITP Nelson.

Arrighi, Giovanni. 1994. *The Long Twentieth Century: Money, Power, and the Origins of Our Times*. London: Verso.

Babad, Michael, and Mulroney, Catherine. 1998. *The Buck Stops Here*. Toronto: Stoddart.

Baran, Paul, and Sweezy, Paul. 1966. *Monopoly Capital: An Essay on the American Economic and Social Order*. New York: Monthly Review Press.

Barnes, Trevor. 1996. 'External Shocks: Regional Implications of an Open Staple Economy' (48–68), in *Canada in the Global Economy* (ed. J. Britton). Montreal: McGill-Queen's University Press.

Battle, Ken. 1993. 'Lowering the Safety Net and Weakening the Bonds of Nationhood: Social Policy in the Mulroney Years' (381–416), in *How Ottawa Spends* (ed. Susan Phillips). Ottawa: Carleton University Press.

Battle, Ken. 1994. 'Poverty: Myths, Misconceptions, and Half-truths' (148–73), in *Continuities and Discontinuities: The Political Economy of Social Welfare and Labour Market Policy in Canada* (ed. A. Johnson, S. McBride, and P. Smith). Toronto: University of Toronto Press.

BC Checkup. 2003. http://icabc.hurrah.com/pdfs/cacheckup/bccheckup/bccheckup_2003/bccheckup_2003.pdf.

Beck, Ulrich. 1992. *Risk Society*. London: Sage.

Becker, Howard S. 1986. *Writing for Social Scientists*. Chicago: University of Chicago Press.

Bell, Daniel. 1987. 'The World and the United States in 2013' (1–31), *Daedalus* 166 (3).

Berle, Adolph, and Means, Gardiner. 1967. *The Modern Corporation and Private Property*. New York: Harcourt, Brace and World.

Berman, Marshall. 1982. *All That Is Solid Melts into Air*. New York: Penguin.

Bhagwati, Jagdish. 2004. *In Defense of Globalization*. New York: Oxford University Press.

Bienefeld, Manfred. 1992. 'Deregulation: Disarming the Nation State' (31–48), *Studies in Political Economy* 37.

Block, Fred, and Burns, Gene A. 1986. 'Productivity as a Social Problem: The Uses and Misuses of Social Indicators' (767–80), *American Sociological Review* 51 (December).

Bordo, Michael, and Krajnyak, Kornelia. 1997. 'Globalization in Historical Perspective' (112–16), *World Economic Outlook*. (May). Washington, D.C.: International Monetary Fund.

Brenner, Robert. 1977. 'The Origins of Capitalist Development' (25–92), *New Left Review* 104.

Brenner, Robert. 1998. 'The Economics of Global Turbulence' (Special Issue), *New Left Review* 229.

Brenner, Robert. 2002. *The Boom and the Bubble: The U.S. in the World Economy*. New York: Verso.

Brodie, Janine. 1990. *The Political Economy of Canadian Regionalism*. Toronto: Harcourt Brace Jovanovich.

Brown, Lester, Lenssen, Nicholas, and Kane, Hal. 1996. *Vital Signs 1995*. New York: W.W. Norton and Company.

Cameron, Rondo, and Neal, Larry. 2003. *A Concise Economic History of the World: From Paleolithic Times to the Present* (4th ed.). New York: Oxford University Press.

Canada. 1924 'Trade and Commerce' (10–29), in *Sessional Papers. Third Session of the Fourteenth Parliament*. Vol. 60. Ottawa.

Canadian Global Almanac. 1999. *The Canadian Global Almanac, 2000*. Toronto: Macmillan Canada.

Chossudovsky, Michel. 2003. *The Globalization of Poverty and the New World Order* (2nd ed.). Shanty Bay, Ont.: Global Outlook.

Clark, Christopher. 1998. *Income Security Programs*. Ottawa: Canadian Council on Social Development.

Clarkson, Stephen. 2002. *Uncle Sam and Us: Globalization, Neoconservatism, and the Canadian State*. Toronto: University of Toronto Press.

Clement, Wallace. 1975. *The Canadian Corporate Elite: An Analysis of Economic Power*. Toronto: McClelland and Stewart.

Clement, Wallace. 1988. *The Challenge of Class Analysis*. Ottawa: Carleton University Press.

Cohen, Marjorie Griffin. 1997. 'From the Welfare State to Vampire Capitalism' (28–67), in *Women and the Canadian Welfare State: Challenges and Change*. Toronto: University of Toronto Press.

Conference Board of Canada. 2004. 'Canada Is Losing Its Advantages as a Destination for Foreign Direct Investment.' 3 June. http://www.conferenceboard.ca/press/2004/fdi_report.asp.

Courchene, Thomas. 1994. *Social Canada in the Millennium*. Toronto: C.D. Howe Institute.

Cox, Robert. 1994. 'Global Re-structuring: Making Sense of the Changing International Political Economy' (45–59), in *Political Economy and the Changing Global Order* (ed. R. Stubbs and G. Underhill). Toronto: McClelland and Stewart.

Daly, Herman E., and Cobb, John B., Jr. 1994. *For the Common Good* (2nd ed.). Boston: Beacon Press.

Daniels, Patricia, and Hyslop, Stephen. 2003. *National Geographic Almanac of World History*. Washington, D.C.: National Geographic.

Davies, Scott, and Guppy, Neil. 1997. 'Globalization and Educational Reforms in Anglo-American Democracies' (435–59), *Comparative Education Review* 41 (4).

Dehli, Kari. 1993. 'Subject to the New Global Economy: Power and Positioning in Ontario Labour Market Policy Formation' (83–110), *Studies in Political Economy* 41.

Deloitte and Touche. 2004. 'U.S. Manufacturers Decrease Overseas Investment for Third Consecutive Year.' http://www.deloitte.com/dtt/press_release/0,2309,cid%3D49618%26pre%3DY%26lid%3D1,00.html.

Derrida, Jacques. 1994. *Specters of Marx: The State of the Debt, the Work of Mourning, and the New International*. New York: Routledge.

Dicken, Peter. 2003. *Global Shift: Reshaping the Global Economic Map in the 21st Century* (4th ed.). New York: Guilford Press.

Dobbin, Murray. 2003. *Paul Martin: CEO for Canada?* Toronto: James Lorimer.

Drucker, Peter. 1996. *The Pension Fund Revolution*. London: Transaction Publishers.

Eagleton, Terry. 1991. *Ideology*. New York: Verso.

Ernst, Alan. 1992. 'From Liberal Continentalism to Neoconservatism: North American Free Trade and the Politics of the C.D. Howe Institute' (109–40), *Studies in Political Economy* 39.

Esping-Andersen, Gøsta. 1990. *The Three Worlds of Welfare Capitalism*. Princeton, N.J.: Princeton University Press.

Estevadeordal, Antoni, Frantz, Brian, and Taylor, Alan M. 2003. 'The Rise and Fall of World Trade, 1870–1939' (359–407), *The Quarterly Journal of Economics* 118 (2).

Featherstone, Mike, and Lash, Scott. 1995. 'Globalization, Modernity, and the Spatialization of Social Theory: An Introduction' (1–24), in *Global Modernities* (ed. M. Featherstone, S. Lash, and R. Robertson). London: Sage.

Ferguson, Niall. 2003. 'Globalization in Interdisciplinary Perspective' (555–62), in *Globalization in Historical Perspective* (ed. M. Bordo, A. Taylor, and J. Williamson). Chicago: University of Chicago Press.

Findlay, Ronald, and O'Rourke, Kevin. 2003. 'Commodity Market Integration, 1500–2000.' (13–64), in *Globalization in Historical Perspective* (ed. M. Bordo, A. Taylor, and J. Williamson). Chicago: University of Chicago Press.

Firestone, O.J. 1958. *Canada's Economic Development, 1867–1953*. London: Bowes and Bowes.

Fraser, Nancy, and Gordon, Linda. 1997. 'A Genealogy of "Dependency"' (121–50), in *Justice Interruptus* (ed. Nancy Fraser). New York: Routledge.

Friedman, John. 1995. 'Global System, Globalization, and the Parameters of Modernity' (69–90), in *Global Modernities* (ed. M. Featherstone, S. Lash, and R. Robertson). London: Sage.

Galbraith, John Kenneth. 1995. *Money*. New York: Houghton Mifflin Company.

Garraty, John, and Gay, Peter. 1972. *The Columbia History of the World*. New York: Harper and Row.

George, Susan, and Fabrizio, Sabelli. 1994. *Faith and Credit: The World Bank's Secular Empire*. Toronto: Penguin Books.

Giddens, Anthony. 1984. *The Constitution of Society*. Berkeley and Los Angeles: University of California Press.

Giddens, Anthony. 1985. *The Nation State and Violence*. Cambridge: Polity Press.

Giddens, Anthony. 1990. *The Consequences of Modernity*. Stanford: Stanford University Press.

Giddens, Anthony. 1994. *Beyond Left and Right*. Stanford: Stanford University Press.

Giddens, Anthony. 2002. *Runaway World: How Globalisation Is Reshaping Our Lives* (2nd ed.). London: Profile Books.

Glyn, Andrew. 1995. 'Social Democracy and Full Employment' (33–55), *New Left Review* 211.

Gordon, David M. 1988. 'The Global Economy: New Edifice or Crumbling Foundations?' (24–64), *New Left Review* 168.

Gough, Ian. 1979. *The Political Economy of the Welfare State*. London: Macmillan.

Guest, Dennis. 1985. *The Emergence of Social Security in Canada*. Vancouver: University of British Columbia Press.

Guppy, Neil, and Davies, Scott. 1998. *Education in Canada: Recent Trends and Future Challenges*. Ottawa: Ministry of Industry.

Hacker, Andrew. 1997. *Money: Who Has How Much and Why*. New York: Scribner.

Harris, Richard. 2003. 'Old Growth and New Economy Cycles: Rethinking Canadian Economic Paradigms' (31–68), in *Governance in a World without Frontiers* (ed. T. Courchene and D. Savoie). Montreal: Institute for Research on Public Policy.

Harvey, David. 1982. *The Limits to Capital*. Chicago: University of Chicago Press.

Harvey, David. 1990. *The Condition of Postmodernism: An Enquiry into the Origins of Cultural Change*. Cambridge, Mass.: Blackwell.

Harvey, David. 1995. 'Globalization in Question' (1–17), *Rethinking Marxism*, 8 (4).

Harvey, David. 2003. *The New Imperialism*. New York: Oxford University Press.

Heilbroner, Robert. 1980. *The Worldly Philosophers*. New York: Simon and Schuster.

Helleiner, Eric. 1994. 'From Bretton Woods to Global Finance: A World Turned Upside Down' (163–75), in *Political Economy and the Changing Global Order* (ed. R. Stubbs and G. Underhill). Toronto: McClelland and Stewart.

Helleiner, Eric. 1995. 'Forum: Debt and Disorder in the World Economy' (149–64), *Studies Political Economy* 48.

Helliwell, John. 2002. *Globalization and Well-being*. Vancouver: University of British Columbia Press.

Henwood, Doug. 1996a. 'Antiglobalization,' *Left Business Observer* 71. http://www.leftbusinessobserver.com/Globalization.html.

Henwood, Doug. 1996b. 'Globalization Revisited,' *Left Business Observer* 72. http://www.leftbusinessobserver.com/Globalization_sequel.html.

Henwood, Doug. 1997. *Wall Street*. New York: Verso.

Hirst, Paul and Thompson, Grahame. 1996. *Globalization in Question*. Oxford: Polity Press.

Hobsbawm, Eric. 1994. *Age of Extremes: The Short Twentieth Century, 1914–1991*. London: Abacus.

Holmes, John. 1996. 'Restructuring in a Continental Production System' (230–54), in *Canada in the Global Economy* (ed. J. Britton). Montreal: McGill-Queen's University Press.

Howlett, Michael, Netherton, Alex, and Ramesh, M. 1999. *The Political Economy of Canada* (2nd ed.). Toronto: Oxford University Press.

Human Development Report. 2003. http://hdr.undp.org/reports/global/
2003/indicator/index_indicators.html.

ILO (International Labor Organization). 2004. 'Global unemployment remains
at record levels in 2003.' http://www.ilo.org/public/english/bureau/inf/
pr/2004/1.htm.

Industry Canada. 2004. Trade Data Online. http://strategis.ic.gc.ca/sc_mrkti/
tdst/engdoc/tr_homep.html).

Iversen, Torben. 2001. 'The Dynamics of Welfare State Expansion: Trade Openness, De-industrialization, and Partisan Politics' (45–79), in *The New Politics
of the Welfare State* (ed. Paul Pierson). Toronto: Oxford University Press.

James, Harold. 2001. *The End of Globalization: Lessons from the Great Depression.*
Cambridge, Mass.: Harvard University Press.

Jessop, Bob. 1993. 'Towards a Schumpeterian Workfare State? Preliminary
Remarks on Post-Fordist Political Economy' (7–40), *Studies in Political Economy* 40.

Kasper, Wolfgang. 1993. 'Spatial Economics' (82–5), in *The Fortune Encyclopaedia of Economics* (ed. D.R. Henderson). New York: Warner Books.

Keil, Manfred, and Pantuosco, Louis. 1998. 'Canadian and U.S. Unemployment
Rates: A Comparison Based on Regional Data' (38–55), *Canadian Public Policy*
24.

Kontradieff, Nikolai. 1984. *The Long Wave Cycle.* New York: Richardson and
Snyder.

Korpi, Walter. 1983. *The Democratic Class Struggle.* London: Routledge and
Kegan Paul.

Krugman, Paul. 1994. *Peddling Prosperity: Economic Sense and Nonsense in the
Age of Diminished Expectations.* New York: W.W. Norton and Company.

Kumar, Krishan. 1994. 'Modernity' (391–2), in *The Blackwell Dictionary of Twentieth-century Social Thought* (ed. W. Outhwaite and T. Bottomore). Oxford:
Blackwell.

Kumar, Krishan. 1995. *From Post-industrial to Post-modern Society: New Theories
of the Contemporary World.* Cambridge, Mass.: Blackwell.

Kurtzman, Joel. 1993. *The Death of Money: How the Electronic Economy Has Desta-
bilized the World's Markets and Created Financial Chaos.* Toronto: Simon and
Schuster.

Kuznets, Simon. 1966. *Modern Economic Growth.* New Haven Conn.: Yale University Press.

Langille, David. 1987. 'The Business Council on National Issues and the Canadian State' (41–85), *Studies in Political Economy* 24.

Lash, Scott, and Urry, John. 1994. *Economies of Signs and Space.* Thousand Oaks,
Calif.: Sage.

Laxer, Gordon. 1995. 'Social Solidarity, Democracy, and Global Capitalism' (287–313), *Canadian Review of Sociology and Anthropology* 32.

Laxer, Gordon. 2003. 'Stop Rejecting Sovereignty: Confronting the Antiglobalization Movement' (29), *Canadian Dimension* 37 (1) (Jan./Feb.).

Laxer, James. 1973. 'Introduction to the Political Economy of Canada' (26–41), in *(Canada) Ltd.: The Political Economy of Dependency* (ed. J. Laxer). Toronto: McClelland and Stewart.

Laxer, James. 1984. *Rethinking the Economy*. Toronto: New Canada Publications.

Leacy, F.H. 1983. *Historical Statistics of Canada* (2nd ed.) Toronto: Macmillan of Canada.

Lenin, Vladimir I. 1939. *Imperialism: The Highest Stage of Capitalism: A Popular Outline*. Moscow: Progress Publishers.

Levitt, Theodore. 1983. *The Marketing Imagination*. New York: Free Press.

Luke, T.W. 1995. 'New World Order or Neoworld Orders: Power, Politics, and Ideology in Informationalizing Glocalities' (91–107), in *Global Modernities* (ed. M. Featherstone, S. Lash, and R. Robertson). London: Sage.

MacPherson, Alan D. 1996. 'Shifts in Canadian Direct Investment Abroad and Foreign Direct Investment in Canada' (69–83), in *Canada in the Global Economy* (ed. J. Britton). Montreal: McGill-Queen's University Press.

Macpherson, C.B. 1977. *The Life and Times of Liberal Democracy*. New York: Oxford University Press.

Maddison, Angus. 1995. *Monitoring the World Economy, 1820 to 1992*. Paris: OECD.

Maddison, Angus. 2001. *The World Economy: A Millennial Perspective*. Paris: OECD.

Mandalios, John. 1996. 'Historical Sociology' (278–302), in *The Blackwell Companion to Social Theory* (ed. Bryan Turner). Cambridge: Blackwell.

Mann, Michael. 1997. 'Has Globalization Ended the Rise of the Nation-state?' (472–96), *Review of International Political Economy* 4 (3).

Marchak, Patricia M. 1988. *Ideological Perspectives on Canada* (3rd ed.). Toronto: McGraw-Hill Ryerson Limited.

Marchak, Patricia M. 1991. *The Integrated Circus: The New Right and the Restructuring of Global Markets*. Montreal and Kingston: McGill-Queen's University Press.

Marx, Karl, and Engels, Friedrich. 1968. *The German Ideology*. Moscow: Progress Publishers.

Marx, Karl, and Engels, Friedrich. 1986. *Manifesto of the Communist Party*. Moscow: Progress Publishers.

Marx, Karl, and Engels, Friedrich. 1989. *Manifest der Kommunistischen Partei*. Stuttgart: Reclam.

Massey, Doreen 1994. *Space, Place, and Gender*. Minneapolis: University of Minnesota Press.

McBride, Stephen, and Shields, John. 1993. *Dismantling a Nation: Canada and the New World Order*. Halifax: Fernwood Publishing.

McMurtry, John. 2003. 'The New World Order: The Hidden War of Values' (23–39), in *The New Global Order* (ed. G. Yovanovich). Montreal: McGill-Queen's University Press.

McQuaig, Linda. 1998. *The Cult of Impotence*. Toronto: Penguin Press.

McQuaig, Linda. 1995. *Shooting the Hippo*. Toronto: Penguin Press.

Merriam-Webster. 1991. *The Merriam-Webster New Book of Word Histories*. Springfield, Mass.: Merriam-Webster.

Mimoto, H., and Cross. P. 1991. 'The Growth of the Federal Debt' (3.1–3.18), in *Canadian Economic Observer*. Ottawa: Statistics Canada.

Mishra, Ramesh. 1984. *The Welfare State in Crisis: Social Thought and Social Change*. Brighton: Wheatsheaf Books.

Mishra, Ramesh. 1990. *The Welfare State in Capitalist Society*. Toronto: Harvester and Wheatsheaf.

Mullaly, Robert. 1994. 'Social Welfare and the New Right: A Class Mobilization Perspective' (76–94), in *Continuities and Discontinuities: The Political Economy of Social Welfare and Labour Market Policy in Canada* (ed. A. Johnson, S. McBride, and P. Smith). Toronto: University of Toronto Press.

Mulvale, James. 2001. *Reimagining Social Welfare: Beyond the Keynesian Welfare State*. Aurora, Ont.: Garamond Press.

Myles, John. 1988. 'Decline or Impasse?: The Current State of the Welfare State' (73–107), *Studies in Political Economy* 26.

Myles, John. 1989. *Old Age in the Welfare State*. Kansas: University of Kansas Press.

Myles, John, and Pierson, Paul. 2001. 'The Political Economy of Pension Reform' (305–33), in *The New Politics of the Welfare State* (ed. Paul Pierson). Toronto: Oxford University Press.

National Council of Welfare. 1995. *Social Security Backgrounder 1*. Ottawa.

National Council of Welfare. 2004. *Fact Sheet: Welfare Recipients*. http://www.ncwcnbes.net/htmdocument/principales/numberwelfare_e.htm.

Naylor, Tom. 1972. 'The Rise and Fall of the Third Commercial Empire of the St Lawrence' (1–41), in *Capitalism and the National Question in Canada* (ed. G. Teeple). Toronto: University of Toronto Press.

Nederveen Pieterse, Jan. 1995. 'Globalization as Hybridization' (45–68), in *Global Modernities* (ed. H. Featherstone, S. Lash, and R. Robertson). London: Sage.

Norcliffe, Glen. 1996. 'Foreign Trade in Goods and Services' (25–47), in *Canada in the Global Economy* (ed. J. Britton). Montreal: McGill-Queen's University Press.

Norrie, Kenneth, and Owram, Douglas. 1996. *A History of the Canadian Economy*. Toronto: Harcourt Brace Canada.

Nozick, Robert. 1974. *Anarchy, State, and Utopia*. New York: Basic Books.

Obstfeld, Maurice, and Taylor, Alan. 2003. 'Globalization and Capital Markets' (121–90) in *Globalization in Historical Perspective* (ed. M. Bordo, A. Taylor, and J. Williamson). Chicago: University of Chicago Press.

O'Connor, James. 1973. *The Fiscal Crises of the State*. New York: St Martin's Press.

OECD. (Organisation for Economic Cooperation and Development). 1997. *OECD National Accounts, Main Aggregates*. Paris: OECD.

OECD. 2001. Education: Tables. http://www.oecd.org/dataoecd/26/45/2672042.xls.

OECD. 2003a. Education at a Glance: Tables. http://www.oecd.org/document/34/0,2340,en_2649_34515_14152482_1_1_1_1,00.html.

OECD. 2003b. *OECD National Accounts, Main Aggregates*. Paris: OECD.

OECD. 2003c. 'Trends and Recent Developments in Foreign Direct Investment.' http://www.oecd.org/dataoecd/52/11/2958722.pdf.

OECD. 2004. Frequently Asked Health Data. http://www.oecd.org/document/16/0,2340,en_2649_34631_2085200_1_1_1_1,00.html.

Ohmae, Kenichi. 1995. *The End of the Nation State*. New York: Free Press.

Olsen, Gregg M. 2002. *The Politics of the Welfare State: Canada, Sweden, and the United States*. Toronto: Oxford University Press.

O'Rourke, Kevin, and Williamson, Jeffrey. 1999. *Globalization and History: The Evolution of a Nineteenth-century Atlantic Economy*. Cambridge, Mass.: MIT Press.

Panitch, Leo. 1994. 'Globalisation and the State' (60–93), in *Socialist Register 1994* (ed. R. Miliband and L. Panitch). London: Merlin Books.

Pierson, Paul. 1994. *Dismantling the Welfare State? Reagan, Thatcher, and the Politics of Retrenchment*. Cambridge: Cambridge University Press.

Pierson, Paul. 2001. 'Post Industrial Pressures on the Mature Welfare States' (80–106), in *The New Politics of the Welfare State* (ed. Paul Pierson). Toronto: Oxford University Press.

Piven, Francis Fox. 1995. 'Is It Global Economics or Neo-laissez-faire?' (107–14), *New Left Review* 213.

Piven, Francis Fox, and Cloward, Richard A. 1993. *Regulating the Poor: The Functions of Public Welfare* (2nd ed.). New York: Pantheon Books.

Polyani, Karl. 1944. *The Great Transformation*. Boston: Beacon Press.

Porter, John. 1965. *The Vertical Mosaic*. Toronto: University of Toronto Press.

Pulkingham, Jane. 1998. 'Remaking the Social Division of Welfare: Gender, "Dependency," and UI Reform' (7–48), *Studies in Political Economy* 56.

Ritzer, George. 2000. *Classical Sociological Theory* (3rd ed.). Toronto: McGraw-Hill Higher Education.

Ritzer, George, and Stillman, Todd. 2003. 'Assessing McDonaldization, Americanization and Globalization' (30–48), in *Global America? The Cultural Consequences of Globalization* (ed. U. Beck, N. Sznaider, and R. Winter). Liverpool: Liverpool University Press.

Robbins, Richard. 2002. *Global Problems and the Culture of Capitalism* (2nd ed.). Toronto: Allyn and Bacon.

Robertson, Roland. 1985. 'The Relativization of Societies: Modern Religion and Globalization,' in *Cults, Culture and the Law* (ed. T. Robbins, W.C. Shepherd, and J. McBride). Chicago: Scholars.

Robertson, Roland. 1992. *Globalization: Social Theory and Global Culture*. London: Sage.

Robertson, Roland. 1995. 'Glocalization: Time-Space and Homogeneity-Heterogeneity' (113–36), in *Global Modernities* (ed. M. Featherstone, S. Lash, and R. Robertson). London: Sage.

Robertson, Roland, and Khondker, Habib H. 1998. 'Discourses on Globalization' (25–40), *International Sociology* 13 (1).

Rosenberg, Justin. 2000. *The Follies of Globalisation Theory*. New York: Verso Press.

Rostow, Walt W. 1978. *The World Economy: History and Prospect*. Austin: University of Texas Press.

Rostow, Walt W. 1990. *The Stages of Economic Growth* (3rd ed.). Cambridge: Cambridge University Press.

Saul, John Ralston. 1997. *Reflections of a Siamese Twin: Canada at the End of the Twentieth Century*. Toronto: Penguin Books.

Scott, Alan. 1997. 'Globalization: Social Process or Political Rhetoric' (1–24), in *The Limits of Globalization*. New York: Routledge.

Shannon, Thomas. 1996. *An Introduction to the World-System Perspective* (2nd ed.). Boulder, Colo.: Westview Press.

Skocpol, Theda. 1986. 'Bringing the State Back In: Strategies of Analysis in Current Research' (3–37), in *Bringing the State Back In* (ed. P. Evans, D. Rueschemeyer, and T. Skocpol). Cambridge: Cambridge University Press.

Smith, Dorothy. 1990. *Texts, Facts, and Femininity: Exploring the Relations of Ruling*. New York: Routledge.

Smithin, John. 2004. 'Can We Afford to Pay for Social Programs?' (163–76), *Studies in Political Economy* 71/72.

Smythe, Elizabeth. 2003. 'Canadian Sovereignty and Global Trade and Investment Rules' (325–44), in *Reinventing Canada: Politics of the 21st Century* (ed. J. Brodie and L. Trimble). Toronto: Pearson Press.

Sossin, Lorne. 1998. 'Salvaging the Welfare State?: The Prospects for Judicial Review of the Canada Health and Social Transfer' (141–98), *Dalhousie Law Journal* 21.

Sowell, Thomas. 1996. *Migrations and Cultures*. New York: Basic Books.

Stanford, Jim. 1995. 'Forum: Debt and Disorder in the World Economy' (113–35), *Studies in Political Economy* 48.

Stanford, Jim. 1999. *The Paper Boom*. Toronto: James Lorimer and Company.

Starr, Amory. 2000. *Naming the Enemy: Anti-corporate Movements Confront Globalization*. London: Zed Books.

Statistics Canada. 1870–1987. *Canada Yearbooks*. Ottawa: Statistics Canada.

Statistics Canada. 1952. *Trade of Canada*. Ottawa: Statistics Canada.

Statistics Canada. 1993. *Canada's International Investment Position, Historical Statistics, 1926–1992*. Cat. No. 67-202. Ottawa: Statistics Canada.

Statistics Canada. 1993. *Public Finance Historical Data*. Cat. No. 85-512 Occasional. Ottawa: Statistics Canada.

Statistics Canada. 1995. *Public Sector Statistics*. Cat. No. 68-212-XPB. Ottawa: Statistics Canada.

Statistics Canada. 1997a. *Canada's Balance of International Payments, Historical Statistics, 1926–1996*. Cat. No. 67-001 XPP. Ottawa: Statistics Canada.

Statistics Canada. 1997b. *Canada's International Merchandise Trade*. Cat. No. 65-001-XPB. Ottawa: Statistics Canada.

Statistics Canada. 2004. *National Balance Sheets*. Cat. No. 13-214-PPB. Ottawa: Statistics Canada.

Stearns, Peter N. 1993. *The Industrial Revolution in World History*. San Francisco: Westview Press.

Steger, Manfred. 2003. *Globalization: A Very Short Introduction*. New York: Oxford University Press.

Stehr, Nico. 1994. *Knowledge Societies*. London: Sage.

Stern, Robert. 2004. 'Comment' (494–7), in *Challenges to Globalization* (ed. R. Baldwin and L. Winters). Chicago: University of Chicago Press.

Stewart, Walter. 1982. *Towers of Gold – Feet of Clay: The Canadian Banks*. Toronto: Totem.

Stewart, Walter. 1997. *Bank Heist*. Toronto: HarperCollins.

Stiglitz, Joseph. 2002. *Globalization and Its Discontents*. New York: W.W. Norton and Company.

Stiglitz, Joseph. 2003. *The Roaring Nineties*. New York: W.W. Norton and Company.

Stubbs, Richard. 1994. 'The Political Economy of the Asia-Pacific Region' (366–77), in *Political Economy and the Changing Global Order* (ed. R. Stubbs and G. Underhill). Toronto: McClelland and Stewart.

Tabb, William K. 2002. *Unequal Partners: A Primer on Globalization*. New York: New Press.

Teeple, Gary. 2000. *Globalization and the Decline of Social Reform* (2nd ed.). Toronto: Garamond Press.

Therborn, Goran. 1986. *Why Some Peoples Are More Unemployed Than Others.* London: Verso.

Therborn, Goran. 1995. 'Routes to/through Modernity' (124–39), in *Global Modernities* (ed. M. Featherstone, S. Lash, and R. Robertson). London: Sage.

Thurow, Lester C. 1980. *The Zero Sum Society.* New York: Penguin.

Torpey, John. 1998. 'Coming and Going: On the State Monopolization of Legitimate Means of Movement' (239–59), *Sociological Theory* 16 (3).

Turner, Lowell. 1991. *Democracy at Work: Changing World Markets and the Future of Labour Unions.* Ithaca, N.Y.: Cornell University Press.

Urmetzer, Peter. 2003. *From Free Trade to Forced Trade: Canada in the Global Economy.* Toronto: Penguin Canada.

Urmetzer, Peter, and Guppy, Neil. 2004. 'Changing Income Inequality in Canada' (75–84), in *Social Inequality in Canada: Patterns, Problems, Policies* (3rd ed.) (ed. J. Curtis, E. Grabb, and N. Guppy). Scarborough, Ont.: Prentice Hall Canada.

Urquhart, M.C. 1993. *Gross National Product, Canada, 1870–1926: The Derivation of Estimates.* Kingston: McGill-Queen's University Press.

Urquhart, M.C., and Buckley, K.A.H. 1965. *Historical Statistics of Canada.* Toronto: Macmillan of Canada.

Vidal, Gore. 2004. *Imperial America: Reflections on the United States of Amnesia.* New York. Thunder's Mouth.

Wade, Robert. 1996. 'Globalization and Its Limits: Reports of the Death of the National Economy Are Greatly Exaggerated' (60–88), in *National Diversity and Global Capitalism* (ed. S. Berger and R. Dore). Ithaca, N.Y.: Cornell University Press.

Wade, Robert. 2001. 'The Rising Inequality of World Income Distribution' (37–9), *Finance and Development* 38 (4).

Wallerstein, Immanuel. 1974. *The Modern World System: Capitalist Agriculture and the Origins of the European World-economy in the Sixteenth Century.* New York: Academic Press.

Wallerstein, Immanuel. 1991. 'The National and the Universal: Can There Be Such a Thing as World Culture?' in *Culture Globalization and the World-System* (ed. Anthony King). New York: State University of New York.

Wallerstein, Immanuel. 1997. 'Eurocentrism and Its Avatars: The Dilemmas of Social Science' (93–108), *New Left Review* 226.

Wallerstein, Immanuel. 2002. 'The Eagle Has Crashed Landed' (61–8), *Foreign Policy* (July–Aug.).

Wallerstein, Immanuel. 2003. *The Decline of American Power: The U.S. in a Chaotic World*. New York: New Press.

Waters, Malcolm. 2001. *Globalization* (2nd ed.). New York: Routledge.

Watkins, Mel. 1992. *Madness and Ruin: Politics and the Economy in the Neoconservative Age*. Toronto: Between the Lines.

Weiss, Linda. 1997. 'Globalization and the Myth of the Powerless State' (3–27), *New Left Review* 225.

Williams, Glen. 1986. *Not for Export: Toward a Political Economy of Canada's Arrested Industrialization*. Toronto: McClelland and Stewart.

Williams, Raymond. 1983. *Keywords*. London: Fontana.

Wood, Ellen. 2002. *The Origin of Capitalism: A Longer View*. New York: Verso.

Zweig, Stefan. nd. *Die Welt von Gestern: Die Geschichte eines Europäers*. Stuttgart: Knopf.

Index

Studies in Comparative Political Economy and Public Policy

1 *The Search for Political Space: Globalization, Social Movements, and the Urban Political Experience* / Warren Magnusson
2 *Oil, the State, and Federalism: The Rise and Demise of Petro-Canada as a Statist Impulse* / John Erik Fossum
3 *Defying Conventional Wisdom: Free Trade and the Rise of Popular Sector Politics in Canada* / Jeffrey M. Ayres
4 *Community, State, and Market on the North Atlantic Rim: Challenges to Modernity in the Fisheries* / Richard Apostle, Gene Barrett, Petter Holm, Svein Jentoft, Leigh Mazany, Bonnie McCay, Knut H. Mikalsen
5 *More with Less: Work Reorganization in the Canadian Mining Industry* / Bob Russell
6 *Visions for Privacy: Policy Approaches for the Digital Age* / Edited by Colin J. Bennett and Rebecca Grant
7 *New Democracies: Economic and Social Reform in Brazil, Chile, and Mexico* / Michel Duquette
8 *Poverty, Social Assistance, and the Employability of Mothers: Restructuring Welfare States* / Maureen Baker and David Tippin
9 *The Left's Dirty Job: The Politics of Industrial Restructuring in France and Spain* / W. Rand Smith
10 *Risky Business: Canada's Changing Science-Based Policy and Regulatory Regime* / Edited by G. Bruce Doern and Ted Reed
11 *Temporary Work: The Gendered Rise of a Precarious Employment Relationship* / Leah Vosko
12 *Who Cares? Women's Work, Childcare, and Welfare State Redesign* / Jane Jenson and Mariette Sineau with Franca Bimbi, Anne-Marie Daune-Richard, Vincent Della Sala, Rianne Mahon, Bérengère Marques-Pereira, Olivier Paye, and George Ross
13 *Canadian Forest Policy: Adapting to Change* / Edited by Michael Howlett
14 *Knowledge and Economic Conduct: The Social Foundations of the Modern Economy* / Nico Stehr
15 *Contingent Work, Disrupted Lives: Labour and Community in the New Rural Economy* / Anthony Winson and Belinda Leach
16 *The Economic Implications of Social Cohesion* / Edited by Lars Osberg
17 *Gendered States: Women, Unemployment Insurance, and the Political Economy of the Welfare State in Canada, 1945–1997* / Ann Porter
18 *Educational Regimes and Anglo-American Democracy* / Ronald Manzer